2nd Edition

Threshold: A Memoir

FAITH A. COLBURN

DEDICATION

To Grandma Hazel who carried me over the mud puddles when my legs were too short.

ACKNOWLEDGMENTS

Thanks first to Grandma Hazel, who started me on this journey with her stories of family members, both living and long dead. Not only did she tell me stories about where I come from, she also helped me see, through those stories, that other people have come, successfully, through much worse traumas than mine.

In addition, I'd like to thank Tom Bass, who helped me believe I could do this when my life was in chaos, and Dennis Held, who did the first edit of the first of these stories, years ago when they were a mere germs. Dr. Mike Stricklin from the University of Nebraska-Lincoln deserves credit for encouraging me to do the research and write the skeleton of this story and Dr. Timothy Mahoney, also from UNL, helped me track down the generations before Grandma's memory. Thanks to Dr. Allison Hedge Coke who guided this process through a finished manuscript, as well as Drs. Robert Luscher and Robert Ficociello of the University of Nebraska-Kearney, who served as beta readers on my graduate committee as I earned my master of arts in creative writing.

And I'd like to thank the generations of my family, some of whom are mentioned in this book, for "passing it on," that is, serving as examples of surviving and even thriving under trying circumstances. I hope I can live up to their courage.

INTRODUCTION

Why?

As a journalist, I always start my writing process with a question and *why* is the most frequent question that arises. I am interested in everything. I cannot help myself. I simply have to ask how everything works, how everything happens. So I read written history to help me understand why things are the way they are. I read all sorts of history. I have read natural history, about whales, elephants, and chimpanzees. I have read about quantum physics and about the geology of the Grand Canyon. I do not fully understand everything I read, but everything I read informs my thinking and my writing.

About fifteen years ago, when Grandma and I began digging through the box of old photos she had found in her closet, I asked all the questions I had learned in journalism school decades before. Who is that? When was that photo taken? Where was it taken? What on earth is she doing? And, inevitably, *why* is my family the way it is? Does this person in this photo have anything to do with it?

Together we wrote names and places onto the backs of the photos. Some of them were dated. Most of them were posed; people just standing in front of the camera. My family didn't have television until I was in high school, so I grew up on static images, but by the time we found the photos, I had grown accustomed to pictures that move. I wanted to see these people in motion, to know them, to see them in action. After all, I shared their DNA and all its complexities.

So Grandma and I made a date, actually a series of dates to record her stories. We met once a week for about five months and sat down each time with a tape recorder between us. I asked questions and Grandma told stories. She was glorious. Ninety-eight then, she had Technicolor™ memory of seven generations, three before hers and three after. She remembered not only events, but also colors and sounds. Each person who moved through her stories was an individual with her own oddities and quirks.

As a trained journalist, I started out to report only facts. I had no intention of inserting myself into Grandma's stories at all, but three things happened on the way to a manuscript. First, I began to discover squishy facts, things that might or might not be true, but that made a huge difference in how we saw the world, because we believed them to be true. Those "facts" had deeply affected me, so I had to write about me. Secondly, those times when Grandma pushed away things she didn't know (and sometimes didn't want to know), I realized that my quest for *why* had to go beyond what Grandma knew; that some of the answers would have to come from my own interpretations. Thirdly, as I learned how members of my family dealt with their own crises, I discovered my quirky responses to challenge and began to fathom *why* I respond the way I do. I began to believe that my new discoveries might help others trying to find a way to think about our nation of strangers and our inability to care for one another.

That inability has never been clearer than when my friend, Majda Obradovic, once stopped me cold the day she commented on her neighbors. Majda and her daughters left the Bosnian portion of Yugoslavia during the genocide there, with what they could carry in a backpack. In the U.S. she was learning her fifth language, but Majda's a keen observer and she nailed the culture she had dropped into. She barely knew her neighbors' names, she said. They just left their apartments, jumped in their cars, and went to work. They would return home and close themselves in their apartments with their air conditioners and rarely see each other. She contrasted this image with Sarajevo, before the war, when the people walked the streets in the evening, greeting each other and talking. Religion did not matter then and being together was more important than being cool.

I was very young and I only witnessed the end of an era when rural Americans lived that same way, so I have depended on Grandma to fill in the blanks. I hope, between us, we have revealed something of what it was like.

Sometimes, though, we've had to guess and that's created a dilemma for me. Pat Murphy addressed this guessing part in her short story "One Odd Shoe."

"I wasn't around for this next part. But that's okay. My grandmother tells the story of how Coyote brought the people fire, and she wasn't around for that. So I'll tell you how I think it was, and that will be good enough."[i]

I do believe, on the deepest level, that words matter. I believe that truth matters. This has been my dilemma, time after time, as I have stumbled into missing facts and stories that contradict themselves or each other. Each time I have worked my way through such a morass, I have attempted to make clear that I am wading in a swamp and I have done my best to describe my landmarks. I have provided those landmarks within the text and expanded on them with endnotes because I am acutely aware that the same landmarks I see may lead someone else to a different place.

Although Murphy was writing fiction when she wrote the above lines, and although as a journalist, I cringe at that statement, I have found that "how I think it was" often has to be good enough. While I realize that my considered opinion "ain't the facts, Ma'am," I have realized that it is my considered opinion that moves me when the facts have been obscured.

I sought guidance in reading Lee Gutkind's *The Art of Creative Nonfiction*. As a journalist, I was almost immediately annoyed by Gutkind's assumptions about journalists.

"Traditional journalists learn early in their education that creativity or imagination in newspapers and magazines are basically disallowed."[ii]

This statement could not be farther from the truth. Although deadlines and the pressure of the news cycle sometimes make it difficult, the best journalists do bring both imagination and creativity to their work. We do recognize that we cannot be objective and are aware of the difference between subjectivity, which we try to minimize, and editorializing.

After discussing journalists' lack of creativity and imagination, Gutkind describes a series of techniques that *creative* nonfiction writers use, techniques I had personally learned in journalism school. Gutkind employs some of the exact terminology taught in colleges of journalism, like "lead."

As a former teacher of technical communication, I appreciate the way Gutkind helps his audience, me, by using many heads and subheads and listing even the subheads in his table of contents. Under the subhead,

"How to Sound Objective While Being Subjective," I found this advice: ". . . balance and objectivity are certainly permitted and sometimes desirable, but they are not required."[iii] Normally I would take exception to that advice, and the subhead, but I found in Gutkind's examples that he was discussing focus and keeping to the subject, although the subhead implies dishonesty.

In my case, writing about my own family, including its dysfunction, I darn well better present a balance, I decided, even if I cannot be objective. My dad was the one person who would have no voice because he died long before I started asking questions. I came very close to overcompensating for that loss, but I hope, by reading every scrap of his surviving letters and everything Grandma said about him, as well as studying the context of the Depression and war years, that I have reached my sought-after balance.

In order to deal with the empty spots, not just my dad's but many others', I have looked at context. So when I found my uncle, several generations back, was kidnapped and adopted into the Shawnee nation, I searched for autobiographies and biographies of other children similarly captured and adopted. Their stories helped fill in blank spaces. When I stumbled upon a great aunt who died in childbirth, an unwed mother, I looked at the institution where she died and the rules she had to live with as a criminal, because pregnancy outside of marriage was a criminal offense then.

Year after year, as I have heard our communal language descend into doublespeak, I have felt an increasing need to use language responsibly. Our political and economic discourse has become a catfight, full of suspicion and accusation, and I find myself struggling to remember that the catfight is not the total of our human potential. My grandmother's stories and the love underlying them have served me as an antidote. Her moment in time, immersed in a loving family and community, in a place alive with possibility, provide a respite from the wars and domestic upheaval that came both before and after.

Because I am a sixth generation Nebraskan and every inch a plainswoman, I have lived in community with a place in ways many people cannot even imagine. The great winds on the Great Plains excite me and I have stood upon the front step watching a tornado form, unable to take my eyes off the clouds. I love to sit by my window and watch snow, driven by blizzard winds, filling the landscape with white. The energy of those events electrifies me and fills my writing, even in the gentlest of passages.

When I was little, I lived with my grandparents for a year or more. When they were busy and I was troubled, I "*drove*" their rusting Model A Ford out across the prairie, maybe trying to escape feelings I simply didn't understand. Even now, the smell of wet, rusty metal and moldy leather feels like a perilous journey through wild country.

Sometimes, Grandma took me in charge and we walked around the pastures where she introduced me to native wildflowers—a purple vetch she called buffalo beans, purple prairie coneflowers, the tiny white flowers of daisy fleabane, broad, composite heads of ironweed, the splashes of white on snow-on-the-mountain, and lavender spikes of verbena. Later, I think it was she who taught me to swing a machete, and although I chopped weeds with everyone else in the family, I mostly remember summer mornings working my way through the fields with her, slicing the thick, peppery stems of sunflowers and cockleburs and sneezing on the pungent smell.

Afternoons, I would lie in the grass under a tree, by myself, listen to thousands of insect chirps and creaks, and chew on a grass stem carefully pulled from a whorl of leaves. Except on the most brutally hot days, the sun, filtered through the leaves of a seventy-foot cottonwood tree, would feel warm and comfortable. I have only begun to realize what a gift those unscheduled, unobserved hours represent. In some ways I grew up almost a wild thing, poking around in creek bottoms and under bridges. I had limits and I knew them, but as long as I turned up at mealtime and did my assigned chores, I was a free spirit. Those days are never far from my mind as I write.

Nebraska naturalist and author, Loren Eiseley, captured my imagination with his musings about a skull he found in his search for prehistoric bones.[iv] That essay, entitled "The Slit," led me into several volumes of Eiseley's essays and changed my perspective on nature forever. As Eiseley thought in writing about animal consciousness, I went along for the ride, wondering with him about animal experience. That, too, has seeped into my description of prairie and our relationship with it.

Another influence in this manuscript, is my own work life. I worked for the Nebraska Game and Parks Commission for more than a decade. During those years, I camped out with buck skinners, canoed the Dismal, rode with dog trainers in the Sandhills, camped in the Pine Ridge, and floated the Missouri's Sunshine Bottoms region. That is where I honed my attention to detail, watching wildlife artist Bud Pritchard as, each month, he prepared a painting of some native Nebraska creature. He used study skins most of the time to get every hair or every feather right. There, I learned to identify ducks by the pattern of feathers on their wings—the powder blue shoulder patch of a blue-winged teal, the row of iridescent green on the edge of the mallard wing, the white splash on the male bufflehead.

There, I also discovered the awful vacancies on the Plains, where countless wild things used to be. Although I have spent some time watching prairie dogs, and even killed some when they invaded the pastures, I have never seen a black-footed ferret or a burrowing owl. I have never seen the "gray and white avalanches"[v] of cranes swooping out of spring clouds like Sandy Griswold described in his 1890s sports columns in the *Omaha World Herald*. I have seen pretty fair numbers of buffalo in the Black Hills, but I have never seen tens of thousands of them migrating to new pastures in the fall.

I brought those images (those I have seen and those I have only read about) with me when I started a degree program in creative writing at the University of Nebraska–Kearney. By then I was desperate for feedback. I had been working when I could, while my life happened in a pretty chaotic fashion. Probably the most useful courses I took during my first year were the poetry classes taught by poet, Don Welch. Although I rarely write poetry, those two courses made my prose line denser as I peeled away at my normally complex sentences. But that peeling came in the context of Derek Walcott's elegantly complex poetic sentences that sometimes ran for pages. And that was a lesson in pacing. Those long sentences without end stops force readers into a breathless reading that heightens excitement.

More recent poetry courses with Allison Hedge Coke have reinforced and built upon that base, making me more aware of the music of poetry, a music I attempt to bring into my prose with vocabulary that not only has meaning that sets a mood, but also sounds that bring out the emotional setting. I occasionally turn to a poem when a story fragment is dense with meaning, but short on action and I have wavered back and forth between poem and scene to tell Elsie Robeson's story within this manuscript.

In my creative nonfiction class I read other students' nonfiction and received the feedback I had lacked for more than a decade. Not only did we review each other's work in class, several of us also met outside of class to critique other stories we didn't have time for in regular sessions.

The texts in the formal class included Laura Wexler's book, *Writing Creative Nonfiction.*

"Creative nonfiction writers are in an ideal position to be one-person 'truth and reconciliation' commissions,"[vi] wrote Wexler in her essay "Saying Good-Bye to 'Once Upon a Time,' or Implementing Postmodernism in Creative Nonfiction." Unfortunately, the people who most needed the truth and the reconciliation had to find it themselves, right at the end of my father's life. ". . . creative nonfiction is a particularly well-equipped genre to deal with events that have been forgotten or understudied by official histories, and to unearth lives at the margin of bigger events,"[vii] Wexler continued. As I discovered more and more members of my family, I began to realize that they had been at the margins of all the big events in American history, but they were just ordinary Americans going about the business of pursuing happiness wherever they could find it. I even considered calling the memoir, *Ordinary Americans.*

Dennis Held, my first editor for this memoir, gave me permission as he commented on what I had written by then, to look more closely at my "squishy facts." He also told me I needed to add in the "wisdom." I do not know if I have that wisdom yet, because I don't feel very wise. However, in the process of writing down what I have learned about my family, I have found some causes and effects that have had profound results, not only for the people directly involved, but also on people far removed from the initial action.

Since I began this project, only a couple of years before Grandma's death, I have read numerous memoirs. I have done my best to forget them all so I don't copy them, but the techniques of telling stories has remained with me. William Kittredge's *Owning it All,* a series of essays about living in the American West, has probably influenced my thinking more than his memoir. In a chilling central scene, he focused on his grandfather, baiting, trapping, and killing magpies, "because they're mine."[viii]

I have thought about and reread that passage many times because it really emphasizes the significance of my own grandfather's claim that "We don't own the land, we're just give it to take care of for the next generation." The contrast couldn't be more stark.

As I thought about my mother's struggle to understand the concept of extended family and a community existing in a particular place, I was drawn to Susan Schaller's book, *A Man without Words,* about a man who was, not only deaf, but also without knowledge of language.[ix] The idea of growing to adulthood without knowing that language exists seemed roughly parallel to my mother's maturing without a clear concept of a placed family and her resulting handicap.

I am still digesting newly discovered mental illness in my own family, guided by Allison Hedge Coke's *Rock, Ghost, Willow, Deer*[x]. Even as I child, I thought my mother struggled with some secret fear that I couldn't place. Now I can see how my great-grandmother's paranoid schizophrenia brought chaos, not just to her immediate family, but to generations going forward. I suspect I will be writing about it for some time.

Futurist Alvin Toffler has had an enormous influence on my thinking, particularly in his book, *The Third Wave*. In his concepts of the "prosumer" and the "electronic cottage" he stirred my imagination. If he's right about our potential new future society, and many of his predictions have already come to pass, then my family can serve, at least in part, as a model. Put simply, Toffler's prosumer is a producer/consumer, someone who produces at least a portion of what he or she consumes.[xi] Farm families have always been prosumers, but I haven't spent a great deal of attention on that aspect of my family history. On the other hand, in Toffler's electronic cottage, families work together as they did on my grandfather's farm. One person may have the computer-based job, but all members of the family participate in the work, depending upon each person's computer literacy.[xii] I have tried to discover in this memoir how those things worked because I am not sure families know how to be intensely together anymore.

In the late 1990s Brazilian journalist, Gustavo Said, and I corresponded regularly, by email, about that living together thing. We called our discussion something like "the nature of time in a globalized society" and we characterized time by the kind of society that exists within it. For example, when we talked about slow time, we talked about the very things I have focused upon in this memoir, that is, extended families living in close proximity and surrounded by familiar communities living in relationship with the place they occupy. Quick time, on the other hand, is the time of single-parent households, often moved from place to place by economic necessities, and almost completely lacking the support of grandparents, aunts and uncles, neighbors and long-term friends. My friend, Molly Klocksin, has pointed out that there is a flash time, too, in which single women and men get shunted from one corner of the world to another because their employers do not have to feel guilty about disrupting families. She wondered how one forms a family when she cannot remain in any one place for more than a few months or a year or two.

I found one more precedent for the way in which my family solved its own problems without the help of the government sector. In his novel, *Plainsong*, Kent Haruf has revealed ways in which stable communities can support their members in need. As Haruf describes his fictional characters, he shows his readers some unconventional responses to very conventional situations, even when families do not function.

I had drafted a beginning-to-end version of my memoir and a friend, Dennis Held, who was teaching creative writing in Idaho, had done a first edit, but I had kept doing research and writing and I felt I needed more feedback. That's when I began my degree program in creative writing at the University of Nebraska–Kearney.

The response has been wonderful. Not only was I able to work on several chapters in classes, I was also able to read them to small groups of classmates during out-of-class sessions. I got ideas from other students and, of course, through our class readings. Every course made me a better reader-who-writes, in that I notice how writers accomplish their ends. Often that amounts only to noticing something I like about a story or a book and then going back after I have finished reading to look again. For example, I loved the way Stephen King built the relationship between Jake and Sadie in *11/22/63* around dance. But I am a sucker for a story and I can't stop until I know what happens. So I have taught myself to read and read and read and then go back and look at the mechanics.

When I started this project, I did not expect to understand my parents better. My dad had been dead for a very long time and my mom had refused to answer a lot of my questions. Then she had Alzheimer's. I have been amazed at how much I have learned, particularly at how significant the tiniest hint could be. One hint that didn't register at the time it appeared, has grown huge since. Grandma was talking about my mom's first pregnancy. She told me the doctor recognized that my mom was too small to give birth and that she would need a caesarian section. Then she said, "She took a lot of treatments. She told me they took a thing with a whole lot of towels and things and went in there and tried to stretch her," and Grandma went on without pause to talk about the car that burned up. I missed it, even when I transcribed it. What the doctor had done to my mother soaked in over a period of a decade, a bit at a time, until the enormity of those "treatments" became real when I described them to my friend B. J. Wheeler. Without an instant's thought, B.J. said, "In other words, he raped her."

For now, in this thesis manuscript, the story is merely a sample of my mother's stoicism. I will be writing a lot about it in the future, though. From her, I learned to ignore pain in the hope that it will go away.

In conclusion, I have done an excruciating amount of research and taken almost a decade and a half to write these stories. I have attempted to collapse time and space in stories from diverse times and locations. I have described times and places that were more gentle and more genial to families and communities than most of the places we inhabit now. In so doing, I hope I have provided hints about how to reconstitute our communities.

I have been thinking for a very long time about the tree that falls in the forest when there is no one there to hear its final squeal. Like the soundless tree, a story that is never told goes unheard. So eventually a writer has to stop writing and allow readers to judge whether or not she has accomplished her goals. I have many more stories to tell, but I'll have to save them for the next volume.

TABLE OF CONTENTS

DRAMATIS PERSONAE

You don't need to know these names right at first and trying to remember them is not good for you. So just go on with your reading and they'll make sense to you later.

Hazel Izetta Colburn, the storyteller and matriarch. In her late nineties at the time of the interviews.

David Erin Klein, her great-grandson. His accident and Hazel's stories served as the impetus for the memoir.

Joseph Ulrich Swope, Hazel's grandfather, six generations removed, followed the frontier west of the Allegheny Mountains. Persisted on the frontier after Shawnee raids drove most settlers east of the mountains.

Joseph Ulrich Swope, Jr., Hazel's uncle, five generations removed, kidnapped by Shawnee during the French and Indian War. Lived with Indians for nine years.

Hokolesqua, called Cornstalk by the Whites, Joseph's captor and adopted brother. Chief leader of all Shawnee villages. Assassinated by Whites while imprisoned at Fort Randolph.

Sicily Hendricks, Hazel's great-grandmother, a midwife and folk healer. Sicily and her husband, Hiram, settled in the Nebraska Territory with nine of their children as soon as it opened for settlement.

Philip Thomas Hunt, a Canadian who settled in Otoe County and befriended Hazel's father, as well as her grandparents, Thomas Jefferson Smith and Catharine Hendricks Smith, Sicily's daughter.

Thomas Jefferson Smythe, a Scotsman who came to the United States with his wife and children and settled in Otoe County. He Americanized his name to Smith.

Elsie Robeson Smythe, Thomas Jefferson's wife. Divorced by husband after arriving in Nebraska. She succumbed to some kind of old age dementia, but not before she burned down the house Thomas and his second wife occupied.

T.J. Smith (Thomas Jefferson, Jr.), Hazel's grandfather and Philip Hunt's neighbor. Arrived in the U.S. in time to serve in the Civil War, married Hendricks daugher.

Catharine Smith, Hendricks daughter, Hazel's grandmother. The last generation to serve as midwife (assisting M.D.)

William James Carpenter, Hazel's father who migrated from Ohio in the early 1890s. Married T.J. and Catharine's daughter. Lived with Philip Hunt until after the birth of his fourth child.

Frank Aurilla Smith Carpenter, T.J. and Catharine's daughter. Married William J. Carpenter. Lived with Philip Hunt.

George Albert Colburn, Hazel's husband. Arrived in Nebraska in 1912 during a blizzard and a prison break at the state pen.

Johnny Bivens, Hazel's great-uncle. Travelled with George the winter they arrived in Nebraska to visit Johnny's sister, Sarah Ann Bivens Carpenter, Hazel's grandmother.

William and Sarah Ann Bivens Carpenter, Hazel's grandparents on her father's side. William and Sarah moved to Nebraska after their son, William James settled there.

Eva May Colburn, George's sister who emigrated to Nebraska after her brother settled there. Lived with George and Hazel briefly after their marriage.

William Merle Colburn, Hazel's father-in-law, Eva May's father. Family has very different memories of him.

Sarah Jane Green, Hazel's mother-in-law, George's and Eva May's mother.

Doc Hostetter, delivered two generations of Hendricks/Carpenter/Smith children. Took over Sicily Hendrick's practice.

Frank Arterburn, Hazel's and George's neighbor after they moved to Webster County, Nebraska.

Carl and Edna Marie Carpenter Meents, Lawrence Finley and Emily Reeve Carpenter, Hank Meents, Hazel's siblings, their spouses and a brother-in-law. Traveled with Hazel and George to California in 1928.

Ollie and Ella Lease, Hazel's aunt and uncle who took care of the farm so Hazel and George could travel.

Cecil William Colburn, Hazel's and George's son. Served in New Guinea during World War II. Married Ella Mae (Bobbi) Bowen and Margo Goodman.

Ella Mae (Bobbi) Bowen, grew up in Akron and Cleveland determined to marry money. Married a Nebraska farmer instead and spent the rest of her life trying to adjust.

Paul David and May Ford Bowen, Bobbi's mother and father. Divorced when Bobbi quite young.

Faith Ann Colburn, Hazel's granddaughter; Ella Mae and Cecil's daughter. First person narrator of memoir.

Jo Ann Colburn Klein, Hazel's granddaughter; Ella Mae and Cecil's daughter.

Nina Marie Colburn, Hazel's and George's daughter, never married. Served various family members during birth, deaths and illnesses. Intensely centered on family.

Margo Goodman, Cecil's second wife, crowded out by the first.

Linda Murphy, Hazel's granddaughter; Cecil and Margo's daughter. Visited sisters once.

Jenifer Dawn Klein, Hazel's great-granddaughter; Ken and Jo Ann Colburn Klein's daughter.

Ella May Shank Ford, Ella Mae's grandmother, suffered with paranoid schizophrenia, probably the source of much chaos in succeeding generations.

Mildred Ford, the real girl in the madhouse.

. . . the emigrants . . .were talking about one particular elephant, the Elephant, an imaginary beast of fearsome dimensions . . . . It was the poetic imagery of all the deadly perils that threatened a westering emigrant . . . . Of turnarounds it was said . . . that "they had seen enough of the elephant."xiii -- Merrill J. Mattes

Running in Place

By the time Dad picked up the turtle, my mother had deserted him and Margo, carrying his second child in her belly, had asked him to take her back to Tennessee. Right then, it was just my father and the turtle, trying to make sense of the alien worlds they'd somehow wandered into. The turtle in the bathtub was very much a product of my father's world view and a symptom of the chasm between his and my mother's. During their six-week courtship, my parents hadn't even peered over the edge of the gulf. Only when she settled into the little cottage at the base of a tall hill in a howling prairie wilderness, where she "died a thousand deaths of loneliness," did my mother realize she might be lost.

It's hard to think of the divide where I grew up as a watershed. The creeks are dry most of the year, rainfall is undependable at best, and folks in one river system are always trying to steal water from another.

People have lived in this country since prehistoric times, between drought cycles. The site of a Pawnee village that far outdates White documentation lies unexcavated beneath hundreds of years' dust devoid of pollen near the Little Blue

River. The remains of a large Pawnee village are buried under generations of wind-blown dust on a hillside sweeping down to the Republican.[xiv]

Even now, my imagination wanders to the ruins of old farm houses smelling of wet plaster and wallpaper glue, such as Aunt Edna's and Uncle Carl's crumble-down place that I haunted when I was a kid. As an adult, I've looked into the bewildered faces of men and women torn from the land during my generation's farm crisis in the 1980s. I've seen them trying to imagine their lives, watched them struggle to conceive of living without their hands and their minds in the soil.

I think it's my father's DNA that makes me look at the land-forms and imagine the prairie without houses and trees, without fences and fields. In my mind's eye, I see it covered only with rippling grasses that run before the wind. I hear it in swishing, whistling silence that feels like standing in the warm breath of God—or like having your breath torn from your lungs. I try to visualize the free people that lived in this cradle of land before my white ancestors arrived. I think about how the wind that sometimes drove white women crazy might have affected them.

Thinking about prairie wind reminds me of my first writing assignment for NEBRASKAland magazine back in the 1970s and my first argument with my editor. I began a story about the Nebraska Territory with the land.

"Too passive," said Fred. He wanted cavalry and Indians in the lead.

"But they weren't there," I said. "The pioneers died mostly of accidental gunshot wounds and diseases like cholera."

"Not interesting," Fred said.

For Fred, the prairie was a mere stage for the larger-than-life deeds of brave men in blue. It's only been during the last few years that I realized why I insisted on pulling my by-line from my first professional feature story. For me, the prairie is active. It is the lead actor in an endless drama. People are the supporting actors. I've stood on the front doorstep and watched a tornado form in boiling clouds of deep purple, green and blue-black. I've seen a little tongue lick out of those clouds and the twisted sheets of steel that used to be my neighbor's grain bin, strewn up the ravine for a mile from his farmstead.

When I'm quiet, I hear insect songs in my head. My friend tells me its tinnitus, but I think it's a summer hayfield where grasshoppers fiddle sweet, sad songs. I can remember drifting off to sleep in my father's old bedroom at Grandma's house with the wind singing in the screens. This place is as alive to me as our neighbor, Otto Miller, with his tub of iris bulbs that he gave to Grandma so his divorced wife couldn't have them.[xv] Cattle graze Fred Sundermeier's old place and on quiet evenings, the windmill screams dry bearings. I've been exiled from where I grew up. I can't make a living there. But my imagination soars like a mouse-hunting falcon following the creases of dry creeks.

I grew up here. It's my home and I won't apologize for it. Though I recognize the occasional danger, I'm excited by the prairie's tantrums. But my mother, a strong, brave woman, cut and ran. She said she couldn't even recognize herself here.

More than a century ago, my father's people crossed the prairie afoot or ahorseback at six miles per hour or less. They saw its breath in the bending, shimmering oceans of grass. They heard the insects, smelled the rains, felt the blast furnace of summer winds and tasted the dust. Unlike some of the people headed for Oregon who "seen the elephant," and turned around when the dust, wind, storms, runaway animals, and simple fatigue got to be too much for them, my people headed their prairie schooner off the trails and found a place to stay. Like a lover, the prairie embraced their first breath in the morning of their lives and cradled their last in the evenings.

Generations of chasms opened and drawn shut preceded my parents' struggle to find common ground. Grandma told me about a lot of those generations. I found some of them in old county histories and archives of all sorts. In 1989, I was team-driving a semi tractor-trailer with a poet from Vermont. I remember Virginia where the first of my traceable Carpenter ancestors stepped off the boat to become George Washington's neighbor.[xvi] That was more than two-and-a-half centuries ago. Sometimes, silver mists lit by Virginia moonlight and brilliant reds, golds and greens lit by sunlight must have taken his attention from the job at hand. I remember mists and maples in Ohio, where the Shawnee took five-year-old Joey Swope in 1756, to become the foster brother of a war chief.[xvii] I imagine members of my family, years later, walking those same woods and tall-grass prairies in search of medicinal herbs they would use in their new places.

A century later, in 1856, they ferried across the Missouri at Nebraska City. They waded the Little Nemaha and settled within its curves on the south bank of the South Fork. Two generations later, in 1918, they moved on across the Big Nemaha, the Big and Little Blue rivers and settled on the divide between the Little Blue and the Republican in Webster County.

By the time Grandma Hazel came to live with my youngest son, Ben, and me, we had sorted and identified all the photos and recorded all the stories she could remember in a kind of extended seánce. She was one hundred years old. I'd pestered her, not only for all the stories about the old days, but also for some kind of perspective on those chaotic months or years when my dad and mom struggled to be together—or apart. I've never been quite satisfied with her answers, when she gave any. I grilled my mother and my Aunt Nina, too, and they both tried to give me some kind of answers. When I met Margo for the second time in 1988, she gave me another unsettling perspective. My dad had died before I could ask for his side of the story, but Margo allowed him to speak for himself by sharing many of the letters with which he'd courted her. She'd kept them for forty years.

4

Grandma had moved in with us when she left the hospital following an attack of congestive heart failure. She'd awakened struggling to breathe, used her Life Alert necklace to summon a neighbor who called the ambulance for her. For more than a decade, she'd lived alone in a little yellow house near the Methodist Church in Blue Hill. Before that, she'd lived at the home place tending to her daughter, my Aunt Nina, who had Lou Gehrig's disease. Grandpa was long since dead then and Grandma was well into her eighties and wearing out.

Sometime during her ninety-ninth year, Grandma had had a car accident. Her doctor wasn't sure whether the accident caused her stroke or the stroke caused her accident, but her strength never really returned. She'd begun feeling off balance when she walked. She hated that walker, but it had kept her motoring. Once we'd added saddle bags so she could carry things, she was better able to accept it.

She'd given up her driver's license on her own and rode the Handi-bus to the nursing home, another inconvenience that tried her patience because it wasn't always available. The night she couldn't breathe, I think she "saw the elephant" because she never stopped fearing that she would smother. She couldn't sleep with the bedroom door closed. When it was open, my study light kept her awake. She wanted to sleep with the window open, although temperatures were dipping below zero at night.

I tend to look for scientific explanations of supernatural things, but I'd read something about entangled particles by then and my world view had begun to change. If a particle light years away from another particle that's entangled with it "knew" to change orientation the instant its partner changed, anything seemed possible.[xviii] Mostly I remain a skeptic, but I still can't deny the overwhelming sense I had of my grandfather's presence hovering in my living room those nights when Grandma couldn't sleep. I remembered an essay by Loren Eiseley called "The Bird and the Machine." He wrote that he'd captured a little falcon for a zoo. The falcon's mate had escaped and he thought she was long gone. In the morning, he took the little hawk out of the box where he'd imprisoned it.

"I saw him look that last look away beyond me into a sky so full of light that I could not follow his gaze," Eiseley wrote.

Without any real intention, he laid the hawk on the grass. The bird didn't move for a second or two, then, without seeming to move, he was gone into the sun where Eiseley couldn't see him. But from somewhere in that sunlight, a cry of "unutterable and ecstatic joy" came ringing down.

"Straight out of the sun's eye, where she must have been soaring restlessly above us for untold hours, hurtled his mate . . . . I saw them both now. He was rising fast to meet her. They met in a great soaring gyre that turned into a whirling circle and a dance of wings."[xix]

By the time she moved in with me, Grandma Hazel was all "played out," but not done struggling, and my sense of my grandfather, dead more than forty years by then, was one of hovering in hope and despair, like the falcon. He seemed full of deep sorrow that he couldn't be there to help Grandma along, as she'd cared for him in his last days at home.

Grandma and I hadn't visited his grave that year as we'd always done in the past. Like elephants, my grandma, my son, and I visited our family bones. Unlike elephants, we can't handle the bones, so we placed vases of peonies. And, with our fingers, we read the stones, as if we were blind, touching the names etched there—Cecil, George, Sarah, William, Hiram, Jasper, Olive, Mae. We even visited Doc Hostetter, who'd delivered three generations with Sicily's help.

Once when I was little, in a quiet little corner near Great-grandma Sarah and Great-grandpa Will, Grandma pointed out a tiny, unfinished, stone—red granite, I think. It was Dan Erven's arm. Dan lost it in a corn picker accident, she said.

6

That arm always excited my imagination. I wondered if Dan's family helped him bury his arm. How did he come to have it? Did the doctor hand it to him after he sawed it off? Did he have to ask for it? Did he bury it himself as part of learning to cope with the missing part of himself? I even tried to visualize how he could hold the spade, one-handed, and leverage dirt out of his arm's grave. It was my first introduction to the concept of living after losing a big piece of yourself.

Grandma and I both thought of Dan's arm when my nephew, David, lost his leg. David's resemblance to my father is striking. Dad had played center on his high school's state championship basketball team in 1933. David was sixteen, sixty years later, playing varsity basketball as a sophomore for the same high school and being scouted by a major land-grant university, when he had his accident. We found ourselves wincing as he limped, remembering all the fluid elegance of his body running down the court. I've often thought, since then, of the contrast between the cold green lights of the operating theater where they took his leg, labeled it hazardous waste, and disposed of it, and the warm glow of candlelight in my great-great-great grandmother's birthing rooms.

David's recovered as much of his life as possible now, I think. Grandma didn't live to see him pick up the threads and march forward. But he comes from tough stock, she said. She described pathfinders and explorers, men and women who opened the frontiers and filled in the maps. One generation would gobble up a few hundred miles of prairie and stay for a while. Then the next generation would gobble up a few hundred more. I'm sure Grandma had some awareness of the massive theft and genocide that took place those years, but not necessarily of how I would be a receiver of stolen property when I inherited the home place from her. Somehow, we seldom talked about that, or about the generations of relationships, both peaceful and violent, between my ancestors and the Indians.

Her mother talked about baking bread when she was a girl. She'd feel like she was being watched, then look up and see Indians peering in the windows. Grandma Frank said they always gave bread to the wandering remnants of the tribes. Grandma Hazel remembered that, when she was a girl, her dad always allowed wandering Indians to take as much of his sweet corn as they wished. That's all I learned from Grandma. She could talk about seven generations in vivid detail with some cloudy, painful spots. When it came to the generations before Nebraska, I was on my own. The rest of what I know came to me from books, archives, and Aunt Nina's notes.

I've thought a lot about the scattered people and my grandparents who recognized them as suffering human beings. I wonder how their grandparents justified the theft that led to that suffering. I've come to cherish the prairies where I grew up and I think maybe that helps me to understand how the First People must have felt about those same hills and winds and wildflowers.

As Grandma told me about the folks I never met, she ignited my imagination. Day after day, she would collapse time and space for me, speaking in the same tense and the same breath of people long dead or far away and those right in front of her. She always knew the difference, but it didn't matter. We were all equally immediate to her. I could almost hear the voices. Sometimes they would whisper like the shuffle of bare feet crossing the kitchen in nighttime silence when the cows have their calves and the womenfolk peer at dark skies, looking for funnels. Sometimes they'd mumble like my grandma's Uncle Jasper whose lower jaw was shattered and part of his tongue blown away by a rebel miniball.

I could almost see her Aunt Ada tearing across the prairie ahorseback, skirts flying over the animal's rump, trying to end yet another pregnancy. Grandma said Ada never rode a horse unless she was pregnant, and it never worked. But who could blame her? She had a bunch of kids— Gaylen, Alva, Merle, Darrel, Vera, Berdean, and Juanita—and no apparent aptitude for discipline. The kids ran wild and Ada had no control. That lack of control resulted a little bit of frontier justice that caused a fight between Hazel's mother, Frank, and her sister-in-law.

"Uncle George lived right down the hill from us," she said. "The boys were climbing the windmill. Mom told them to get down out of there and just about that time Gaylen ran by behind my mom and hit her on the butt.

"Her left hand just came around like that and hit him before she even thought. She knocked him down. They wouldn't speak to us for a month. I'll bet he remembered that, though. It was just what he needed."

Through Grandma Hazel's stories, I attended Grandma Sicily Hendricks' ninetieth birthday party in March 1902, in Uncle Wesley Hickok's maple grove near Douglas. Slender and delicate, Sicily wore widow's weeds, with a cape trimmed in tassels and lace, and a white lace bonnet. I could imagine the sun filtering through the trees, the sawhorse-and-plank tables with bright tablecloths, the dozens of children tearing through the trees in games of hide and seek.

Grandma Hazel claimed that Sicily never lost a mother during all the years she practiced midwifery as she moved over and over across the eastern half of the continent. Given the terrible risk of infection, called milk fever, hemorrhage, and carrying a baby that's simply too big to deliver, Grandma's claim seems hardly credible. One trait that's passed down through generations of my family may have made some difference, though. We really don't touch each other. Grandma Hazel told me that her mother, Frank, did not want people "slobbering over" her babies. Perhaps our reluctance to touch saved some mothers' lives. Grandma says that's the "Scotch" in us.

I visited Sicily's daughter, Catharine Smith, her legs swollen by dropsy, baking her husband's favorite sugar cookies and struggling to breathe in a room full of her husband's and son's tobacco smoke. Catharine's daughter, Great-Grandma Frank, harrowed fields with a tree limb and curled her daughter's long, blonde hair around her fingers, while her husband, Will, whistled at his work behind the draft horses. I saw Sarah Colburn, with legs galled like cottonwood trunks from too much childbearing and too many buckets of water. She baked soda biscuits for her family every morning, including mornings after giving birth.

We even visited my mother when she arrived from the nightclubs in the cities, learning how to wash on a washboard, use catalogue pages in the outhouse, and wring a chicken's neck—until Grandma had mercy on the chicken. I saw my father, back from the Pacific with his new city bride, raising hybrid tea roses and watering a weeping willow tree, a misfit on the prairie, kind of like my mother.

Those months when Grandma lived with me, Ben was barely thirteen, struggling in school and enduring abuse from his classmates. I was finishing a graduate degree and running out of money. My assistantship was about to end. Although Grandma's Social Security paid all of her expenses, I needed a job. My son desperately needed my attention. So I decided that Grandma really had to live somewhere else, a place where she would have people to take care of her while I looked for work and attended to my son's needs.

My mom, my sister, Jo Ann, and I made arrangements for her to take a room at the assisted living center in Blue Hill. Grandma had lived in Blue Hill for sixty years, we reasoned. She knew almost everyone there so she wouldn't be lonely. The assisted living folks promised a salt-free diet, so I thought she would be safe. I knew Grandma hated leaving my home and that she felt abandoned. I knew the move would be hard for her and I knew that family and community meant everything to her. But I felt I had to do this. So I did, hoping community would help take the place of family.

A month later, she was back in the hospital because her heart became too congested to pump oxygen. I learned that her salt-free diet had included green beans with bacon and Polish sausage. Once out of the hospital, she went to the local nursing home where Nina had lived for more than a decade. This was to be temporary, but she folded her hands over her chest and quit breathing very early in the morning of June 6, 1997.

We make choices in our lives that we struggle with for as long as we live. Moving Grandma killed her. Before her time? She was one hundred years, six months and twenty days old when she died. It's impossible to know how long she could have lived in my home. I chose the next generation over the previous, something I've no doubt she'd have done, too. Still, I have this little niggling doubt that haunts me. When I was a small child, living with Grandma and Grandpa, waiting for my parents to decide to be married to each other and to be parents to me, Grandma carried me over the mud puddles when it rained. I promised her then that I would carry her over the mud puddles when I got big. I've only broken two sacred oaths in my life. I still struggle with both.

Grandma herself, a day or two before the funeral, told me to let go of that. In the most vivid dream I've ever had, I met her in a parking lot somewhere. She wore her short gray coat with the big turquoise pin on the shoulder and she had no walker. Her balance was fine and she didn't look worn out. Startled to see her, I stood and let her walk toward me in her old, slightly-bowlegged gait. She touched my arm with her crooked fingers, damaged in a pump jack, and said, "You done everything you could."

Then I was awake, disoriented.

Maybe George had stopped somewhere waiting. Maybe the entangled particles of George and Hazel had met somewhere in a falcon dance. Maybe he told her that she couldn't care for Nina forever, "Hazel, you worry about things that will never be. You done what you could."

As I wrote Grandma's eulogy, I called my sons, my nephew and niece, a cousin or two, my mom and my sister. Each contributed a story, a line or two. My sister gave me Walt

Whitman from "Song of Myself." I used his lines to end my last tribute:

"I depart as air, I shake my white locks at the runaway sun,
I effuse my flesh in eddies, and drift it in icy jags.

I bequeath myself to the dirt to grow from the grass I love,
If you want me again, look for me under your boot-soles.

You will hardly know who I am or what I mean,
But I shall be good health for you nevertheless,
And filter and fibre your blood.

Failing to fetch me at first, keep encouraged,
Missing me one place, search another,
*I stop somewhere waiting for you."*xx

"Until white people realize that we have a race and a racial history, we'll never solve the racial problem of this country. It's not only a matter of dealing with facts we would like to ignore because they're uncomfortable; it's also coming to an awareness of a fact that isn't part of our consciousness."xxi -- Martha Collins

Kidnapped

"I stop somewhere waiting for you . . ."

Missing them one place, I've gone looking for my family, the ones I've known, the ones my grandma told me about and the ones neither of us ever met. I've sought connections that span generations, time and space. How did they make communities? How did they make their lives work?

I've found them, too, stopped waiting somewhere. Young Joseph stopped, waiting, in a history of Monroe County, West Virginia, though he couldn't have known his niece many generations removed, would even go looking for him. He couldn't know his story would have an impact on her life.

Caught on the hook of a dream, I do not want to wake, not until I can set the dream right. In utter blackness, I search for some sign of my vanished son. I feel the muscles in my legs gather. I will run. I will find him wherever he is. I love to run. I can run until I find him. But I don't know which direction. I don't know if he's wandered off or if someone has taken him. I come fully awake and feel my way into his bedroom, leaning over him in the dark to feel his breath on my cheek.

"What's the matter, Mom?"

"I just came in to see if you're all right."

"I'm all right, Mom."

"I know. Go back to sleep,"

When my youngest son, Ben, was small, I saw ads about missing children on milk cartons and on the sides of big trucks. Mostly I noticed and forgot them, but an item in USA Today about a six-year-old boy kidnapped, raped, smothered with a pillow and thrown into a dumpster, grabbed me somehow. Usually I defend myself against kidnap stories because they don't happen here. They don't happen to people like me, like my children. But that particular little boy somehow left me defenseless. I saw his big, surprised eyes. I saw his silent tears, heard his muffled cries and smelled his limp, gray body.

I think that's where the nightmares started, with a newspaper item that was too real.

Those years, I often sought diversion, if not comfort, in Grandma Hazel's stories. In her memories I discovered that people I never knew endured many of the traumas I only imagined and I was embarrassed by the intensity of the nightmares that woke me night after night. Digging back into the generations Grandma never knew, I've found hints of myself. Sometimes those hints have more resembled revelations, a kind of déjà vu moment.

Anna Swope's nightmares must have begun when she learned about the defeat of Braddock's Army in July, 1755, at the beginning of the French and Indian War.[xxii] The Swopes didn't see any milk cartons or fliers tacked on telephone poles, but they would have heard about the storm of raids led by the Shawnee, Hokolesqua, that followed. She heard stories of husbands and children tomahawked before their wives' and mothers' eyes, a baby smashed to death against a tree.[xxiii] Those were the kinds of stories Joseph's mother knew. No one told the stories of white raids against the Indians.

Although Draper's Meadows was a couple of days away, farther back in the mountains, the Swopes would have heard about the raid there a less than a month after Braddock's defeat. On July 30, 1755, Shawnee raiders had captured four-year-old Thomas Ingles, his two-year-old brother, George, his mother and several other white settlers. Five people had died, including Tommy's grandmother and his infant cousin. The Ingles cabin had burned.[xxiv]

On August 12, thirteen settlers had died at Henry Baughman's Fort on the south bank of the Greenbriar, just a few miles from the mouth of Wolf Creek[xxv] and only a couple of hours' walk from the Swope cabin. They'd have seen the smoke from the burning fort.

Those facts were undoubtedly embellished with blood and flames and shrieks. The terror of my nightmares seems well ordered and sane in comparison with my images of the Ingles cabin and the inside of Baughman's Fort. Like Anna, I imagine what I don't see. I imagine the pandemonium of men's bodies, thrown against each other with clubs and tomahawks, swords and rifle butts, in a confusion of limbs that's impossible to sort out from the shouts and grunts and the screams of women and children unable to escape.

The raids into Greenbriar were thorough. The settlements were wiped out and the survivors moved back to the east side of the Allegheny Mountains.[xxvi] Some of the settlers, however, did not leave the colony. "The pioneers were willfully careless. While serving as militia they could not be counted upon to obey their officers or serve out their terms. They disliked to be cooped up in the stockades . . . they took imprudent risks . . ."[xxvii] Oren Morton wrote in The Annals of Bath County.

15

I wasn't there during the French and Indian War, so I can't imagine why Joseph's father remained on the deserted frontier, more vulnerable than ever. Maybe he thought the Indians would never notice one family, all alone on Wolf Creek. Maybe he thought he could outsmart them, as he had when he'd staked his claim. Maybe he was just a risk taker; the settlers almost had to be. Anna may not have shared his optimism, but she and her sons were trapped because, back then, the husband truly ruled the roost and roost he did.

Anna's nightmares came true when her son, little Joey Swope, was just five years old. In fall, 1756, a small band of Shawnee swept out of the forest and grabbed him.[xxviii] His capture is more than two centuries and a half a continent away, yet it's as immediate to me as the news. Sometimes I imagine that little boy's terror as he's carried off into deep woods, far from his family.

When I think of that child, my granduncle generations removed, I remember a morning with Ben. He was in the garden with me when a robin landed a few feet away, pecking and scratching in the overturned soil. Ben began walking toward the bird. He would walk a few steps and the bird would hop away. They kept to this game for several minutes, with Ben stepping and the robin hopping.

What if someone had slipped around the corner of the house when my back was turned? It would be easy to take a child. He might even stand and stare, round-eyed, wondering who the strangers might be. That's how I imagine Joseph in the moments before his capture, focused on a bird when the Indians broke out of the trees. He might have been fascinated by the raiding party, men who looked very different from his father. He might have stopped and stared. And then, it was too late to run.

I wasn't with Joey when the Shawnee picked him up and carried him off, but I've read many accounts of Shawnee raids and captives' years among the Indians, including anecdotes from Joseph's own life. From those stories, I've woven a fabric of survival and of a very personal clash of cultures in war and peace. That history, a combination of myth and truth, helps me to deal with my fear of the sudden, senseless traumas that circumscribe our lives.

I imagine that, when Hokolesqua's band raided the Wolfcreek settlement, Anna scooped up her three-year-old son, Michael, and ran for the cabin. Somehow, they escaped. Perhaps she cowered in the cabin while her husband chased the raiding party away. Maybe she hid in the woods, covering her baby's nose and mouth with her hand to keep him silent. Joey never saw what happened to them. The raiders snatched him up and swung him onto a horse in front of one of the riders and took off whooping. Within seconds, he was deep in the woods, moving fast, too terrified to think, maybe screaming for his mother.

That fall, the Shawnee took at least thirty captives from the Jackson River settlements, northeast of Wolfcreek back in the mountains, including five members of the John Byrd family and twenty-two of their neighbors. Many others died in those raids.[xxix] As they swung south and then west, Hokolesqua's band joined up with the New River, maybe spreading out along the Greenbriar and Wolf Creek to hunt. By then, they were several days away from the settlements. They probably didn't expect to find any whites on Wolf Creek, but when they saw Joey, they grabbed him. Maybe they thought taking him would discourage any whites who might intend to stay. Maybe they wanted to adopt a little boy to fill the place of someone who had died.

The Indians fled down Wolf Creek to the Greenbriar River and then joined up with the path they had taken the previous year. They followed a short distance along the New to the head of the gorge where boulders tumbled down the banks of the river, blocking passage. Here they followed a faint trail, leaving the river and climbing the cliffs where the forest opened up into thickets of shrubby mountain laurel. From their vantage point

17

at the top of the ridge, they could see any pursuing party. It was a good place to stop for the night. Game was available and both captors and captives had travelled hard all day without food. A year before, they had camped by a little brook where the advanced guard had brought down a woods buffalo and had it skinned by the time the rest of the party arrived. Then, they had been traveling fast for two days and thought they were far enough ahead to take time to hunt.[xxx] When they took Joey, they were several days' ride from Jackson River and Joseph's father didn't pose any threat. They had plenty of time.

Life on the frontier bred a certain stoicism that extended even to the children. I've witnessed that stoicism in my grandmother with awe. Joey may have survived simply as a young heir to that silent endurance. It may have literally saved his life. His captors couldn't tolerate a whining, crying child during the long march of more than two hundred miles.

Riding single file, they moved through the woods along the rivers, traveling up the New to the Kenawha and up the Kenawha to the Ohio. It took the Ingles party a month to get that far, with time for hunting and a stop to make salt at one of the natural salt springs along their route.[xxxi] The Indians took Joey in the fall, though, and they didn't have as much time to mosey on home.

Joey was an early victim of European immigrants' centuries of land theft. When he founded Wolfcreek, Joey's father, Joseph Ulrich Swope, must have realized the border territory was someone else's home, for when he encountered a Shawnee hunting party, he didn't approach them; he hid in a hollow poplar tree until they were gone. Later, he described crawling up into that tree and listening to the Indians murmuring together and walking around the tree as they looked for him. When they finally left, still puzzling over his disappearance, he staked his tomahawk claim by ringing a tree at each corner of his land so that the tree would die, leaving a permanent mark of his territory. Then he walked back across the mountains to get his wife, Anna, and their year-old son,

Joseph, Jr.^{xxxii} If he had any qualms about the danger to which he was subjecting his family, they didn't stop him.

I don't know if my grandmother Swope crossed the mountains willingly. There were no wagon roads over the mountains then; and I wonder if they had a pack horse or a mule. Perhaps her son was able to ride on top of the packs. Perhaps Grandma Swope carried her little boy most of the way. I remember the heft of my sons at that age. I carried them at the zoo. I carried them to the garden and the grocery store. But I never carried one of them over a range of mountains or into wilderness where people driven from their homes waited in hostile silence.

They had settled at Wolfcreek about five years before the Shawnee came for Joey and Swope was still a squatter on someone else's land. That was the crux of the matter for the Shawnee. That's why they allied themselves with the French. It was the British colonists who, more often than not, treated them with contempt and who kept gobbling up land. But in 1755 and 1756, the Shawnee were taking it back and Joey was their prize, an adaptable little boy who would become one of them.

When Tommy Ingles told about his captivity, he remembered them flashing to each other over the campsite and wafting away over the river.^{xxxiii} Once the initial shock of captivity had worn off, Joey may also have had time to get caught up in the wonder of those luminescent insects. I'm reminded of my own childhood, two hundred years later and half a continent west, chasing fireflies with my little sister while our parents tried to close the gap in their separate world views, views that were not nearly as divergent as those of White captives and their captors. Their differences had more to do with living in city and country cultures and their respective traumas came from different sources, though they had a lot in common.

Gradually Joey adjusted to his nights in captivity. He had plenty of distractions, a scurrying chipmunk to watch or a squirrel scrambling around a tree to keep the trunk between itself and the riders. He might distract himself in the evening, as he drifted off to sleep, by listening to the familiar hoot of an owl, or the drawn-out howl of a wolf in the distance. As the weather cooled, massive flocks of passenger pigeons darkened the skies for hours.

When they reached the Ohio, he could watch the fascinating work of making a raft like they did when the Ingles party crossed. The Shawnee gathered driftwood logs from piles along the river, lay them side by side, and wove them together with vines they gathered from the woods. They split driftwood poles to make paddles. Then they loaded all the gear the horses had been carrying onto the raft, along with Joey and any other whites still with that raiding party. As the white men poled and paddled the raft, the Shawnee swam the horses across.[xxxiv] Joey was already learning the ways of his captors.

As he adjusted to the Shawnee during those first days and weeks, his mother had to make her own adjustments. I can imagine her hanging onto a dream after her son disappeared, refusing to wake until she changes the end, trying to will her child safe. Maybe she'd intentionally hang somewhere between waking and sleeping. She might replay the raid, thinking faster, running swifter, rescuing him this time. But she would always find him gone. At first, she may have jumped out of bed to check; to make sure she hadn't dreamed the raid. But soon, she would know. The minute she awoke, she would know. She had no television or radio where she could make appeals to her son's kidnappers. There were no letters home like those my Grandmother Hazel received when my father was fighting in World War II. No letters, no word, only worry.

As a mother, I've imagined Anna Swope coping with the loss of her first-born son and I'm reminded of my recurring dream. My own son kidnapped from the men's room of an Interstate rest area as he proudly goes in alone for the first time. I would wake with a start and go into my son's room to check on him before returning to bed, semi-conscious, to somehow catch up to my nightmare kidnappers before they escaped with my child. But Grandma Swope had no way to know that her son was still alive, except perhaps an occasional rumor about a little boy glimpsed among the Shawnee.

Meanwhile, her little boy crossed the Ohio River and entered a deep forest where oaks, hickories, birches and tulip trees crossed overhead to form a dark ceiling. In just a few days, the captives reached the Big Scioto River, site of the main Shawnee Village. By then, Joey had become relatively comfortable with the Shawnee. They had taken good care of him, shared whatever food and water they had and made sure he hd a blanket to curl up in at night.

In the village, Joey began his transformation into a Shawnee. After a ritual scrubbing in the river and a change to the skin clothing of his new family,[xxxv] he became the adopted brother of Hokolesqua, great grandson of Thomas Pasmere Pasmore Carpenter.[xxxvi] His adopted mother would later save his life.

As he grew up, Joey played with the Shawnee kids, planted corn and beans with his new mother and learned to hunt and fish from his new father, Akulusska, and his brothers, Hokolesqua and Silverheels. When the Shawnee had their councils, he's have found himself among Hokolesqua's several wives, including two Shawnee women, an adopted mulatto woman and later, Catherine Vanderpoole See, along with their many children.[xxxvii]

He may have had to fight his way to acceptance, and another kid's prank, along with his own response, nearly cost him his life. He'd been with the Indians for years when a larger, stronger Shawnee boy scented him with skunk musk, as a practical joke. Joseph responded with his own joke. He put several grains of gunpowder into the kindling the other boy was blowing into a flame. He probably expected to singe the Shawnee's eyebrows and maybe his forelock. Instead, he blinded the other boy. The Shawnee Nation went into council and sentenced Joseph to death. That's when his foster mother stepped in and saved his life. She told the tribal leaders that they were only teaching intolerance—and she took him back to her lodge.[xxxviii]

21

During those hours and days when Joey was on trial for his life, Joey may have tugged on his connection with his birth mother like my mother connected with hers in crisis. When my father died, my mom had not seen or heard from her mother for ten years. But Grandma May called the day after Dad's death.

"Ella Mae, what's wrong?" she asked without preamble.

Maybe Anna drifted from one task to another the day of Joey's trial, unable to settle down, like my mother did the day of my sister's accident. I wonder if I will be able to sense trouble if one of my sons is in mortal danger.

At the end of the French and Indian War, the sides exchanged prisoners, whether the prisoners wanted to be exchanged or not.[xxxix] They had to tie John McCullough's feet under his horse and his arms behind his back to drag him home.[xl] He loved his adopted Indian family and he didn't want to leave them. That was not unusual and I wonder if they had to restrain Joseph, in order to take him back to his mother. Like McCullough, he was fourteen when they brought him back.

Baffled white leaders tried to understand why the captives refused to return to their families. Over and over they compared Indian captives among the white and white captives among the Indians. Even Ben Franklin expressed his concern about whites' refusal to leave their Indian friends and families.

"When an Indian Child has been brought up among us, taught our language and habituated to our Customs, yet if he goes to see his relations and makes one Indian Ramble with them, there is no perswading him ever to return,"[xli] he wrote.

"No Arguments, no Intreaties, nor Tears of their Friends and Relations could persuade many of them to leave their new Indian Friends and Acquaintances; several of them that were by the Caressings of their Relations persuaded to come Home, in a little Time grew tired of our Manner of living, and run

22

away again to the Indians . . ."[xlii] wrote Cadwallader Colden in 1747 as he noted, like Franklin, that white captives prefer to remain with their captors.

Joseph had lived with the Shawnee in a large, extended family that gave him complete acceptance. He'd grown up among them. So Anna did not get her little boy back. It had been nine years. Little Joey was a young man—a young Indian man, a stranger who disappeared at times, who always seemed a little wild, a little unsettled and a little unsettling.

The History of Monroe County describes Joseph's father as a man embittered by the capture of his son. Apparently, he never passed up an opportunity to harass any Indians he could find or to secure a scalp. He died of injuries sustained when he fell from a horse, apparently while his son remained with the Shawnee, so the two never had to reconcile their views of the Indians and that's probably fortunate for both.[xliii]

No one has written about how difficult it must have been for Joseph to live between two warring peoples. One history indicated that he was given to moody silences and to wandering off. Another history, though, says he learned to read and write and that he prospered despite those difficulties, marrying a fiery Irishwoman, Catherine Sullivan, and fathering nine children.[xliv]

Catherine turned out to be a good match for her husband. She was unruffled when six Shawnee braves arrived at her home and ate everything in sight, then immediately brought her a freshly-killed buck to restore her larder. She's said to have taken the rifle and the dog and wandered off to hunt in the middle of the night by herself on occasion.[xlv]

Catherine Sullivan Swope was a midwife and folk doctor, maybe the first in a long line that reaches forward to my great-great grandmother, Catherine Hendricks Smith. One of her neighbors, later, told about running to her for help. When he got to the cabin, she called out a "dashing, dangerous-looking stallion." She used a man's saddle, mounted astride and galloped up hills and down hollows to get to her patient. He said she was nearly sixty years old at the time.[xlvi]

Perhaps she took the opportunity of close proximity to learn alternative healing arts from her husband's Shawnee friends and family. Perhaps her sister-in-law, Mary Eleanor Ellison Swope, Michael's wife, learned from her and passed that knowledge down. Most of those cures disappeared when doctors took over medical practice, but we know that Native Americans all across the North American continent would steep bee balm to make a tea that soothed coughs and sore throats and comforted nausea. They also knew that birch tea relieved headaches. Blue cohosh must have been especially useful to Catherine in her midwifery.[xlvii] It has been used for uterine cramps and delayed menses. In addition, there's a salve my great-great-grandmother made with beeswax and other mysterious ingredients. It healed a burn Doc Hostetter had been treating unsuccessfully for months.

The peace sputtered along with whites continuing to squat on Indian land, killing any native people they encountered. Early in 1774, an unprovoked attack on a peaceful band of the Leni Lenape set the frontier ablaze. The Whites summoned Hokolesqua to Fort Pitt for peace talks. Eager to prevent mass hysteria, Hokolesqua complied. But, as he and his delegation, including his sister, Nonhelema, who was as tall as Hokolesqua at six foot six and his brother Silverheels, approached the fort, a mob of settlers attacked the seven Shawnee. Although the White chief stopped the attack almost immediately, Silverheels was badly injured, with one knife wound in the shoulder and another deep in his chest.[xlviii]

And the wars went on despite the natives' attempts to keep the peace. By spring, 1774, attacks and counter-attacks were constant. Although Hokolesqua urged peace, a Pennsylvania militia attack destroying seven Mingo villages inflamed the frontier. Lord Dunmore sent one thousand soldiers deep into Shawnee territory to establish a fort at Point Pleasant, the confluence of the Ohio and Kenawha rivers. Joseph Swope's brothers, George and John, marched with Dunmore's force, led by Colonel Andrew Lewis.[xlix] Hokolesqua, against his better judgment, met Lewis at Point Pleasant. In a battle lasting nearly all day, Hokolesqua and Colonel Lewis conducted a seesaw action between the rivers until Hokolesqua received intelligence that five hundred military reinforcements were on the way.

The Indians made a careful, gradual withdrawal, floating their dead, including Hokolesqua's friend and war chief, Pucksinwah, across the river in the canoes they'd floated into battle. In a few days, the Shawnee agreed to the previous Treaty of Fort Stanwix.[l]

Joseph's mother-by-choice, though she saved Joseph's life, could not hold her own son-by-blood, or her grandson, safe. Years had passed since Joseph's return to his White family. Hokolesqua had kept the peace since the treaty. The tall, commanding Shawnee had led his people away from war with the whites whenever he could. I've found no hint that Joseph ever took part in scouting or warring against the Indians, but his brother, Michael, served as an Indian scout during the Revolutionary War, in addition to fighting with Lewis at Point Pleasant. Perhaps the qualities he'd seen in his adopted brother gave him hope that the whites could behave like civilized human beings, but the expansion war between whites and natives was just beginning. In 1777, Hokolesqua returned some horses stolen from the settlers. Later he visited Fort Randolph, at the Point Pleasant Battle site, with his son, Elinipsico, his sub-chief, Red Hawk, and another brave. For Hokolesqua, it was a matter of honor to warn the Whites that he could no longer keep his word to hold his young men in check. Again, peace was possible, but Captain Arbuckle returned the favor by imprisoning the Shawnee.[li]

Then, while Hokolesqua was still in the stockade, other Shawnee warriors killed a settler named Gilmer during a raid. Gilmer's companions knew immediately where to find some

Indians. They rushed to the fort and shot down all four captive, unarmed Shawnee, without apparent intervention from the soldiers there. According to the Monroe County historian, White settlements around Fort Randolph "did not prosper for many years afterwards and many believed it lay under a curse."[lii]

Perhaps it was guilt that hung over the community. Perhaps the hex was Joseph's. Perhaps when he learned of his brother's murder, he called a plague on the settlement. Pasmere Carpenter Okowellos may have added her keening to the wind that swept the settlers' homes and fields with her own curse.

Weyapiersenwah, son of Pucksinwah, took leadership after the two older leaders' deaths.[liii] Twenty years after Point Pleasant, he met another member of my family in battle at Fort Recovery, Ohio. June 10, 1794, a supply column lost thirty-two killed and thirty wounded when attacked by the Shawnee. During an attack on the fort the next day, another of my grandfathers, David Thompson, carried dispatches to General "Mad" Anthony Wayne through two thousand attacking Shawnee. Reinforcements under Wayne's command drove the Shawnee away and finally defeated the Indians in the Battle of Fallen Timbers.[liv] Once again, in the Treaty of Greenville, Whites took over Indian land—most of Ohio and parts of Indiana.

The generations now occupying land taken by theft and genocide still live with the Fort Randolph hex. We still try to own land. As a receiver of stolen property, I struggle to imagine a way to repay the awful debt of my forebears and I feel that a piece of my soul remains with the Shawnee family that befriended young Joseph Swope and with both women who mothered him. Those mothers are with me in my dreams, waiting for their sons, willing them safe. They used to make me get up and look at my son in his sleep. Will they stay by my side as I struggle to find the lost part of myself?

"We abuse land because we regard it as a commodity belonging to us. When we see land as a community to which we belong, we may begin to use it with love and respect."lv -- Aldo Leopold

Sicily

I once knew a man who said, frequently, that "everything has to be somewhere." I didn't think much about it at the time, but he was right. Since we do not live in a quantum world, if we exist, we have to exist in a place. We can choose our places and change our places, but we have to be somewhere.

Like it or not, we live in relationship with a place, although most of us are probably not aware of it until our place comes to knock us about, as in a flood or tornado. Hiram and Sicily Hendricks' daily survival, however, depended upon their awareness of place. As they ferried across the Missouri River in 1854 and walked out on the Great Plains, they crossed a transition zone, the boundary between North America's eastern and western plant communities. It is a zone of enormous diversity, not only plant diversity, but also in the variety of animals that depend upon those plants. After generations of learning about the plants and animals of the eastern range, the Hendricks were about to take a baby step out of that safe zone.

In the bluffs and hills along the Missouri, Sicily encountered plants she didn't know. They might be poisonous or safe to eat. Their lives could depend upon their choice of new plants to eat and to heal. Perhaps that's why they stayed very close to the Missouri where they could find most of the plants they'd used in the past.

Sicily's had long been a restless family. When her great-great grandfather, Yost Swope, left Germany for America, he had started a chain of moving that lasted for generations. His descendants moved halfway across the continent, leaving all the places they knew, as well as the graves of their grandparents, their parents and some of their children. When Hiram and Sicily crossed the Missouri, two of their grown daughters, Mary Jane Morgan and Louisa Saunders had come too, along with their husbands, Thomas and Joseph. Hiram and Sicily, themselves, had uprooted four times, wandering westward in stages. Maybe they were searching for home, that ancestral place that was known and safe. But each successive move took them farther from the once-familiar forests and farms of Europe. So, they tried to recreate them on the North American prairies.

I try to imagine what it would be like to select any place you fancy on greening prairies, where last year's reddish-golden plumes of big bluestem, golden Indian grass, needle and thread, and switch grass grew chest high. Sometimes the way would be bald and level as a floor. Then it would dip and dive through gullies and swales. When the skies cut loose, torrents of water would pour down the hills into draws lined with tangled grasses and creeping vines.

During those first days in the new territory, amid millions of buzzing and chirping insects, waking and whispering their spring love songs in the long grass, they ambled west, looking for the perfect spot. They crossed the Little Nemaha and settled about thirty miles into Nebraska Territory on the divide between the Little and Big Nemaha Rivers. They got to know something about their new place. I wonder if they had time to really know it.

The pre-emption law of 1841 had provided for settlers to select land from the public domain for $1.25 per acre.[lvi] The

Territory's opening had made new lands available and Hiram had hurried to take advantage of the new lands. He pre-empted land and immediately set out to "tame" it, which always seemed to mean to transform it, usually without really understanding what it had been.

When my family stepped off the ferry, it must have been very like Grandma's description of it, as it was some fifty years later. Grandma described an orgy of wild things she remembered from her childhood in eastern Nebraska. Listening to her filled my head with color, colors I'd seen in bits and pieces, but in her telling I saw splashes, like a Claude Monet painting with a blue Nebraska sky as background, perhaps. Sometimes I think my search for my forebears is as much a search for that abundance of place as a search for people.

"When the wildflowers bloomed, they'd be so thick, the draws would be colored with them," Grandma said. ". . . so many violets . . . Johnny jump-ups. We had lots of wild daisies and wild asters . . . oxeye daisies . . . blanket flowers . . . butterfly milkweed—great big clumps of them. Bright red. Red-orange. We had black-eyed Susans. When the ironweed bloomed, it would . . . just purple the draws. Bushels of ironweed."[lvii]

"We had geese and ducks, all kinds of ducks," Grandma said. "Teal. We had mallards."[lviii]

Grandma's mention of waterfowl reminds me of the years I worked in the field for the Nebraska Game and Parks Commission and a spring on Harvard Marsh in particular. More than a century after Hiram's and Sicily's arrival, I saw flocks of waterfowl for the first time, before fowl cholera broke out in the Rainwater Basin, reducing e already-depleted numbers. It seemed to me then that the marsh was full of ducks, chattering and clamoring. I saw strings of pintails wavering over the muskrat domes and mallards settling in among them. By then I'd learned to identify ducks, the streamlined silhouette of pintails, the high forehead of redheads, and the big bills of shovelers. I remember the speckle-bellies, the white-fronted geese, too. I haven't seen any white-fronts or heard their squeaky gabble for decades.

The Hendricks moved onto the Great Plains amidst that abundance of clamoring waterfowl, although they had no time to just watch them as I did. At the end of each westward move, the Hendricks had had to start again with the work of building an agricultural unit with houses and cellars, barns and chicken coops. In the Nebraska Territory, with only a tent, or the wagon, for protection, they began building. During the migration seasons in spring and fall, Hiram and his sons undoubtedly shot ducks and geese for the pot. That may have been their first native provisions in the new territory as they began to set up housekeeping in yet another new home.

About forty years before the Hendricks arrived, fur traders who moved up the Missouri in 1812-1813 had killed bear, deer, turkey and rabbits to provision themselves[lix]. Probably those animals remained in the 1850s and Hiram must have killed big as well as small game to keep the family fed for the enormous task of establishing their farm. During the nights, a black bear, fresh out of hibernation might wander up the nearest creek bed. The meat wouldn't have lasted long with three working men and their wives, as well as seven children, to eat it. Bear grease would recondition harness, saddles and shoes nearly worn out during the trek west. A plains grizzly might also roam up the rivers from the west and into camp, but the Hendricks families would not celebrate its arrival. The killing power of a grizzly was awe inspiring and the Hendricks must have worried about a nighttime incursion, at least until they had a cabin where they could be secure. At night, the howl of prairie wolves reminded them that they weren't in Iowa any more where they had had the security of other settlers surrounding them and discouraging wild beasts from coming too close.

That summer, the Hendricks prepared for winter. The three families cut logs for cabins, maybe something temporary until they could properly dry logs for permanent structures. The oxen dragged them from one of the Nemahas or some nearby creek bottom because frequent prairie fires swept trees from the high ground.

Hiram's permanent cabin, built of hewn walnut logs, still stands south of Douglas, although it's been moved to higher ground, one log at a time when the local Natural Resource District built a little dam that would have flooded it. It's an amazing structure, two stories high. It appears to be two cabins joined by a breezeway.

Sicily and her daughters did their part, of course, at first living out of the wagons and tents. They kept chickens, fed stock, milked, gathered wild fruits, preserved them, and cooked. They made pots of boiled meats, greens wilted in vinegar and hot grease, bear grease, perhaps. They made and pans of biscuits slavered with fresh-churned butter and wild jellies. They fried venison steaks and maybe cured some hams. They might have made tiny gardens, but breaking up the roots of grasses that were six feet deep was daunting at best and their crop ground, even garden ground, increased in small increments.

Sicily meandered over the hills with her daughters as I have with my sons. The Hendricks women gathered food and medicinal plants. We just looked, picking an occasional asparagus stalk or a morel. Sicily may have noticed the buffalo beans and wild onions as she inventoried what the mountain men called "possibles"—those things that made it possible to live in the wilderness. The women may have gathered Jersey tea leaves or maybe young leaves of leadplant to dry for tea. As they'd ventured out on the prairie, they had left behind most of the Kentucky coffee trees, although a few of them may have followed up the Big Nemaha for a way. Settlers used the beans for coffee. Sicily had known coffee trees all her life. She knew how to use them safely, probably using the wood pulp for fevers and headaches.

Back then, they all carried stout sticks, hoes, or shovels to kill any rattlesnakes that they might surprise. They probably dug the fleshy roots of sunflower-like Jerusalem artichokes and breadroot, a wild alfalfa, to supplement the garden, especially that first year when they tore the garden plot from fierce, tough prairie grasses. Wild strawberries grew in the wooded areas and gooseberries along the creeks. That fall, Sicily

31

probably made gallons of wild plum butter and maybe some currant jelly.

Often they worked in gale force winds that took their breath away and filled their noses and mouths with dirt. They had to carry all of the water they used for cooking or washing clothes. I never got the hang of carrying water buckets, forty pounds on a side, splashing in my shoes. I never developed the neck and shoulder muscle to hold them away from my legs, so I wouldn't trip on them, but Sicily must have.

Once they'd provided shelter from the storm, the three men would have begun breaking sod. Big, muscular oxen pulled the plow, but men had to hold the plow steady in the ground. My father-in-law told me once about riding a Percheron when it was pulling a Model T out of the mud. He said he could feel the muscles swell and ripple. As the horse stretched out, George's feet nearly touched the ground. Both man and animal made that kind of effort as they broke old and tough and fibrous and deep roots. From sunup to sundown, the men had to hold the handles of the wooden moldboard plow, requiring every ounce of strength a big man could muster.

In Otoe County, rocks complicated the task of opening a furrow. During the Ice Ages many centuries before the Hendricks family arrived in Nebraska, the westernmost edge of the glaciers had scoured into Otoe County and ground to a halt. When they melted there, they dropped tons of rocks crumbled from mountains elsewhere. In those early days, Hiram might cut only a few feet before the plow slammed into a rock, tearing at tendons in neck and shoulder. He often had to stop and dig a rock from his field before going on.

Grandma remembered the rocks, even during her childhood when the fields had been cleared numerous times.

"We picked up enough rocks . . . to make a foundation for the house . . . We picked them up by the wagonloads. If you strike them with a hammer, the fire would fly," she said. "We made a cellar. The old guy that made it made an arch over the top of it. Pete Anderson was plowing with horses," she said, "and he struck a rock. It was a gangplow, they call it, with more than one blade. It was such a big rock, it throwed him off the plow. Knocked him unconscious. It had finally come up to the surface enough so it was just there. They tried to blast that rock out of there, but I don't think they ever did get it. Just farmed around it. It was just kind of offspring of some mountain somewhere."[lx]

Trees got in the way, too. Hiram and the boys would clear them, but then "suckers," new little trees that grow up from the stumps, would grow in their places, so they had to clear trees almost every year, chopping and cutting over and over. They learned that prairie fires often scoured the hills of native trees, but they feared the fires and couldn't imagine letting them burn. I used to wonder why, at the end of his fifth year in the Territory, Hiram only owned forty acres of cultivated cropland.

The oldest boys, David and George, at sixteen and twelve, would have made hay, the swishing bite of scythes punctuated by bubbling calls of a meadowlark, if the boys even heard them. Again, this was hand labor. These days, not too many people can say they've used a scythe, but I have. The hours of twisting and slicing are man killers for anyone unaccustomed to the labor and exhausting for anyone who is, but prairie grass provided winter feed for livestock, as well as currency to buy winter provisions. That first year, it was undoubtedly their only cash crop, but by the third year, they were harvesting up to seventeen tons of it. It continued to be a cash crop for generations, including my grandmother'.

"We had a big prairie," Grandma said. "I remember Dad taking a load of prairie hay to town to pay a doctor bill. At Christmas time he took a load of hay into town and he bought us all a present."[lxi]

These were no big, expensive presents, maybe an orange or a banana, fruits that wouldn't normally be available. He might buy some rock candy or some new Sunday shoes.

As spring passed into summer, the work continued and the Hendricks' high-protein diet changed. David and George varied their workdays and the family diet with a little hunting. Grandma said flocks of prairie chickens still strutted their stuff when she was a girl in southeast Nebraska.

When I worked for the Game Commission, there was an isolated little "booming grounds," in that area where prairie chicken males still danced and sang their mating song, amplified by the bright orange air sacs along their necks. When the Hendricks arrived in Nebraska, they numbered in the hundreds of thousands. I've seen photos of dead prairie chickens by the wagonload. They're not hunted like that anymore and they're making a comeback in some areas, but the only live ones I've seen have been isolated individuals, maybe reconnoitering their old territory to see if we humans have left yet.

By fall, the Hendricks, Saunders and Morgans were ready for the coming storms. They had shelter and provisions for the cold months. They had enough hunters and ammunition in their party to assure a supply of protein. In the spring, they would break more sod and plant more crops, but for the winter, they were secure.

As it turned out, though, they were able to work long into the winter months. Their first two winters in Nebraska were balmy and spring-like, leading many settlers to believe they'd found the land of milk and honey, a land of perpetual summer. That was until the winter of 1856.

"The terrible cold winter . . . began on December 1, 1856, freezing into ninety solid blocks of ice all the days of that month and the succeeding ones of January and February, 1857. Deep snow covered the whole earth and game . . . perished from cold and hunger. Deer ran through the streets of Nebraska City seeking safety from wolves . . ."[lxii]

The wolves may have been the most abundant wildlife during that starving winter because they could run on the icy crust. Deer couldn't, so the wolves ate well that winter. Fortunately, Hiram was not a stockman. He only had a yoke of oxen, three milk cows, three beef cows and five hogs and he, along with his sons and sons-in-law, had had the better part of two years to build sufficient shelter for their few head of livestock, to protect them from predators.

They survived that winter and prospered until the summer of drought in 1859 with its reduced crop yields and profits. Even in a drought year, though, Hiram had raised five hundred bushels of corn, two hundred bushels of buckwheat, and one hundred bushels of potatoes. His biggest cash crop was still prairie hay and he had put up seventeen tons of it. The family also made and sold three hundred pounds of butter and they had six bushels of beans in the larder.[lxiii] Short crops or not, they needn't worry about food for the winter.

In addition to being a secure shelter and larder, the Hendricks' double home served several public purposes. The family led church development in the new community and, as a few more families moved into the area, they held church services at their home whenever they could secure a minister.[lxiv] The Hendricks were founders of Douglas, Nebraska, which was originally named Hendricks. "When the county organized, Hendricks became justice of the peace and their home served as a polling place . . . convenient . . . since he was a judge over voting procedures from 1859-60."[lxv]

By then Hiram was all played out. An encyclopedia of Nebraska Towns editor speculated that the unremitting labor contributed to his death "on November 21, 1861, at the age of 53, leaving his wife and 11 children to work the farm. By this time many settlers had arrived, which provided some measure of protection for the family."[lxvi]

I've wondered what they needed protection from in those years. Wolves and grizzlies maybe, claim jumpers willing to kill for a prime piece of real estate, perhaps, Indians possibly. In their minds, however, the land itself may have produced the greatest fear.

As the Hendricks had walked across the continent, they'd crowded out the people who knew the prairie. They were bold and they were brave and they thought they were on a God-given mission. When they met oceans of grass in the middle of the continent, they saw it as an enemy to be feared and conquered. They didn't seek to understand how a prairie works because they owned it, or at least their little corner of it, and they would bend it to their will. They never thought of conserving it, because they never thought it could be depleted. As Aldo Leopold said, "Conservation is . . . incompatible with our Abrahamic concept of land [ownership]."[lxvii]

Like generations of Whites both before and after them, the Hendricks altered the land, as if it were deficient. They didn't recognize that the prairie had supported a rich, diverse plant and animal community, including humans, for thousands of years. Somehow the rich abundance of everything they needed escaped their notice. The grasses and forbs they ripped with their plows had supported millions of the largest land mammals in the world. The people who lived there before had adapted sustainably to what they found. The Whites tore it up and transformed it.

My grandfather checked fence every Sunday. It was his worship time and his manner of worship was the study and appreciation of the few acres of which he had custody. Since he never really believed he owned the land he'd bought, he took care of it to the best of his ability. That meant knowing something about it. His practice involved observing every detail, the health of every creature, domestic or wild. He was a meticulous farmer, but his insistence that every crop row must be perfectly straight, even to the point of staking them, gave way to cropping systems that followed the land's contours as he

36

learned how to conserve the rich soils he'd been "give to take care of." He's been dead more than fifty-five years and people still tell me that they can see his stewardship on the land he left behind.

My dad wanted to turn all six-hundred forty acres then in the family farm back to grass. In a letter dated only June, 1949, he wrote, ". . . if we are going to feed this country, the soil must be saved." He thought the future of the Great Plains ". . . lies in cattle."[lxviii]

He had a reverence for wild things, as well. Among the conservation measures dearest to his heart was a little "game preserve" just below the spillway of the big dam. It grew up in a tangle of Russian olive, floribunda roses, Ponderosa pines, and ash trees. In the understory were shrubs grandma called buck brush and bridal veil. Dad's trees, north and west of the little house where I grew up, was a haven for wild things, too. I can't remember waking up there, except in the very dead of winter, without a cacophony of bird songs.

Four generations and 100 years after Hiram and Sicily arrived in Nebraska, almost as soon as I could walk, my Grandma Hazel took me walking. She pointed out a purple-flowered legume she called buffalo beans. We found daisy fleabane and poppy mallow. We found tiny, pink wild onion flowers that smell so sweet they make your ears ring. There was a little clump of them just outside the corral every spring.

I inherited my dad's camera bug and I have folders of wildflower photos, close-ups mostly, some with bees mining them for pollen. I also inherited my dad's desire to turn the farmland back to grass. Since my entire income doesn't derive from the farm, I've managed to eliminate some more acres, leaving only about seventy of the two-hundred forty acres I inherited in crops.

I cherish in my mind a vision of the prairie as it was before my family arrived. It's built on a lifetime of thinking about one little piece of land in the mid-grass prairie, on years of kicking around in Nebraska's back country and on working with the scientists who spend their days and nights managing wild lands.

When I think of spring, I think not just of waterfowl, but of wading birds like killdeer, dowitchers, and avocets. I love the piercing cry of a killdeer across the fields, but my favorites are phalaropes. I've spent hours sitting by a roadside puddle watching them twirl around on their flower-stalk legs, making little whirlpools that stir up tasty aquatic insects. They allowed me to get amazingly close, but they valued their privacy and a shutter click sent them skittering.

With my kids, I've spotted bald eagles, wild turkeys, cardinals, deer, and antelope. My middle son turned out to be an excellent road hunter of wild asparagus, while the older one bested me when we looked for morels. All of us have stopped still in the middle of whatever we're doing when we hear Sandhill cranes. I've stalked the big birds in the Platte Valley, belly crawling through wet corn rows to get close enough for a photo. And I envy the Omaha World Herald sports writer, Sandy Griswold, who wrote in 1890 of hunting the "gray and white avalanches" of cranes that flew down out of the north in March. I imagine a sky filled with the indescribable wild cry of millions of cranes and I wish, just once, I could witness such an avalanche of feathers.

I find my relationship with the land in concepts I've stolen from quantum physics that leave me stunned. The continuum of matter and energy and the entanglement of subatomic particle, which dictates that, when one particle changes its aspect, its partner simultaneously makes the same change, even across light years of space, remind me of mater awareness studies completed decades ago. They lead me to a universal consciousness some might call God. For me, that consciousness encompasses every vibrating subatomic particle in the cosmos—every speck of soil, every molecule of rock, every plant cell, every neuron that ever existed. So when I walk attentively on this earth, I feel welcomed here, a part of the conscious silence of stones and of the whirling fury of storms.

And that, in those moments, is enough.

Between August 4 and 24, 1787, [Martha Ballard]
performed four deliveries, answered one obstetrical
false alarm, made sixteen medical calls, prepared three
bodies for burial, dispensed pills to one neighbor,
harvested and prepared herbs for another, and doctored
her own husband's sore throat . . . . In twentieth
century terms, she was simultaneously a midwife,
nurse, physician, mortician, pharmacist and attentive
wife.--Laurel Thatcher Ulrich

Grandma Hendricks

Wind howls over treetops, bends trees and clatters
branches. Golden candlelight flickers in bits of breeze that pick
their way through tightly-chinked logs of a cabin in the
southeast corner of the Nebraska Territory. In a far corner of
the room, driven snow spits through an unseen crack, building
a tiny, glistening drift. The cabin fills with bustle and chatter
as a small group of women wait.

In a scene I frequently imagine, Grandma Sicily Hendricks
arrives sometime after midnight, well before her young
neighbor's crisis. She waits with her young patient, I'll call her
Mary, her mother and two sisters. At eighteen, Mary's mature
enough. She'll be just fine. Not like some of the fifteen- and
sixteen-year-olds Sicily's tended—too narrow and still too firm
to give. Their babies have to force their way out. Sicily can only
imagine being desperate enough to marry off a daughter that
young.

But in the St. Deroin Cemetery, fifty miles southeast of Grandma Hendricks home in Douglas, an old grave lies separated inside a wrought iron fence. Dulcina Bratton, wife of John, fifteen years, nine months and twenty days, is buried there with her infant daughter who died with her on December 12, 1873. By that time, doctors had opened practices in many southeast Nebraska communities, but perhaps the nearest doctor was just too far away and John started after him too late. Maybe a doctor was there and he just couldn't save Dulcina and her baby.

Before the doctors, women made do with midwives like Sicily. They would almost surely have brought robust good health to their births. During the Civil War years, frontier women actually had better chances of surviving childbirth than their urban sisters, despite—or maybe because of—the lack of medical attention. Midwives just intervened much less frequently in the birthing process than doctors and so passed on fewer infections.[lxix] Without x-rays and sonograms, though, women had no way to recognize a baby too large to bear until it tore through the birth canal, perhaps ripping into the urethra or the bowel, leaving the mother forever incontinent—prey to infection. Such tears could result in immediate death from hemorrhage or within days of septicemia. If the mother survived, she would sustain permanent disability, avoided by husband and children because she would smell terrible.[lxx]

As Mary labors, Sicily makes sure plenty of fuel waits by the fireplace to keep the room warm. To avoid lethal drafts, she gives orders that no one should enter or leave. No one will. Young Mary's husband went to work in Nebraska City for the winter so he can buy some seed and a mule to pull the plow. Their horse, alone, can't break through the sod.

Sicily encourages Mary to walk, while the other women prepare the bed with worn-out sheets and quilts to soak up blood. Mary's mother has brought extra clothes, so she can stay for a couple of weeks. A new mother would never leave her childbed in less if she could get any help. She needs to regain her strength for the enormous effort of running a household, as well as nursing and caring for the new child.

In order to spend these long hours helping her neighbors, Sicily needs help, too.[lxxi] Her own household is in seventeen-year-old Sarah's hands now, with help from ten-year-old Catherine. They can keep up with the two younger children and the cooking, but Hanna's death the first year in Otoe County was a terrible loss, not just emotionally, but also practically, as Sicily lost dependable help. Two of her older daughters, Mary Jane and Sarah Louise, had already married and left the nest, Mary Jane to Tom Morgan in Iowa in 1852. She's already lost two infant daughters. The first, Sicily after her grandmother, died about the same time Sicily's year-old baby, John. The second, Sarah Louise, died in the territory at about the same time as Hanna. The family has had three years of loss, although Louisa's marriage, just before the family moved from Iowa hasn't sustained any losses yet.

As her contractions come closer and harder, Mary becomes frightened. Like many women facing childbirth, she's told her sisters which of her things she wants each of them to have.[lxxii] Her older sister will take care of the baby, if it survives and Mary doesn't. Now nothing's left to arrange and the intensity of her contractions frightens her. Grandma Sicily soothes her with chamomile tea, reassuring her that all is going well.

My grandmother, Hazel, has described Sicily as little, fine-boned, not necessarily a woman to inspire confidence. Midwifery was hard work, leaning over a bed, lifting a baby or working between contractions to turn a breech. But her daily work, carrying her own babies, moving baskets of fuel and food, walking and harvesting herbs, hoeing a garden and picking vegetables, provided plenty of muscle-building exercise.

She leads the women in a brief prayer. With medical knowledge still at the blister, burn and purge stage, sometimes prayer is the best anyone can do. Perhaps Joseph Swope, a Shawnee captive from generations ago, managed to pass something of Shawnee belief about healing down through generations of nieces and nephews. For Native Americans, religion and healing are inseparable, part of the great mystery of life.[lxxiii]

Through all the strain of birthing, Sicily has plenty of spiritual as well as physical help. Each woman holds Mary and her child safe in her mind, willing them well by holding a vision of them, safe and well. The fire in the hearth pops and sparks, conquering the cold wind that blusters outside. Faces appear ruddy and damp.

The five women wait and murmur together in the warm cabin, shadows flickering over their tired faces. As the end of labor approaches and Mary gets drowsy in the warm room, Grandma leads her to the bed and gets her settled, partly reclining against her sister, who sits behind her. Her mother and other sister gather around and as Mary begins bearing down, they help her sister hold her upright and offer hands to hold, to squeeze and to pull, combining all of their strength and courage with hers in the final moments.

As Mary's crisis overwhelms her, Grandma's quiet voice coaxes the baby out into the golden candle glow.

"Easy," she says. "Breathe. Don't push yet. You'll tear yourself. He's coming. Give him time. Ah, now, there she is. You've got a little girl to help you with your work."

Grandma lays the baby on her mother's collapsed belly and holds the cord, feeling Mary's blood, still pulsing to her child. A few more moments and the pulse stops. Near the baby's belly, Grandma ties the first knot. She ties the second about two inches away. Then she snips the cord between the knots. As the other women wash and wrap the baby, sponge Mary with warm water and make sure she stays warm, Grandma waits for the placenta. When she finally has it in a basin, she lays down on a pallet the women have made for her on the floor, to wait for daylight and a break in the storm so she can go home.

Lying there dozing, she may remember curling up with her own mother after a nighttime delivery, waiting for the new mother and baby to wake from their exhausted first sleep—just to be sure all was well. She might think of all the new lives she's seen and about how all of those people are building a country all the way across a continent. She probably doesn't think about all the people killed or displaced so they can.

She remembers the rumble of wagons and all of the times she's packed her household in it. She remembers the hundreds of miles she's walked beside it, looking for the herbs she left behind in Indiana. Some of them are hard to find in Nebraska. She and her husband have gone where doctors haven't yet, settling for a while in Illinois where her boys went to school and then into Jackson County, Iowa, where John died. He only lived for a year. Hiram and Sicily still pushed west.

I've seen Sicily's kind of stoicism in my own Grandmother and I'm in awe. I remember thoughtlessly remarking to her, a woman who had outlived both her sons, that I didn't think I could survive the loss of a child. Her answer was immediate and forceful,

"Of course you could."

"How?"

"You just do." That's all she said. "You just do." And she turned away.

I can't quite get my mind around that, yet nearly every family lost children back then—to fevers, accidents and diseases that didn't even have names yet. What did that do to their humanity? Wouldn't it have made them more able to empathize, even with people very different from themselves? Or did it harden them to anything or anyone different who might pose yet another threat?

As Sicily drifts off for a brief nap, she feels her own baby move. She's forty-eight this year. She suspects this will be the last one. Eleven is probably enough . . . but then her grandmother had sixteen. Grandma's little rest after a birth must have been a luxury. By the time young Hiram's born, she'll have been pregnant more than eight years and she'll have nursed a baby at least eleven. Only eleven years of adulthood without a baby in her womb or on her breast.

She dozes, well satisfied. This is the work she has come to the Territory to do. She does the other, too, but it's often more difficult and more likely to drain the life out of her, taking care of deadly injuries and fatal illnesses.

The other might involve cleaning and bandaging wounds that resulted from runaway livestock and mishaps with farm equipment. She probably would have sent amputations and gunshot wounds to the nearest doctor. But it was a while before a doctor opened his practice nearby. So Sicily would probably pack the wounds to staunch bleeding as much as possible and send the patient in some kind of wagon behind a fast team for the nearest doctor.

Often settlers moved west ahead of epidemics that swept the cities, and their isolation helped remove those diseases from their environment. Sicily's own granddaughter, Frank, would suffer increasingly severe hearing loss throughout her life because of a childhood case of scarlet fever. A grandson would develop mental retardation as a result of the same "fever" epidemic. But they were still alive.[lxxiv] Sicily undoubtedly helped families nurse—and sometimes bury—victims of various fevers.

When a doctor finally settled for good in Douglas, Sicily had already turned her practice over to her daughters. She gave Margaret, "Aunt Mag," the youngest, all of her recipes. I've wondered what folkways she passed on. I know Grandma Hazel learned to use a poultice of bread soaked in milk or water to "draw out" an infection. Before rubbing alcohol, Great-Grandma Frank used turpentine as a disinfectant——except in a horse barn. Something about horses made turpentine dangerous, Grandma said.[lxxv]

Later on, it would be one of Sicily's concoctions that cured Frank's burns when she dropped a skillet of hot grease on her foot. Sicily was in her nineties by then, but her daughter, Aunt Mag, brought the beeswax salve when Doc Hostetter couldn't cure the foot.

I wonder about other concoctions. Since childbearing posed a serious danger to women and more children meant more work, perhaps she passed on some information about avoiding pregnancy. Sicily, herself, may have used rhythm or a primitive diaphragm made of cocoa butter and boric acid[lxxvi] during the six years—1847-1853—when her parents died in Indiana and her family moved to Iowa, by way of a year or two in Illinois. That six-year hiatus in births, compared to her record of a baby about every other year, may also have been a result of the enormous stress of losing her parents and the several moves. She couldn't just hire a moving van and drive to the new house.

Whatever recipes she used, all died with Margaret. As doctors took over birthing rooms, their medicines seemed better than the old folkways, so Aunt Mag didn't pass them on to her daughters. But Sicily had taught her daughters and they had helped the doctors when their sisters had their babies.

In '02, for Sicily's ninetieth birthday in March, the family gathered at Aunt Mag and Uncle Wesley Hickok's home.

"We had it up to Hickok's and we eat out under the trees," Hazel said. "They had a big grove of maple trees. There was about a hundred of us there, the kids [great-grandchildren] all running around playing tag and hide and seek out under the trees. I don't know if they was them silver maples that was there when Grandma come or if Wesley got some sugar maples from back East somewhere.

"They had sawhorses out in the yard and put planks over them. Everybody brought their own dishes and things. Everybody brought food. There was plenty of food—always plenty of food when the family got together.

"Grandma Hendricks was in a wheelchair, one of them big wooden ones. Caned, I think. She had on a little white bonnet and a shawl. Dressed all in black except for her bonnet and that shawl with tassels on it. She was just little—fine boned—with her hair all smoothed back in a bun."[lxxvii]

When Grandma Hendricks died four years later, in '06, the earth moved—just a little.

They didn't have seismometers then, but the day they buried her, chandeliers swung, dishes rattled in pantries and doors banged. A little bit of plaster fell off the walls. News of the earthquake lined up beside Grandma's obituary and the story of a woman scalped in a bakery accident—like triple tombstones. [lxxviii]

Grandma Hendricks had made herself an icon in Otoe County. By the time she died, doctors trained back East had taken over her practice. But by then she'd delivered hundreds of babies from Ohio to Nebraska. Her obituary didn't even list her eleven children, nine of them still living.

"She leaves living fifty-eight grandchildren, eighty-four great-grandchildren and a number of great-great grandchildren," reported the Nebraska City Tribune. "She has been a consistent member of the Methodist Church (of Douglas, Nebraska) for sixty-two years and was closely identified with that church in its infancy in western Otoe County, being a class leader. She and her husband were the principle movers in church work."[lxxix]

I know she delivered most, if not all, of the grandchildren. Doc Hostetter delivered most of the great-grandchildren probably with help from Sicily's daughters. Her granddaughters helped Doc with the great-greats, including my father, Cecil, and his sister, Nina.

Sicily certainly did her share to populate the wilderness, helping to make ever more manifest the whites' destiny—to own the continent.

Sicily almost never treated strangers. By the time she died in 1906, she was known throughout Otoe County as

Grandma Hendricks. When she helped the sick or injured or delivered a baby, she had the assistance of her patient's family, friends and neighbors, unlike healers today who try to heal relative strangers. Technically, medicine has advanced beyond anything the Native American shaman, the midwife and the frontier doctor could have imagined. But I wonder how much we've lost in the process.

If the First Peoples were right, if healing is half spiritual and half science, then modern medicine may have lost an important ingredient. If the communal nature of Sicily's folkways made a difference to people moving through dangerous passages, how does healing take place now? Except for minor illnesses and accidents, it no longer takes place in our homes. Birth has been moved almost entirely to hospitals, as if it's pathological. Our families, friends, and neighbors no longer help deliver our babies. A husband or a friend may be allowed into the delivery room to coach us, as if our bodies don't know what they're doing. But the loving support of a community of women is denied us.

We may have a relationship with a general practitioner, but she's rarely more than an acquaintance. When we enter a hospital to bear a child or to seek healing for a serious illness or accident, we do it on faith. But it's an entirely different kind of faith than Sicily's patients had in her. Now we have to believe in incomprehensible procedures done with mysterious instruments by perfect strangers. We sign indecipherable forms and hope for the best as we enter an impersonal world that appears efficient, but certainly not warm or comfortable.

In that world, we stop being human.

The people Sicily cared for in sickness and injury, in bringing new life and ending it, were human. Her family grew to include a whole county as she became everyone's Grandma Hendricks. Her healing touch had more to do with recognizing the individual patient than any medicine or procedure.

I saw it happen with my Grandma Hazel when we visited the local nursing home together. She would cross the great room, wandering from lost soul to lost soul, asking about their children, about their crafts projects, about their bingo scores, about their health problems and each person she greeted looked a little stronger, a little straighter for her recognition. That's healing.

I'm not sure how we can do it. I know some medical practices and some hospitals are trying new procedures, new types of facilities, in order to bring the human community into their technical world of efficiency. Perhaps there are models in Sicily's birthing rooms and sick rooms.

I am of the opinion that my life belongs to the whole community and as long as I live, it is my privilege to do for it whatever I can. I want to be thoroughly used up when I die, for the harder I work the more I live.-- George Bernard Shaw

Grandpa's Neighbor

It may sound strange, but one of my favorite places is an old family cemetery three miles west of Douglas, shaded by jackpines. It's cool and quiet there and it reminds me of a tiny community that existed more than a century ago. When I remember Solon Cemetery, I think of wind and Catharine and T.J. Smith and Philip Hunt and a tiny pine coffin laying in the grass next to a gaping black hole in the sod. Philip Hunt was not family, yet he stood there with his neighbors, hat in hand, black hair and beard ruffled in the wind. There weren't any jackpines then.

Philip had arrived in Nebraska from Hamilton, Ontario, in 1868. Grandma thinks he walked, but a county history says he accompanied his aunt, Sarah Jenkins.[lxxx] Maybe she walked, too, or perhaps Philip walked along beside her horse. Philip had a cousin who lived near Douglas, so he'd come to check it out. His aunt likely came to be with that cousin—a son or daughter.

Philip's visit to Nebraska lasted more than sixty years. He homesteaded next to Hiram and Sicily's daughter, Catherine, and her husband, Thomas Jefferson Smythe, a Scot who had Americanized his name to Smith. He had arrived two years earlier after a detour in the Grand Army of the Republic fighting the Confederates on their own turf.[lxxxi] The two men practiced a less rough and tumble style of Old World agriculture than many of their neighbors, with diversity and precision.

When T.J. got to the Nebraska Territory in February, 1866, he homesteaded in the Hendricks Precinct.[lxxxii] Very soon, Catharine Hendricks noticed him at a camp meeting and rushed home to announce to her mother, Sicily, that she had met the man she was going to marry. Marry him she did, too, six months later, on August 12, 1866. By the time Philip arrived, Catharine carried their first-born son in her arms and their first-born daughter in her belly.[lxxxiii]

Philip brought his own romance that later enchanted his neighbor's daughters and, four generations later, touches me. Once established next to the Smiths, Philip sent money back to Canada to bring his fiancé and her brother to Nebraska. He hoped to save their lives in the drier Nebraska climate. Both suffered from "consumption," a disease we now call tuberculosis, and the months between Philip's departure and their arrival had severely altered their appearance. Both had become very thin and pale with hollow cheeks and sunken eyes.[lxxxiv]

Still he dared to hope. Philip saw to it that his bride-to-be and her brother took the black, tar-like medicine he kept warm on the back of the stove. But even the open Nebraska skies couldn't fill their damaged lungs. Philip saw to their bloody handkerchiefs and kept his grief to himself as they got weaker. About all Philip's neighbors had to offer was to spell him during the endless hours of watching at his loved ones' bedsides and to help take care of whatever crops he'd established during that first season.

At last, Philip built caskets, one by one, from fresh pine boards and Catherine helped him wash the bodies and dress them for burial. The Smiths stood among the few mourners to share Philip's loss—sustained so far from home.

A couple of years after Philip buried his sweetheart, Catharine delivered her second daughter, a black-haired, black-eyed girl named by her father before her birth. When she turned out to be a girl, his only concession to little Frank's sex was her second name, Aurelia. A little more than a year later, May 25, 1872, Philip shared the Smiths' celebration of another birth, James Monroe, nicknamed Munn. But two years after that, Philip built another, tiny coffin and stood at graveside with T.J. and Catharine. I wasn't there, but I can't imagine a March day in Nebraska when the wind didn't whip Catharine's skirts and the men's beards. The barbed wire fence that kept the cows out of the little cemetery would have sung as the Smiths buried their two-week-old son, Edward Arzie Ezia. The first handsful of dirt they threw on the coffin probably blew back in their faces.

As Catharine gave birth to another seven, Philip got the first cigar and, as the child survived its first weeks, the first tentative smiles of relief. Philip may have seemed like an uncle to T.J. and Catharine's brood, but he was not family, as the first daughter, Ruilla Carsie, knew very well. Rill made eyes at him, as she passed through adolescence, but he didn't seem to notice, even a dozen years after he'd lost his sweetheart.

I wonder sometimes how the neighborhood, and particularly Philip, took the highjinks between T.J.'s dad and mom. Grandma Hazel said that her great-grandmother, Elsie Robeson Smythe, had lost two daughters at sea on the way to the United States. Then her oldest son, John, glimpsing glory, enlisted in the Twenty-seventh Iowa Infantry August 15, 1862, when the family still lived in northeastern Iowa. T.J. wanted to go, too, but he was only fifteen, so Elsie managed to dissuade him—for a while. Shortly after his seventeenth birthday, he headed back to Delaware County, Iowa, from Hendricks, Nebraska Territory, where the family had moved. He enlisted in the Twenty-seventh, also.

Elsie may have received a few letters and, undoubtedly, news of the carnage reached Nebraska Territory. She waited in terror that she might lose another child. By the time they mustered out, John on June 10, 1863, and T.J. on January 20, 1866, Elsie was losing her mind with worry. Then, Grandma said, if that wasn't enough, Elsie lost her husband.

No one alive remembers what happened between old Tom and Elsie. Maybe she blamed him for her daughters' deaths. Maybe it was he who wanted to go to the states. Maybe she had a nasty disposition. Perhaps Tom just had a wandering eye. Whatever the cause, Tom divorced Elsie and married a younger woman and Elsie moved in with T. J. and his wife, Catharine.

"T.J. had a house on top of a hill," Hazel said, "and my great-grandpa, Tom, had a homestead down the hill. Philip Hunt had homesteaded part of that same section. Great-grandmother was one of them people that got so she didn't know what she was doing. Today, they'd probably say she had Alzheimer's."

As she aged, Elsie settled deeper and deeper into dementia. She started wandering away from the house. I imagine that Philip guided her home sometimes, if he found her wandering on the prairie. Maybe she thought she was back in the highlands. Finally, T. J. and Catharine built her a room of her own where she could have her own, familiar things. When they had to be away for a few hours, they would lock her in her room.

Once when they were gone, though, Elsie found her way out. She wandered down the hill to where her former husband lived with his new wife. Old Tom and his bride also happened to be away from home that day, so no one knows how the fire started. When Tom got home, all he found was charred remains and the twisted wreck of the kitchen range in the basement with a pot of stew, a little overdone, still sitting on top.

They found Elsie sitting on a rock, a remainder of some glacier that had edged the Missouri Basin, humming a quiet, random little tune. A jig, perhaps. I wonder if she knew what she had done.

"But Great-grandpa just rebuilt the house," Hazel said. "Finally, after his second wife died, he lived with T. J. and Grandma Catharine, too. All this happened long before I was born, and nobody ever said how they all got along there.

Through all the goings on and carryings on, Philip remained a true and loyal friend. At a time when divorce was unheard of and mental illness shameful, he stood by to help construct another room, to search the hills and creek bottoms for a lost parent, to dig an iron kettle from among the charred ruins of a man's home.

And of an evening, he would stride into T.J.'s yard with his pipe in his pocket. The men would drag some chairs out into the yard and watch the kids chasing fireflies. Catharine, too, may have brought along a chair and maybe a pan of beans to snap or cherries to pit or apples to peel and core. Maybe the old folks, Thomas and Elsie, would come out, too. It think it would be hard to carry on a grudge—or even a case of nerves—into the velvet black of a prairie night when it's hard to see the border between twinkling stars and winking fireflies or hear the difference between chirping crickets and snapping beans.

Philip was still there, still single, when the Carpenter boys, William, George and Jasper, arrived at their cousin's place near Bennett. William James Carpenter, back in Scioto County, Ohio, had put his living together in bits and pieces, farming his father's worn-out land and cutting briars that grew up after every crop. He and his brothers cut long hook poles and split rails for the transcontinental system just spreading out from the coast to coast trunk line. They foraged in the woods for medicinal herbs like ginseng and bloodroot and sassafras to sell at the Daleyville drugstore. Despite all the time in the woods, they did manage to go to school a little bit, but William never got beyond the third grade.

In 1887, encouraged by glowing letters from their former neighbors and friends, the Williamses who had settled at Bennett, near Douglas, the Carpenters loaded a covered wagon and headed their mule team west. Their mother packed a picnic basket for them. I still have it.

"The day they left Ohio, their folks took some pictures of them and William, my dad, didn't even have a coat. He borreyed a coat to get that picture taken," Hazel said. "He was just a kid, just eighteen. He'd never been away from home. Uncle Jasper always told the story that he was so homesick on the way out. They said they learned him to chew tobacco so he wouldn't be so lonesome."

The Carpenter boys arrived in Bennett in early September, at the home of William Henry Williams. The following year, their parents, William and Sarah Jane, as well as a brother, Marion and sister, Ella, moved from Ohio to a place owned by Williams and located just east of Philip Hunt. Within a few years, George had a farm near Burr; Marion had a job in a blacksmith shop; and Jasper was laying track for the Missouri Pacific. Their dad worked for years as a section hand.

Will hired out as a farm hand, breaking virgin sod and preparing it for a first crop. Within his first six years in Nebraska, he established solid employment on Philip Hunt's place. In those days, a hired man might work with his boss as much as under him. Philip taught Will to bud and graft, how to plant a grape arbor and how to breed horses. That's where he got started breeding Percherons, the big heavy-muscled work horses. T.J. and Philip continued to trade work, including community projects like the Willow Line, the first telephone line in their area, which they hung on willow poles. Will took part in those work parties too. He undoubtedly got to know the Smith girls as he whistled and whittled out in T.J. and Catharine's front yard with Philip and T.J.

The first born, Rill, had already attained the ripe age of eight when Will arrived. In fact, she was a couple of months older. The young stranger out whistling in the fields soon caught her eye and "because he was good-looking and all, she kind of made a play for him," his sister, Ella, later confided in Grandma Hazel. Will's interests were elsewhere and Rill didn't marry until she was thirty-five years old. She worked around for people like all girls do, attending births with her mother who was taking over Grandma Sicily's practice and staying for a couple of weeks to help the new mother.

"Some way or another," Hazel said, Will became interested in "that little black-eyed girl," the second girl, Frank. Perhaps Will liked Frank's toughness that took her into the fields with her brothers, planting corn and walking behind the horses, harrowing the fields with a tree limb. Or maybe he admired the intelligence and persistence that led her to earn her teaching certificate from Bennett Academy. Before she taught even a semester, though, she got sick with the scarlet fever that Grandma blamed for her progressive hearing loss.

As she recovered, she kept house for her older brother, Charlie and Will tried to persuade her to forget about teaching school and make her career teaching him. Starting September 6, 1893, she did. That Wednesday, Will and Frank, along with her brother Charlie and Nellie Sutton, drove a team to Lincoln. At the courthouse, Will and Frank began a life together that lasted almost sixty-two years. Charlie and Nellie were married in a nearby Seventh Day Adventist Church.

Hired men often lived in their employers' houses then. Hazel remembers a succession of men her father hired after he got his own place. Usually, they bunked with her brothers, except one old guy who couldn't stay away from the bottle. He bunked in the barn. When Will and Frank returned to Douglas on their wedding night, they returned to Philip's house. That was exceptional and Philip's hired couple gradually filled every nook and cranny of the lower floor. In addition to a farm laborer, Philip got a cook, housekeeper, laundress and gardener, although none of them seemed to think of it that way. In return for Will's and Frank's labor and that of the children who arrived at about two-and-a-half-year intervals, Philip provided generously. They all had the use of the frame house he had built with his own hands for the bride who never really shared it. There were two gambrel-roofed barns, a bricked cave, a sweet well, a magnificent orchard Philip had planted and grafted, his grape arbors and about three quarter sections of farm land.

In addition to Frank and Will and their family, Philip took in others who needed a place to go. For a time when there was only one child, Will's grandfather, old Henry Carpenter, lived there. Senility had robbed him of his mind and, like Elsie, he would wander away.

"Mom couldn't take care of him for more than a few months," Hazel said. "She couldn't chase him down because she was pregnant with me. So Dad took him down by Burr to Uncle George Carpenter.

Another time, Will's brother, Jasper, was the guest.

"Jasper was a guy that wandered around a lot," Grandma said. "Next year after he and Dad and George come out here, he went back and got Aunt Mollie and brought her out and got married. One year, they thought Arkansas would be a great place to go. So they got them a team of mules and a covered wagon and went to Arkansas. They went broke down in Arkansas and they come back with a team of pretty yellow, maybe sorrel, horses and a baby colt. They come back in the fall . . . and Philip had a great big granary out there. Two rooms. I don't know how it come that it wasn't full of grain. Must have been a poor year and they hadn't shelled the corn yet.

"'Course they had everything they owned in that covered wagon—stove and everything. They moved in that granary and lived in there all winter. That winter, Mollie's sister come from Denver. She had a daughter, Pearl . . . they come and stayed with Aunt Mollie for a while in the granary."

58

Grandma said that Philip's family in Canada also sent him a nephew, John, to nurse. Like Philip's sweetheart and her brother, John had consumption. Frank helped with the doses of "tar" kept on the warming oven. For Philip it must have seemed a terrible task. He'd already lost his most beloved sweetheart to the same scourge. This time, though, the patient recovered. How Philip and the Carpenter family avoided infection remains unexplained.

"He was always helping somebody out," Hazel said. "Any of the Smith boys, if they needed a little help or something financial, he was always helping them. He didn't make a big thing of it or anything. He never expected it back."

"Philip's house was our house, only we wasn't allowed to go into his rooms," Hazel said. "There was a crawl hole back over the top of the kitchen and he had a lot of stuff stored in there. I think us kids snooped once in a while. We had a woodshed. Us kids prowled around there one time and found a tin can with a lot of money in it. Believe me, we put it back in a hurry. We knowed who it belonged to."

"We had peaches and applies and cherries," Hazel said. "There was three big apple trees. They was yellow transparent. They was early summer apples. Real early. We set up in them trees and eat apples. They was a beautiful place to set up in there and eat apples.

"We eat them and we made pies out of them and made applesauce, but they wasn't a canning apple. We couldn't get them out of the top of the tree, but they'd fall on the ground and the ground would be covered and we always were barefooted. And we'd get stung with the bees. Philip always had bees. He probably had ten hives. We always had honey."

"He had all kinds of fruit. He had apple trees that he grafted two or three different kinds of apples on. We had lots of apples. Just gorgeous apples. I can still taste them. The apples on the ground in the winter—a lot of times the leaves would cover them up and we'd go out and dig them up and eat them froze. He had all kinds of berries and everything you ever heard of. He had blackberries and grape vines.

"The garden was fenced with white picket fence. Everything on the place was painted. One time he wanted to paint the barn. He set out there on a stump and broke up bricks. Mixed the brick dust with turpentine and linseed oil and painted that great big barn. He painted all the outbuildings with that. He had us kids once in a while bringing up bricks for him.

"He was a great hand for flowers and shrubs. He had these roses, just a common rose. Seems like I can remember white ones and pink ones and red ones. He probably had yellow ones, but I can't remember them. He kept them trimmed up pretty good. We had tiger lilies, too. During the nine years Frank and Will lived with him, Philip worked less and less in the fields and barns, devoting himself to the orchard and the flower beds."

The family and Philip would sit around the kitchen table in the evenings, reading.

"When us kids were growing up, Mom would send to Sears and Roebuck. She sent for every book she could get ahold of. She was the person that learned us to read. Our evenings in the winter was spent around the kitchen table with the lamp in the middle. Usually we'd pop corn and have a bowl of apples.

In spring and summer, her dad and Philip would sit out on the porch and talk by the hour, "just set there and whittle, out in the sun." Sometimes they didn't say a word. When the evening was particularly hot, the three adults would often drag the chairs out in the yard, watch the air fill with fireflies, and talk, over the sound of snapped green beans clanging into a pot.

Hazel found Philip a bit intimidating.

"Philip Hunt wasn't too good with little kids. He was kind of standoffish. We thought he was cranky. We was kind of scared of him. He wasn't mean or anything, but he would boss us a little bit. As we growed up, though, we growed with him some way or another. We all liked Philip, ever one of us."

Grandma remembers days at Philip's place, playing house in the orchard where she and her sisters marked off rooms with binder twine. They were still at Hunt's place when Uncle Earl was born . . . and Grandma Hazel . . . and Aunt Edna . . . and Uncle Lawrence.

Shortly after Lawrence was born, Philip decided that was just enough children and he moved in with his nephew, James Ratliffe, who lived on another of his farms near Panama, Nebraska. Philip was leaving his own house that he'd built with his own hands to the hired help. I found that incomprehensible, but Grandma said that nobody thought about it that way. She couldn't say exactly how they did think about it except that the Ratliffe house was bigger and the family smaller.

Philip retired then (he was fifty-seven) and turned the place over to Will who bought the equipment and the draft horses. In 1904, Frank had another baby, Norma, in Philip's house. But it was still Philip's land and in summer of 1907, just before Frank had her last baby, Mahlon, the Carpenters bought their own place.

Ten years later, Will and Frank moved half a state away to Webster County. Grown up and married by then, Frank's daughter, my grandma moved with my grandpa onto Will's and Frank's place.

"Philip walked from Panama down to our place. That was about seven or eight miles. He walked there one morning. He said, 'I had to see how you folks was getting along.' Philip Hunt was the walkinest man you ever saw. He could outwalk anybody . . ." Hazel said of him. "I can't remember of Philip

61

ever a'riding a horse. He could walk to Lincoln about as quick as you could drive up there with a horse. He'd start out early in the morning to do some business in Lincoln and he'd be back by dinnertime. You know, he used to own the Post Office block downtown—the Old Post Office on P Street, between Ninth and Tenth."

A walk to Lincoln meant that Philip would have to walk forty miles round trip and still have time to take care of business. She said he would come swinging back into the yard at evening just as fresh as when he left.

"He was a magnificently-built man," Hazel said. "He was probably six foot. His hair was pretty long and it was coal black. He always wore shoes like the railroad men wear, with real thick soles. They was real heavy."

He wanted to buy some land out near Frank and Will, and Hazel thought her Dad helped him look. Sometimes the Carpenters would drive back to Otoe County and bring him out for a visit. Other times he'd walk out. It's almost one hundred twenty-five miles.

At the end, when Philip couldn't care for himself anymore, his nephew took him to Webster County to stay with Will and Frank. They sat with him during his last days after his stroke. When he died June 22, 1930, Frank and Will took him back to Douglas and buried him beside his beloved and near several generations of my family.

In return for their years of friendship and the last few months of caring for him, Philip left the Carpenters a quarter section of land where Grandma Hazel and Grandpa George were living then. Hazel and George bought a second quarter from the estate. Those two quarters became the core of what I now call the "Home Place."

"After he was gone, Grandpa, Dad, and Ratliffe went out to his place. He'd left directions that they found out at the farm.

They went out and dug up two or three cans of money—tin cans, sealed up and buried. I think there was one can of $20 gold pieces, but mostly it was folding money. It seems like money just kinda come to him some way.

"Philip Hunt had a car. It was a two cylinder. He never run it very much. He thought he could walk faster. It hung in the granary at his cousin's. When he died, they sold it for a relic."

As I leaf through the transcripts of my interviews with Grandma, I find Philip time after time, sauntering into and out of my family's daily routines. He died in 1930 after sixty-two years neighboring and mentoring three generations of my family. No better friend is likely to stroll into our lives.

He left us much more than the land. He left us a tradition of community that takes care of its own. Today, communities don't birth our babies any more like they did in Grandma Hendricks' time. Neighbors don't sit with our sick and dying. Hired help don't live in the boss's house, even though the houses are bigger and fewer people occupy them. We don't have hired help.

We have truly become a nation of strangers who wouldn't think to walk a mile just to see how the young folks are getting along. I suspect it's cost us dearly. When I think of the stress the average American faces, I suspect a good portion of it is fear. If we don't have those deep relationships with our neighbors, we have no reason to think that, when we need help, it will be forthcoming like it was when Will Carpenter started out and Philip Hunt ended up and for all those times in between.

Cornbread and butter beans and you across the table/Eatin' them beans and makin' love as long as I am able. -- Anonymous

The Homeliest Man She Ever Saw

George Colburn arrived in Nebraska during a blizzard so strong it blew his breath away. Just a few hours before his train pulled in, a prison break, about twenty miles up the line, had awakened a storm of rumors and fear. Unsuspecting, George, fresh from a winter vacation, was about to walk into an emotional storm that would last his lifetime.

At 2:15, Thursday, March 14, 1912, Shorty Gray escaped from the State Penitentiary in Lincoln. The Warden, a deputy and one guard were dead and another man wounded. Rumors circulated in southeast Nebraska that a riot had broken out at the prison and that one hundred inmates had escaped. Gray and two others headed out through a bellowing snow storm toward the Burlington Kansas City tracks and officials speculated that they had jumped onto a train. They could be anywhere along the tracks heading southeast from Lincoln.[lxxxv]

Douglas was one of those southeasterly communities, about twenty miles from the pen by railroad. George and Uncle Johnny Bivens came from the opposite direction on a Missouri Pacific train late that evening. Once Johnny identified himself as Sarah Carpenter's brother, the section boss allowed them to spend the night in the depot. No sense stumbling across town in the dark during a storm. All section bosses in towns around Lincoln had received telegraph warnings about the escaped murderers so he probably warned the men before he left them alone in the depot. George and Johnny had been hunting and fishing in the Ozarks all winter, so they were well armed and probably looked a little rough themselves with their bearskin coats, shaggy hair and stubble.[lxxxvi]

My grandmother grew up near Douglas. As Shorty Gray, a.k.a. Charles Taylor, was breaking out, she was in school. Because of the storm, she'd been staying in town with her Grandfather Will and Grandmother Sarah Carpenter. It was just too dangerous to drive her little buggy home in a blizzard. No one had quite forgotten the Schoolteacher's Blizzard of 1888 when between forty and one hundred people died out on the prairies, many of them children trying to get home from school. At the end of the day, Hazel waited for her Grandpa, the senior Will Carpenter, to come and get her, breaking trail through the drifts so it wouldn't be such a struggle for her to get to the house. The newspapers may not have been distributed because of the storm, but rumors had already spread. Visibility throughout southeast Nebraska was near zero and the convicts had disappeared. When George and Johnny arrived in Douglas, Hazel had already heard everything she was going to hear about the escape. She was probably asleep.

George had never encountered horizontal snow. In Ohio, snow fell vertically and quietly piled up on fence posts. Wind didn't make the violent threats he heard through the station walls. But the men had Johnny's featherbed to spread out on the stationhouse floor and they both had their bearskin coats. Before they could hunker down to sleep, though, someone spotted them moving around in the station. An investigation was certain to follow.

66

When the local constable waded through the drifts to check on some strangers reported in the stationhouse, he knew about the three dead prison officials. When I think of those three men, all armed, all aware that three desperate murderers were "on the loose," I picture all sorts of dangerous confrontations in that stationhouse and I have trouble imagining how it didn't end in tragedy. Maybe Douglas' town cop peered in the window and satisfied himself that the men were just getting comfortable. Maybe their rifles were sheathed so, I suspect, he may have tapped on the door before entering and quietly inquired about the men's identities and intentions. However it played out, nobody was harmed. After being mistaken for a desperado, though, George probably thought Nebraska a little wild. He may have wondered just what he was doing there.

Next morning, the papers would probably have arrived by train and been distributed. Will tramped off with Hazel to make sure she got through the drifts, then circled back to the house. The school was probably abuzz with excitement about the prison break and someone probably had a paper. There wasn't much news, though. Just more detail about what they'd already heard.

After a night's sleep, George and Johnny shaved and cleaned up. They may have thought they'd be less likely to be mistaken for escaped convicts if they trimmed up a bit. By the time they reached Will's and Sarah's, Hazel was already gone and they had the day to mull over the news. Once they'd disposed of the prison break, there was plenty of news about Ohio. There were the mysterious serpentine mounds, called Long Knob, to talk about. A mile high they said. They thought Indians built them, but what for? No one knew. Some guy was even farming the top of one. George's folks were eking out a living on their seventy acres. The Bivens, too, were just scraping by. Johnny lived with his mother in Daleyville. Much younger than his sister, Sarah Ann, he had formed a friendship with George whose family had moved there not long after the Carpenters left for Nebraska. They'd hunted and fished together and tried to make a buck wherever they could. During the winter if 1911 and '12, they rented a cabin in Peachtree, Arkansas. Sitting in Sarah's warm kitchen, George and Johnny told the "old folks" all about their winter. With snowdrifts piled all over town, the four had a whole day to catch up, until Will bundled up to go get Hazel. Since no new snow fell during the day, that task was easier than in the morning, and he returned with his granddaughter in short order.

Hazel didn't know her grandparents had company because Will didn't tell her when he collected her. So Hazel would have been as surprised as George to find a couple of strangers as she removed her coat at the door.

The first moment he saw my grandmother, Hazel, I believe my grandfather caught his breath, just like he did when he stepped off the train into a blizzard. When I suggest that possibility to Grandma, she shrugs and says, "Well, there's nobody around to say you're wrong."

I suspect George congratulated himself, in the stricken moment when he first saw Hazel stamping snow on her grandmother's braided rag rug, that he'd shaved that morning. He must have greeted Hazel solemnly in an attempt to conceal his numerous decayed and missing teeth. At twenty-one, his mouth was full of snags, brought on, Grandma thought, by the inadequate diet he survived in the poor hill county of southern Ohio.

When I think of Hazel's and George's first meeting, I remember sitting on the blue carpet of Grandma's living room looking through boxes of old photographs. I held a photo out to her. She was tall, blond and slender, unsmiling and thoughtful.

"That's my graduation picture," she said. "I was sixteen." She said she was wearing her first store-bought dress.

I looked at the photo in my other hand. George, shapeless in his bearskin coat, his ears huge for his head, a sober expression making his clean-shaven face appear even leaner than it was.

"You were a good-looking woman," I remarked tentatively.

She grinned. "So how did I end up with such a homely man?"

I couldn't quite look her in the eye. "Something like that."

"I guess he just growed on me."

Grandma doesn't remember what they talked about that afternoon. She had more education than any of the others, so she was the reader when the evening paper arrived. They did learn that there'd been no riot and only three prisoners had escaped. The prison was locked down and Company F of the state militia had been called out. Although Governor Aldrich was in Peru, Nebraska, visiting the state normal school, he'd called Adjutant General Phelps to take charge. Sheriff Hyers, along with newspapermen and assistants, had left immediately for the penitentiary in a sleigh. The convicts had not yet turned up. "Authorities" speculated that the men were lying "under cover" for two reasons. First, they obviously wanted to escape. Secondly, prison officials thought they might not survive if they were out in the open too long. Prison garb was not very heavy, they said.

The Lincoln Daily Star reported that Mrs. May Woodworth of Kansas City, known as Shorty Gray's "friend," had been in Lincoln during the week before the prison break. Mostly, the police were still running around following rumors.

"It must have been a Friday," Hazel said. "Dad come to town in the lumber wagon and I went home. Dad took him home with us."

Hazel said her parents were always like that, taking people in. When her dad's parents followed him to Nebraska, they had nothing to get themselves started. It took everything they made when they sold their place in Ohio to get to Nebraska. Her grandfather, Will, worked as a laborer.

"Whenever he was out of a job, he'd come out and help dad."

Once, when Hazel's Uncle Jasper and Aunt Mollie "went broke," they returned to Douglas. They had their potbellied stove and household goods, so Frank and Will helped them set up housekeeping in their corn crib. They stayed there for a winter, then went on to make their lives elsewhere. It just wasn't unusual for Will to bring home his Uncle Johnny's friend on the spur of the moment.

The country must have seemed wide open to George, with snow drifted over miles and miles of grass. Pristine in white, with the taller grasses glittering like sequins, it may have seemed untrodden, a place of opportunities.

During the following days, Hazel's mother, Frank, would have done the reading. She had her high school diploma and had graduated from Normal School, qualified to teach. She'd always read to her husband and family. The Saturday papers were full of pictures of the dead prison officials and the escaped cons, with no clues to their whereabouts. By Sunday morning, though, the Nebraska State Journal had learned that the convicts had invaded the Dickman home on Van Dorn Street within an hour of their escape. They terrorized the family until late in the evening when they took the family's wagon and left. They abandoned the wagon on the other side of town, not far from the University and disappeared into the snow.[lxxxvii]

Monday morning, Hazel went back to school in town. Not until the following Tuesday would they learn that Shorty Gray had been killed by overwhelming firepower, along with fellow escapee John Dowd and a young, newly-married farmer named Roy Blunt, whom the convicts had forced to drive them in his wagon. No one knew who had fired the bullet that killed Blunt. The third con, Charles Morley had surrendered and was back in prison to face new charges of murder.[lxxxviii]

With the escaped convicts disposed of, the family could focus on the coming spring. George's first Nebraska opportunity came almost immediately. Hazel's dad, Will, offered him a job and George didn't hesitate.

He may have wondered if Nebraskans were a little demented when Frank read about the millions of trees being hand planted in the Sandhills. In Ohio, farmers toiled year after year to remove trees that volunteered everywhere. Like George, my mother had watched trees volunteer in Ohio. Mom said she thought she'd married a madman when my father hand planted a windbreak, hundreds of trees, and watered them in buckets every night when he came in dirty and tired from the fields.

Some men stepping out from the forests onto the savannas have shrunk back into the trees. Even now, when I take people into the Sandhills, where there aren't many trees or houses and the roads have a way of wandering all over the place, they freak out. The emptiness intimidates them and the wind terrifies them. Eastern Nebraska in 1912 was only the edge of that emptiness. The Missouri breaks weren't far away and it wasn't treeless, but home sites were scattered and a lot of empty country still stretched out to the western horizon with little interruption. George had already seen what the wind could do, especially when it was pushing snow. But he held steady.

"He went to work for Dad at $26 a month, his washing, room and board," Hazel said. "That was more than he'd ever made in his life, patching together a living there in Ohio trying to farm. That ground there was so poor."

"That land was just all wore out, back there in Ohio. They couldn't nobody make a living back there. George and his brothers done everything they could. They went out in the woods and dug ginseng. They scraped the bark from little sassafras trees and sold it to the druggists. They made some kind of tea, a medicine tea from it. And they cut trees for railroad ties. But they never could get much money."

It seems ironic that they sold plants said to cure about any illness known to man while George and his brothers teetered on the edge of malnutrition. Research conducted in the 1960s shows that sassafras oil, once used as the flavoring for root beer, causes liver cancer in rodents.[lxxxix] It's probably not coincidental that Grandpa George died of liver cancer shortly after my ninth birthday.

All that summer after George's first blizzard, Grandma's younger brothers and sisters teased her about him. She kept telling them she couldn't fall for him because he was the homeliest man she'd ever seen. I wouldn't have asked him even if he'd lived long enough, but I did ask Grandma if he ever heard the teasing. She didn't know.

Grandma's marriage to the "homeliest man she'd ever seen" had become one of several Grandma stories I cherished. I decided in 1993, when Grandma was ninety-seven, that I should gather all the stories together. I lived in Lincoln by then and Grandma lived in Blue Hill, so almost every week, I drove to Grandma's house and set up the tape recorder on the arm of the couch. Then I sat on the couch and Grandma sat in her red plush recliner and we talked – both looking out the picture window toward the street. I doubt Grandma missed anything that happened on that street during our hour and a half of taping. Afterward, I would return to Lincoln.

Since then, as I've written about those interviews and thought about them, I started noticing a kind of undercurrent. My interviews are something like an oxbow along the Republican River near where I grew up. An oxbow is a loop in the river that gets cut off from the flow of the stream. It's full of algae and mats of watercress. Reeds and arrow weed grow along the shoreline and sometimes become submerged after a spring storm. Sometimes springs feed those deep pools with chilly currents that spread through the sun-warmed water. I think of Hazel and George growing together as one of those cool currents. When I listened to the tapes, I almost felt that Grandma was hesitating, listening to other voices when she answered me, particularly when she talked about Grandpa George. Grandma's way of dropping several generations into the same sentence reminds me of that rich, organic mix of living organisms along a stream.

I listened for the magic that makes people grow eternally together like clumps of prairie grasses, acres of grass joined at the roots. I try to hear my grandfather's voice in the silent waves between the vibrations of Grandma's voice. Try to remember how it sounded. I wonder how he began the conversation with Hazel when he first met her eyes.

I wonder if George ever thought himself unworthy of Hazel because of his appearance. Perhaps he began by believing in her, trusting her imagination, the thoughtful face and penetrating glance he saw that first afternoon. That look may have allowed him to think she might see beyond his ears and his teeth to the man inside. Maybe it was that trust that gave him reason to stay on through the hot, windy Nebraska summer. But he didn't act entirely on trust.

"His front teeth were awfully bad," Hazel said. "Prettinear every tooth in his head was bad. The first thing he done was to go to Lincoln to have his teeth all fixed up. I don't know how many. He had some pulled and some crowned. The dentist capped two and made several bridges. His four front teeth were bridged in. It only cost him $22.50 and them things lasted him for fifty years."

Hearing about Grandpa's teeth gave new meaning to the word courtship. I began thinking about ordinary things.

"He was the cleanest man you ever seen," Grandma said. "When he came in, the first thing he done was went and washed his face and hands and combed his hair. First thing in the morning he'd wash up and shave."

Back then, that was a gift and I try to imagine a man who would willingly carry every bucket of water for all that washing up. It's too bad his cleanliness couldn't make up for the poor diet that ruined his teeth before he grew up.

Now that we don't plow and cultivate as much, the dust isn't nearly what it was back then. In tractors with closed cabs, men can work almost entirely dust free. But in 1912, the wind didn't have to stir very much to fill a man's nose and mouth with grit and adhere to the sweat on every exposed inch of skin. Horses came without power steering and the plows lacked hydraulics. Struggling one year with a garden tiller I couldn't keep on a straight row gave me an appreciation of what it must have been like to handle the horses and hold a plow in a furrow. Grandpa wasn't much bigger than I am and Grandma said my grandfather was obsessive about plowing a straight row.

Things I've taken for granted now seem extraordinary. Grandpa never took Grandma on a Caribbean cruise or a European honeymoon, but he took her to the Old Settlers' Picnic in Palmyra after he'd worked the whole day in the wind and dust. Once they took the buggy and went by themselves. It started to rain as they were coming home. By then the elder Will and Sarah had moved to Montana, but there were other relatives.

"Uncle Jasper and Aunt Mollie lived there in town and we stayed all night with them. 'Course we had to call the folks and tell them where we was. George and Uncle Jasper was pretty good friends, too. George always got along with everybody pretty good – but if he got mad, he was mad!!"

During the eight months before George asked Hazel to marry him, their eyes must have met often over the heads of Hazel's younger brothers and sisters. Maybe Hazel learned love in those glances. Maybe it came from eating together at the same table or from going to bed in adjoining rooms – Hazel with her younger sisters and George with her brothers. They had the summer living in the same house, working together, sitting in the evening on chairs dragged out into the yard. There was the sound of green beans snapping and clanging into a pan as the family talked and watched the sun set, the air fill with fireflies that mixed with stars as they appeared, clear and bright in a deep, black sky.

George was an eager hand and, like Hazel's dad, Will, he learned how to farm the west from a transplant. Grandma has provided a picture of George and Will out in the fields. Will, tall and blond, whistles at the horses, and whistles tunes like Yankee Doodle as he swings along easily behind the plow. George, short and dark, works silent and just a little grim, driven by the poverty of his childhood to grasp his chance under Nebraska's broad, passionate skies.

"He couldn't whistle," Hazel said. "I think it was because of his teeth."

Though George worked like he was driven that summer, Hazel remembers the rare time when he laughed. "When he got tickled and laughed, everybody laughed. He just laughed until tears come down his face. I've seen him get tickled out in the yard and just lay down and roll."

Rolling along was what George needed to do when the men finished their fall work, because Hazel's dad didn't have work for him during the winter.

When he found out an old schoolmate from Ohio, Dave Kokenauer, had moved to Roseland, about one hundred twenty-five miles west, George went to visit. Kokenauer had sheep and George took a job taking care of the sheep.

"Boy!" Hazel said. "He said he'd never have any sheep. All they'd do is beller. You'd go out to feed them and they'd just beller and they'd beller and they'd beller. He'd go out and they'd follow him around and beller."

Hazel and George exchanged a letter or two while he was gone. They'd made up a code so the kids couldn't read it. Grandma saved a note from Grandpa in her steamer trunk. I found it when we sorted out her house after she died. It was written in large printed letters on lined Big Chief paper.

George stayed in Roseland until the ewes were done lambing, then he returned to Douglas. He rented his own farm the next spring.

"He was farming a quarter section," Hazel said. "He bought him a couple of horses and dad loaned him one. He broke a colt that Dad had and then he had three horses. He had an old gray mule and a gray horse and this young horse. And he got a new cultivator."

George had a little house on his quarter with a back door that opened right at the bottom of a little hill.

During their two-year engagement, Hazel and George learned the practice of love from Hazel's parents. By seeing old established love, with all its wrongs and inevitable offenses graced and forgiven, they could learn to trust the ardor and hope of their own growing affection.

"They was always sweethearts," Hazel said of her parents. "Anytime you come in, you might find her sitting on his lap."

Although Hazel's mother, Frank, had come by a man's name through an accident of her dad's stubbornness, it suited her well. She said what she thought and her husband, Will, listened. They had a partnership. "Dad decided what to do," Hazel said, "but it was most often what mom wanted. Dad only went to third grade and he respected Mom's education. But he wasn't no wimp, either."

For George, this grace and respect probably came as a revelation in contrast with his own parents' marriage. Will Colburn ruled his roost, Grandma Hazel said, ignoring anything his wife, Sarah, might say.

"Seemed like whatever she wanted, he wanted to do something different," Hazel said. "And she never . . . she'd just shut up. She'd never say nothing. He was the boss. You know them old bosses. A woman was just another one of their . . . not much more than a horse or a cow. She was just there to do the work and have the kids."

Grandma told me that they once visited George's family in Ohio. A neighbor who'd helped with Sarah's births whispered to Hazel that whenever Sarah had a baby, there was her husband "right there on top of her." Right away. I've always wondered how the neighbor knew anything about that. Was she Sarah's confidant? Did she stay the night when Sarah gave birth?

Hazel says she never knew how it was George turned out different, but he seemed bent on giving his family much more than he'd had. He noticed his wife. He noticed how hard she worked and he didn't want to work her until she was old before her time. Years after he was gone, when I lived in Grandma's and Grandpa's house, I sat in a chair by the window and gazed through swirling snow toward where the windmill used to be. I imagine him gazing at that windmill and making plans. I don't know of anyone who ever tried what he did with that windmill. He ran a pipe to the top of the tower then ran more water pipe from there, suspended over the work area in the yard, to the hog lots west of the orchard. He counted on the windmill to pump water all the way up the tower so Hazel wouldn't have to carry all those buckets of water to the hogs. She could work in the house during the hot summer afternoons when he was in the fields and the hogs needed water, not just to drink but also in slick, viscous wallows to cake their skin with mud. All Hazel would have to do was switch a valve.

In the spring, he called the well man and he ran that pipe. It worked until the Rural Electrification Administration brought power to rural America, and finally allowed him to pump water for the livestock.

"As soon as we had electricity, he put automatic waterers with heaters in the chicken house," Hazel said, "so I wouldn't have to carry water."

I've never figured out how she guessed George would be that kind of husband and she couldn't give me an answer. When she spoke of entering George's house for the first time as his bride, she said she'd been there often before with her younger brothers and sisters. "I knowed what I was agetting into," she said.

On November 17, 1912, Hazel's sixteenth birthday, George asked her to marry him. "I don't remember any dramatic moment or anything," she says. "No. He wasn't that kind of guy. But still he was sometimes. You know, we never had too much time. We had a lot of kids around. My brother and sisters always knowed what was agoing on. Especially Norma and Mahlon. He had to make a big effort just to get me off by myself. He gave me this ring on my finger."

She wore that ring for eighty-four years of planting seeds, picking produce, wringing chicken necks, shucking corn, carrying water and rearing children. I think she left molecules of gold in every corner of the farm.

Once, Grandma mentioned in passing there was no one left to talk to. I was a little hurt. "But," she said, "no one's left knows what I know."

Aunt Eva May

Eva May Colburn grew up poor in the shadow of Long Knob, Ohio,[xc] where mining, drilling and lumbering had squeezed subsistence farmers like her father, William, to the brink of starvation. William had always produced most of what his family consumed. He had raised crops on small areas he'd cleared and his wife always had a big garden. All his life he had hunted deer and squirrels on "common" forest areas and generations of farmers like him had released hogs to forage on chestnuts and acorns, then harvested those hogs for meat. But in the 1880s, when William has a young husband and father, coal mining, gas drilling and lumber companies were rapidly purchasing and denuding all the forest lands that small farmers depended upon.[xci]

They hung on in their Ross County home for several years, even after their first boy, three-year-old Carey, died. Then, in 1891, the Colburns, with their three remaining boys, Edward, Frank and George, retreated one county further south—to Pike County— hoping to escape the effects of all the resource consumption.[xcii] But the same industrial blight soon settled in their new home—little more than a cabin where William and Sarah raised eight children. Eva May was the fifth child; the first daughter and the first born in Pike County. She was closest to her next-older brother, George. By the time he left in fall of 1911, she was the oldest of five siblings at home with an increasingly bitter father and a worn-out mother.

Once George got settled on a rented place in Nebraska, she came west too and arrived in September, 1914. She moved in with George, my grandfather, who was "batchin" just outside Douglas, Nebraska. She kept house for him while she looked for work.[xciii]

Grandma Hazel, still a teenager, and Eva, twenty-one, must have really "got on." Perhaps it was nice for Grandma to have an older "sister." As oldest sisters in large families, they probably had a lot in common. But Grandma only talked a couple of times, briefly, about a woman who was an enormous part of one of the most important events in her life. Then Eva passed out of my consciousness. It didn't occur me to wonder why there were no photos of Eva or why Grandma didn't have more to say about her.

That fall, everybody knew Hazel and George were getting married. They'd been engaged for two years, because Hazel's parents had insisted that she be 18 before they got married. Much later, I realized how important it was then to wait. Teen births now are difficult and dangerous. Back then, childbirth at any age was perilous, the younger the mother the greater the danger. Childbirth was often fatal and there was no reliable birth control to prevent it. Not only did Grandma have enormous respect for her parents, she also must have realized the danger. She waited.

But in September, 1914, Grandma Hazel's 18th birthday was rapidly approaching and only Eva knew about her brother's planned "elopement." Grandma wasn't a giggler, but she and Eva often had their heads together, whispering, as they planned for the big day. Grandma said she and Grandpa slipped away because they wanted to avoid a shivaree. I think they really did it for a lark—not the marriage, they were absolutely serious about their marriage—but the secret planning and the slipping away. The wonderful privacy must have seemed scandalous and exciting—especially when they managed to sneak out from under the very noses of Hazel's younger brothers and sisters, particularly ten-year-old Norma and seven-year-old Mahlon. Eva got into the spirit of all those plans right away; maybe she even instigated the secret. It turns out she was pretty good at secrecy.

Eva was there when Grandma Hazel made her wedding dress. It was complicated and Hazel wasn't an accomplished seamstress, so it took some time. The collar and cuffs and the taffeta trim even required some new skills and Eva helped. I can imagine her leaning over the old treadle sewing machine, watching and reaching in occasionally to smooth a seam. As they put those delicate cuffs together, the two would work side-by-side, each hand-basting a cuff before one or the other sat down at the machine to secure the seam. They spent odd hours together when the eggs were all gathered, the fruit all canned and the garden tended, laughing and talking while they turned the collar and cuffs and smoothed them. They got it all done in plenty of time.

"Cream colored wool crepe. Of course it was long sleeved, a long dress. Just a plain dress," Grandma said.

On November 18, 1914, George, Eva and Hazel celebrated Grandma Hazel's eighteenth birthday, a day late, with a trip to Lincoln. It was about twenty miles away and they arrived mid-morning.

"Steves [a neighbor] had got a brand new Ford car and George hired him to take us up there. Eva went with us. We'd planned for quite a while. We just hadn't told anybody. I put on my wedding dress in my room. Of course I had my coat on. I had a black plush coat and a velvet hat. It was cold. Clear and cold and not too windy."

Eva must have helped Grandma hide that dress under her coat, keeping Hazel's sisters out of the room while Grandma got dressed. I wonder how she kept them busy so that they wouldn't suspect.

"We got married in Lincoln at the same courthouse that my mother was married in. n the judge's chambers. It must have been about 10 or 11 o'clock when we got in there."

"We had something to eat and we wandered around Lincoln and bought a few things. I've got a little sugar bowl that's kind of cracked that I think we bought that day. Just a few things like that. A kerosene lantern. George only had one in the living room. I bought one for the bedroom."

They were an attractive threesome, George and Eva, dark and lean, and Hazel, blond and statuesque, all with just a twinkle of their secret. They may have walked arm in arm down the mains streets of Lincoln, chatting and ducking in and out of shops, examining the merchandise and carrying their little paper packages.

"We started home pretty early. You know, when they had their first automobiles, there weren't very many of them liked to drive after night. I suppose George had paid for everything. I didn't have any money. I hadn't ever earned a penny in my life. And yet to this day, I've never earned a penny for working out. I always had my chickens and things like that, but after we were married, what was his was mine—everything.

"We went back to the folks' and I packed some clothes. Of course, we already had that taken care of, most of it. I had some bags of stuff. Eva and us, we walked home. [We done lots of walking them days.] We'd sneaked off and got married and they didn't know. Didn't none of them know."

I could almost hear a chuckle in her voice, more than eighty years later. "The folks said afterward that they was awatching. 'Yep, she went home with him,' they said. 'They got married.'"

You don't hire a photographer when you sneak off to get married, so Grandma had no wedding pictures. There was no reason to wonder why there's no picture of Eva from the wedding, even though she was, apparently, the maid-of-honor.

The "folks" must have burned up the phone wires that evening, though, because Hazel and George's clever plan failed.

"That night we had the shivaree crowd. The whole neighborhood was there. We didn't avoid it anyway. They come over and they went around the house and pounded tin cans and shot off shotguns in the air and made all the noise they could. And then we invited them to come in. I think we was prepared for them. We had candy bars and cigars. You know, that was just customary. We'd have probably felt bad if they hadn't shivareed us."

Again, Eva helped out, handing out the celebratory candy and cigars, smiling at her brother's pride. He'd made a good catch, coming from dirt poor southern Appalachia and marrying into a solid, prosperous family. And he and Hazel were obviously head-over-heels. Eva hoped she would do as well. The shivaree was a chance to get acquainted with some of the neighbors. She needed a job and one of those celebrating neighbors might hire her or even come "sparking."

"Then we had to give them an oyster supper," Grandma said. "Not that same night, though. When they come back for the oyster supper, they brought me a linen tablecloth. A big, long one. I wore it out. I always used it when we had thrashers and when we had company. They brought some little presents. I had a stemmed jelly dish that Aunt Ada Carpenter give me."

Eva helped make the oyster supper, too. Maybe she helped some of the shivaree crowd with hints about what Hazel and George needed.

"We moved into a little house, was just one big room and two little bits of bedrooms. Just big enough for a bed. One was a storeroom. We had a fold-up couch in the living room. That's where Eva slept. I'd been in that house a lot of times before. All of us kids would go over there. I knowed what I was getting into.

"We had a tall, wooden bed with the scrolled headboard all carved. George had made a little stand out of a grocery box with legs on it. That's where we put the lantern. We had pegs along the wall to hang our clothes up on. We never had a dresser as long as we lived there. Didn't have room for one."

Grandma never indicated any hesitation about sharing her tiny home with her sister-in-law, even during the first nights of her marriage. Life settled back into the everyday almost immediately and Eva was part, not only of Grandma and Grandpa's wedding, but also of their married life. Grandma didn't even remember what she did the first day. Probably went back to her mom's to get the rest of her clothes and the cow, she said. Her parents gave them a cow and a bunch of chickens for a wedding present. Hazel probably took a share of the fruit and vegetables she'd helped to grow and can. And, with her sister-in-law's help, she began work on the house. If Eva hadn't had enough practice cleaning house back in Ohio, Hazel and George provided more experience that she would use when she found a job.

"We just had blinds on the windows. I made some curtains and put up. Board floors. Had to scrub them and scrub them and scrub them.

"The people who lived there before I did had put building paper on the walls. Used to be when they built a house, they put this real heavy paper inside the walls. That was before insulation. They'd papered the walls and the ceilings, even, with this heavy, reddish/pinkish colored paper. Evidently, they'd had it plastered at one time and the plaster got bad. Wallpaper was cheap then and Eva and I papered it, right over the building paper."

For a couple of months, the two women kept busy cutting and sewing, pasting and papering, cleaning and cooking. Then Hazel was on her own. Grandma said that Eva got a job with a neighbor around Christmastime. She moved in with her employer where she worked as a "domestic" doing all the same things she and Hazel had been doing together. They kept her pretty busy, but she still managed to get away for Sunday visits, for the occasional Old Settler's Picnic and maybe even for a secret beau.

She managed to get away for a couple of weeks almost a year later, October 4, 1915, two days before her twenty-second birthday, She was back helping Grandma with a new baby, my father. She took care of household chores, helped to care for the baby and provided the intimate little services women provide for each other. Once again, she took a significant role in one of Hazel's and George's milestones, but Grandma never mentioned her again. I never thought to ask. Family members wandered in and out of Grandma's tales all the time.

I didn't miss her—until I found her death certificate when I was looking for her sister-in-law Eva Colburn. She died May 31, 1916, in an "indigent home" in Milford. She had puerperal eclampsia; she was not married. Apparently she was already pregnant when she helped out with my dad, although even she may not have known it yet.

I can only imagine how Eva became pregnant. Was she a victim of rape? I wonder about the neighbor where she worked. I wonder if he took advantage of a young, single girl. Or maybe he had a grown, or nearly-grown, son. I wonder about all of the neighbors. Who would believe the young newcomer?

His grandchildren describe Eva's father as a gentle, loving man. Maybe Eva thought she'd found that aspect of her father in a beau. But whatever or whomever betrayed her, Eva held her head up and kept working as long as she could. As a first-time mother, she probably didn't "show" until late. But, by the beginning of her seventh month, the trouble may have started. As her blood pressure rose, she'd have began to suffer from blinding headaches. Sometimes she literally became blind; sometimes she saw spots, flashing lights, auras or just blurred vision. And suddenly her hands and face began to swell.[xciv]

In those days, being single and pregnant was a crime, punishable by imprisonment, so there was hardly any place for her.[xcv] Grandma kept her secret so well, I'm reduced to mere speculation. I can't imagine, though, that Eva wouldn't have confided in her brother and his wife. When she got sick, she may have stayed with them for a while as they looked for a place where she could get medical attention. But she may have toughed it out on her own. She could have found the Nebraska Industrial Home in Milford by herself and simply boarded a Burlington and Missouri train alone. Perhaps she hoped that no one would know about her pregnancy and she could give the baby up and live her life.

A rules pamphlet called the Nebraska Industrial Home a place for "homeless, penitent girls who have no specific disease." Back then, it was the only state-supported maternity home in the entire nation. Although the residents were called inmates, the new mothers and mothers-to-be learned domestic skills there. Ironically, they had classes on caring for the babies they were expected to give up for adoption. Eva had already long-since mastered those skills as the oldest sister in a large family. More important for her, since she had not received much education, she got to attend academic classes.[xcvi]

At Milford, she'd have lived in a four-story, brick dorm, rising at five a.m. and going to work by six. She might have arrived in time to go out into the woods and gather wild strawberries or gooseberries, if she felt well enough. If not, she might have been well enough to sit on the back lawn in the evening to stem gooseberries and sing with the other young mothers and mothers-to-be. The girls rotated among several job locations, including the kitchen where they cooked and served meals for the inmates. They canned and pickled and preserved. In the laundry, they washed on a washboard and ironed with irons heated on the stove. They served as nurses in the hospital and took care of all the housework. Some of the girls also worked in the nurseries taking care of the babies. The Home maintained dairy cows and hogs to help provide food for the young women and their babies. There were also chickens and ducks to supply eggs as well as meat.[xcvii]

Between 2:15 and 4:45 every afternoon Eva would have received the instruction that meant the most to her. The girls learned reading, penmanship, spelling, grammar, arithmetic, physiology, drawing and music after the work of supporting the home was done every day.

Eva would have attended chapel at eight p.m., whether she wished to or not. Incoming mail was distributed after chapel and all letters, coming and going, were read by the superintendent. The lights went out at nine.[xcviii]

She was only at Milford for about two months, although a condition of admittance required that she stay for a year. I wonder if she and Grandma wrote. Grandma wrote many letters during the years I knew her. But as a busy young mother, she may have had little time. Eva was only allowed to write letters once every two weeks, but she could receive mail every evening. Grandma was barely able to keep tabs on her friend and confidant by letter.

Grandma and Grandpa may have thought Eva was safe at Milford and that they would help her get started again after the baby and the year in the Home. Even so, there's a good chance Eva spent her short two months in the hospital instead of working. Perhaps she was in and out of the three big rooms the Home had renovated in 1912 for a hospital. With their steel walls and ceiling and fresh paint, the rooms were easy to keep clean and sanitary. She'd have been looked after by other young, unwed mothers or mothers-to-be like herself.[xcix]

Milford is only about forty miles from Douglas, but back then, it was a day's travel. The Burlington and Missouri Railroad had spurs out of Douglas and into Milford, but with train changes it would have been a long day, for my grandma with a seven-month-old baby. The "home" in Milford might as well have been in another state and inmates there were only allowed visitors once every two months on the last Thursday between one and five p.m.[c] Grandma and Grandpa could only have visited once on Thursday, May 25. Maybe Grandpa visited alone.

He must have been alarmed when he arrived. By then, Eva was probably experiencing muscle aches and abdominal pain, right below her ribs. She'd have been severely agitated. Perhaps she'd have had her first seizures by then.[ci] A Dr. Saunders took care of Eva the last five days of her life. I don't know if he was "on call" for the home or if Grandpa called him and stayed around waiting to be sure his sister was safe. He was still there when she gave birth. Grandma may have come at the end, too. No one's left who knows if Eva's baby survived.

I wasn't there, so I don't know, but common symptoms of puerperal eclampsia include seizures, unconsciousness and coma following or during childbirth.[cii] Eva's brother was right there by her side, holding her hand through it all—a surrogate for the man who should have been there—the man who has no name. Decades later, Grandma honored Eva with her name, even as she kept her secret. She was very clear—her sister-in-law's name was pronounced "eh vah," not "ee vah."

I know so little. Eva's a ghost. When I learned about her, I looked back at a booklet my cousins made for a family reunion. I found one picture of Eva at 19, just a year before she came to Nebraska. The photo's black and white, so there is no color reference, but it appears that she's wearing a white blouse with a scarf or tie and a long, black skirt. She's not smiling and looks a bit warily toward the camera. She's facing slightly away and, as in many photos of that time, she's standing with her hands behind her back. She looks like she's handcuffed.

Her story appears only in snippets mixed into Grandma's story. When I knew Grandma, she was indignant about the way women get blamed while men just walk away. Now I know why that indignation is so deep. Grandma knew that some man, probably someone Eva had trusted with her life— literally—had walked away, leaving Eva, young, naïve and away from home for the first time, a criminal and finally, dead. Eva's secret might have been safe forever. Grandma never breathed a word. If I hadn't been looking for her sister-in-law, I'd have never found her. Now, I'd like to know her. I'd like to honor her short life, but no one's left who knows what Grandma knew.

Barn-blind Mules

In the orchard west of the house, Hazel listened to the hens singing as she picked a couple of sweet, yellow cherries. She ate them, just to see if they were ready. Golden and sweet, they were never very juicy but they were ripe. She'd hoped to pick them that afternoon, in case the storm predicted for the night brought hail or high winds. She'd get the kids up in the tree, they were more birds than people anyway . . .

As she followed a narrow, mowed path to check the sour pie cherries, she heard the faint rasp and chirp of insects in the tall prairie grasses and wildflowers her husband, George, allowed to grow among the trees. Over the hill on the southwest hay field, she could barely hear George, and their neighbor, Frank Arterburn, talking over the clatter of the stacker. She smiled as she thought about how upset Frank had been that morning when he came over to help put up hay. She wondered if he'd lost a lot of sleep.

"We shoulda got this started last night," he told George. "I just got too busy and it got dark," he said. "It's bad luck to start anything on a Friday, you know."

She remembered the week before when she and George had gone out at dawn to chop weeds from the cornfield. There was Frank, already clearing firebush along the fencerow. As they walked up, she heard their shoes crunch clods along the corn row and the swish/chop of Frank's corn knife slicing through chest-high cockleburs.

"What're you doing, Frank?" George had asked. "You've got your own work to do."

"Oh, I've got that mess of kids chopping weeds on my place. I knowed you wanted to get this done before any of this stuff went to seed and I want to start cutting hay before Friday," he'd said.

Hazel had gathered up her apron to pick enough bright cherries for a pie when the men's calm voices turned into shouts and the stacker clatter turned into a frantic smashing and banging. In just a couple of seconds, as she realized Frank's mules had taken off for home. She gathered up her skirt and sprinted for the road. If she could get ahead of the mules, she could turn them into the lane and—maybe—get them stopped.

She raced to the road and stopped just east of the driveway. As the mules crested the hill, eyes rolling in terror, she jumped and waved her arms. Unable to stop, the mules veered hard left. Apparently, the car shed reminded them of home and they careened in, barely stopping in time before they punched their way out the back. They were still panting when George and Frank trudged up the hill. Hazel was panting just a little bit, too.

I asked Grandma how she got ahead of those mules running full tilt.

"Oh," she said, "I could run then."

Back then, little stories like these, of mules and men, were a staple of neighborhood get-togethers. And neighborhood get-togethers were a staple of daily life. Until the labor shortage during World War II led to mechanized farming, neighbors shared labor and equipment and their daily lives. Now the whole countryside is industrialized and farms are becoming

90

larger and larger agribusinesses that compete for land and resources. The people like my grandfather are gone and so are the mules. Hardly anyone misses them.

Yet, when I look at the skeleton of the land my grandfather worked, I can still see the pattern of his mind on that land. I don't think that kind of intelligent stewardship can take place at the scale we see now in agriculture. Agribusiness people, managing thousands of acres, don't have the time to pay attention to a little two-acre game preserve here or a one hundred fifty foot waterway there. Alternating crops to control pests gives way to chemicals that kill pests and beneficial insects alike.

My grandmother often quoted her husband, "We don't own the land," he'd say. "We're just give it to take care of for the next generation."

Take care of it he did, and if we'd been able to carry forward the practices he initiated, they'd have stood for the seventh generation.

On still nights when I couldn't sleep, Grandma Hazel would snuggle me next to her warm body and tell me to shush so I could hear the train. Sure enough I'd hear the rattle and whistle of the Burlington Northern and Santa Fe snaking through the hills a mile and a half west and my imagination would carry me into sweet slumber.

Grandma's Trip

One day in spring of 1928, Grandma Hazel dropped a pin. She heard it tinkle when it hit the linoleum. It bounced from end to end, then settled down and rolled. She couldn't see where it rolled and, as she began looking for it, she felt a bit of pressure building behind her eyes.

Although she always found everyone else's needles in haystacks, her pin eluded her. On her hands and knees, she crawled around the corner where she'd been mending, feeling for the pin. She found only dust blown in overnight. The pressure in her head increased as she worried that someone would step on that lost pin, even though her husband wouldn't come in for hours and the kids had just left for school.

It's just a pin, she thought. And then, inexplicably even to her, she began to cry and she couldn't stop.

Month after month the Weather Bureau had reported deficient moisture and deficient wind to bring in the moisture.[ciii] Grandma and Grandpa did not need the weather reports to tell them about the stress on their winter wheat crop. They'd seen the signs since the previous fall. Without realizing it, Grandma Hazel missed the sound of the wind whooshing around the corner of the house and shaking the porch windows in their frames. She hadn't slept well all spring, waiting for sleep, listening to the train, waiting for the high-tension hum of wind across the telephone line, like a bow on violin strings. She'd had no breeze sighing through the screens to sing her to sleep.

When she dropped the pin, the tinkle seemed amplified by the silence. She scrabbled around on the floor, tears streaming, until she just sat down and wept.

Outside, sun poured on crops and fields. All winter, when she'd walked across the wool living room carpet, she'd got an annoying shock.[civ] Already in January, the wheat had shown drought stress.[cv] George had grazed the cows on it because the pasture had dried out early. She could see that the grazed fields looked bleak.[cvi] The first week of February, light rain mixed with snow had teased her into thinking the wheat would be all right, but then the rain stopped and the crop yellowed again. In March, the highs had ranged between seventy-five and ninety degrees and the wheat died.[cvii]

Grandma didn't remember finding the pin and she didn't remember the many other inconveniences that made her cry. Often, she cried because she "just felt like it." Perched on her hill between the Little Blue and Republican rivers, she could see for miles around and it all looked dry. By the end of the day, most days, she felt "all in," like she could barely drag herself to bed, knowing she would have to do her chores all over again the next day. She had no Prozac® or Zoloft® and no psychiatrist's couch where she could lie down and talk about her troubles. She had only her relationship with the land and her family and community, all holding her in mind with loving concern and deep familiarity that comes from living and doing together.

"Hazel just wasn't quite right," said her sister-in-law, Emily. "We could all see that she wasn't herself."[cviii]

Emily's assessment gave me goosebumps when my cousin, Phoebe Larne, relayed it to me. I'd heard the phrase before. "Wasn't quite right" is what happens in the summer when a big wind from the southwest blows up a hailstorm that shatters the windows and smashes the corn. Then something happens. Maybe heat lightning makes a horse shy and he drags a wagon-load of wheat over a man's body. Maybe a kid gets in a hurry to beat the rain and reaches into a baler and his arm gets dragged into it.

This time, the phrase told me something different. Grandma's family was paying attention to her. Close attention. I know those old stoics. They didn't say anything at all and Grandma probably didn't even know they were watching. But they knew she was in trouble and they were ready to intervene, if they could just figure out what to do.

Sixteen years had passed since Grandpa had given her the soft twenty-four karat ring with its little chip diamond and it had already started to wear. After their November wedding, they'd had plenty of time together without much farm work to do. They cut some wood for the cook stove and the heating stove and they read.

A runt pig provided their greatest excitement their first year.

"It was kind of a pet," Grandma said. "George give it to me to take care of and we were gone. She was getting about two hundred pounds. We come home and she'd got the back door open. We always took our corn and wheat to the mill, you know, and we'd just got a fifty-pound sack of cornmeal. It was setting in the sack in that storeroom. She come in the back door and got into that. It was the awfullest mess you ever seen

. . . she had the cornmeal all over the room. I think she probably wet on it or something. It was in the living room, too."

About eleven months after their wedding, Grandma left her husband to shuck the corn on his own, even though she worked faster because of his damaged hand. She couldn't shuck corn in bed and Doc Hostetter ordered that she stay in bed for ten days after she gave birth, October 4, 1915, to a twelve-pound boy, my dad.

"Mom and I had the bed padded down good so it [blood and birth fluids] didn't go through. We used some old quilts that had wore out. She seen about the water and had the cloths and whatever else ready. The doctor did the delivering. Your grandpa was kind of nervous before the doctor got there, but after Mom and Doc Hostetter got there, why, he was all right. He was pretty calm about it. He sat right by my bed and held my hand during the whole time.

"I weighed 110 pounds before I was pregnant. Had to take him with forceps. I had to have a lot of stitches. He was big, long and lanky, but he didn't have a bit of fat. The first thing he does is cries, so that was it. We named him Cecil.

"They wrapped him in a towel and put him in my arms at first. Then they took him out and greased him up and pommed his hair. I had never seen a newborn baby. I never had."

While Eva did the legwork, Grandma sat up in bed with a pincushion at her elbow, keeping the pins under control, and a needle in her hand.

"I suppose I patched and sewed. There was always something I could do in bed. I don't think they needed to keep me down that long, but it gave me a chance to get acquainted with my baby. After a child is born, a family becomes kind of a different family," she said.

"I think fatherhood was a joy to George, but men never used to pay much attention to the kids. I don't think he ever diapered one of his kids, but he took care of Cecil when I weaned him. Nine months. We always weaned the babies at nine months back in them days. And Cecil bawled all night. George just took Cecil in his arms and he held him all night long. Walked around the floor and rocked him and joggled him in his arms until morning. So Cecil wouldn't have to be alone when we took away that comfort."

By the time they weaned Cecil, Grandma was pregnant again. Early in the morning of April 4, 1917, Hazel gave birth a second time to a "little butterball" they named Nina Marie. Again Doc Hostetter attended with Frank's help.

"When I was in labor, I could see in the kitchen. Dad was standing by the window and talking to Cecil. Holding him up there, looking out the window, chattering with him about something. Cecil was a chatterbox. He'd come up after Nina was born and climb up on the bed. Both of my kids talked pretty young. It didn't take him long to call her Nina. He started out calling her Nine."

Since Eva was gone, Grandma hired one of her dozens of cousins to help around the house for a couple of weeks as she got back on her feet.

"Everybody always had a hired girl," Grandma said. "That was the only work young girls had to do. Most of them didn't go to high school, they went out and worked for somebody with a baby. Two and a half a week. We never paid more than two dollars and a half a week for a hired girl."

They had no problem paying that two and a half. Grandma said that they'd done well farming. They worked hard, never bought anything on credit and put money in the bank. Up until then, Grandma's life seemed to be going just like she wanted.

"After the First World War, prices boomed. Everything went up," Hazel said. "I always thought the kids could go to college. Everything was going good and then I started to cry. 1928."

In 1928 her kids were growing up strong and healthy. She had a wonderful marriage. The stock market crash was about eighteen months in the future. The first dust storm was about five years off. Yet she always seemed to be searching for that pin.

"What did you cry about?" I asked.

"Oh, I don't know. I just felt like it. I couldn't do my work very good. I lost my appetite. I got thin. I was just all in. I couldn't stay with anything. I'd start something and it seemed like I couldn't stay with it. I felt like giving up."

Puzzled, I just listened.

"I think it was kind of hard on George, because all at once I'd—over nothing—I'd bawl. He'd come in from the fields and I'd be crying or I'd been crying. He'd hug me and kiss me and talk to me. It would help for a while."

When she said her crying was hard on Grandpa, she reminded me of her gift for understatement. I'm convinced that he was head-over-heels over her on their first meeting as she blew in with the sharp cold following his first blizzard. He'd only grown more in love during the sixteen years following. While she cried, he would have worked the fences on Sundays, distracted, tearing his hands on sharp barbed wire spurs he was hardly aware of, slamming his fingers with the fencing pliers. He might have stopped in the fields sometimes, resting the horses, scratching their withers, maybe looking toward the house and willing his wife to feel better, holding her vibrant in his mind working and watching and waiting for his chance to do something.

"How did the kids cope with all that crying?" I asked.

"I tried not to let the kids know it," she said. "I don't think they ever knowed it. They were in school."

Nina turned eleven in 1928; my dad, Cecil, twelve. They would come home from school and find their mother standing in the kitchen, eyes red and puffy, dragging herself around like a sack of meal. Even a kid notices. They knew. In their own, kids' way, they were waiting too.

"Finally, George made me go to the doctor," she said. "I felt like there was something wrong to cause it, too."

Doc O'Neill told Hazel that she should have been taking medicine since her surgery.

"He said I was probably going through—probably just went through—menopause. That's about what happened. He gave me medicine. It helped. It helped some."

"1928. Menopause?" I said, adding fast. "But . . . you were only thirty-one."

"Well, I had a hysterectomy when I lost that baby. They took everything."

Apparently the baby and the hysterectomy and the breakdown were not secrets. They were just painful and past and no one talked about them. I sort of knew I'd had another uncle who had died as an infant but in a myth-like way that wasn't real to me, like my mother's singing career.

"Winter of 1919, when we moved to Webster County," Grandma said. "I was pretty far along—pregnant. We came on the train. Mom and Dad and I and the kids come on the train. A lot of our stuff was shipped on the train, too. The cattle and the machinery was shipped on the train. We got on in the morning and we got out here in the evening. We took lunch along."

That ride took Grandma and her family whistling and rattling through new little Nebraska towns—Beatrice, Fairbury, Hebron. Trailing sound and steam, the Burlington

Missouri took them to Cowles. Perhaps the ride and the moving wore her out.

"We got the flu. The folks got it first. Earl was in France, World War I, Argonne Woods so Ollie, his wife, come up and took care of them. We had it, too. Anna, George's younger sister, come out and took care of us. She was just eighteen. We was really sick and Anna was the only one that was able to do anything. She done the chores. We had horses in the barn and she took care of the horses. Done the milking and fed the chickens and gathered the eggs. Cecil . . . was only three-and-a-half. Anna took care of him. The doctor at the time said his heart was affected. But later he was all right."

In the spaces of her story, I remembered that she was talking about the 1918-1919 Spanish Flu Epidemic. Later I found a Stanford University Website to fill in the details. It infected a fifth of the world's population; twenty-eight percent of all Americans. In the U.S., 675,000 died—ten times the number who died in World War I. More people died in a single year than in four years of the Black Death [Bubonic Plague].cix I'm sobered by how close I came to never existing.

My family all survived, but surely my grandmother, far along in her third pregnancy, suffered some weakening of her normally robust immune system.

Soon after Grandma and her little family got up and about, Grandma went into labor. On March 19, 1919, not quite two years after her last baby, she gave birth once more. This time, Doc Hostetter was half a state away. Great-grandma Frank saw to the cloths and the water again.

"I had a real short labor and everything. He was a good, strong, healthy baby when he was born. More than nine pounds. But the doctor came from a blood poison case. I think it was one of the Zimmerman boys had blood poison . . . and I got blood poison and the baby got . . . it, too.

"I was so bad they finally took me to the hospital. I think it was a little over two weeks. We drove the buggy to Cowles, got on the train and went to Hastings to the hospital. We had to get a taxi. I had such a high fever, up there where it was awful dangerous. I was out of my head and didn't know nothing. Not unconscious, but I was seeing things that wasn't. I was kind of irrational for a while."

"The baby—you didn't take the baby with you. We left him at home with Mom and Ollie. They was taking care of him and he got pneumonia. They didn't have penicillin; they didn't have anything like that then. Not for years afterwards. Carbolic acid is what they used for disinfectant."

After a week, George came in hanging his head. Their good, strong, healthy baby boy had died overnight.

"I went all to pieces. I cried and cried. George just held me. He said, 'It could have been Nina or Cecil.' That wasn't any comfort, but I could see how it was for him."

After another week of high fever and delirium, "They give me a real good examination and they found out I had what they called a water tumor. They said that sometimes they grow overnight big as a basketball. So that's when they operated. They took everything. They took my appendix and everything. It was all from the blood poison."

The doctor performed a salpingo-oopho-hysterectomy, removing her uterus, fallopian tubes and ovaries. Grandma remembers lying helpless, waiting for the fever to go down and hearing the doctor tell George he was afraid she wouldn't make it. She wanted to tell them she would be all right, but she couldn't speak.

"I never had any idea I wasn't going to make it."

Grandpa George hung around the hospital every hour he could get away from spring plowing and planting. He waited, silent, hour after hour, hoping and watching. He brought her a dozen red roses and hoped she would be able to see them.

She survived and went home.

And that's it. In one long moment in 1919, Grandma lost all of her children-to-be for the rest of her life. I had seen my Grandmother's belly, puckered with every stitch, every time that needle pierced her flesh in an attempt to put her back together. Apparently, they left out some parts—the ones she found herself searching for as she crawled around on the floor after that sharp, tinkling pin. For a year, she couldn't climb the stairs to the second floor where her children slept and I wonder how she got through the nights.

I couldn't invade her pain, and it obviously still hurt, although I had a million questions.

Instead I asked, "How old were you?"

"Twenty-two. I was twenty-three in November."

The abrupt loss of estrogen production with the loss of her ovaries should have crashed her through menopause immediately. I wondered how she weathered those years and if something else changed nine years later in 1928. I asked how she and Grandpa got along after the baby died. I asked if she ever fought with Grandpa and who made the decisions.

"Pop was usually the boss," she said. "I think he was a little smarter than me, although I don't know as I ever told him so. We argued sometimes a little bit. I usually told him what I thought and he told me what he thought and, I'll have to be honest about it, usually he come to my way if I just shut up . . . and didn't say no more about it."

"So you never fought," I asked.

"Heavens no!" she said. "We had our twelfth wedding anniversary and I heard Norma ask George, 'You know, I never have heard you guys fighting.' George says in that slow way of his, 'We never fight.' We didn't either.

"He would always listen. Things usually went his way, but when I made up my mind, things wasn't right, I told him."

She volunteered one of those times when things weren't right.

"Pop would get done in the field and he'd decide he wanted to go to town and play cards. He didn't hardly go very often. But he got so he'd leave the horses for me to unharness and put away. Well, I thought if he wanted to go enjoy himself that was fine, because he worked hard. But I had my work to do and I thought he could take care of the horses first. So one night I left them standing just like they was. Oh, I laid awake all night thinking about them poor horses.

"He never done that again. He took care of the horses first."

But, I thought, even then, she didn't tell him when she thought things weren't right. I'd never heard her say anything in a firm tone of voice and I wasn't sure she had it in her. My neighbor, Walt Witte, set me straight about that, one afternoon standing on Grandma's threshold, reminiscing about the old place when Grandma and Grandpa traded work with his family. He said that, when he was a kid, he'd been working at Hazel's and George's when noon came around, so Hazel fed him. But when his dad came to pick him up, Walt was still eating and his dad had a fit.

"Hazel faced him down," Walt said. "She told Dad that when somebody's at her house at dinnertime, they eat and that's that. He was to leave me alone and let me eat . . . and he did!"cx

I asked Grandma if Grandpa ever said things that hurt her feelings.

"Well, I remember one night I got my feelings hurt or some such thing," she said. "I went out and walked in the pasture in the moonlight. Then I just sat down on the side of the hill. Pretty soon, here come a family of skunks arolling and playing around with their mother. I watched them for a while and then whatever it was that was bothering me seemed kind of foolish. I don't even remember what it was. I just remember the skunks."

Skunks. Grandpa apparently wasn't the problem. He was the solution. Sometimes some serendipitous inspiration born of love and long familiarity saves a person who's wandered into a dark prairie winter. George was looking for that kind of safety. Doc O'Neill's drugs had made Grandma better, but not better enough for her husband. Grandpa George gave his wife a vacation, and their families enthusiastically joined in. It was the opportunity they'd waited for, to do something.

"That was the first time we went to California, that summer after school was out," Grandma said. "George had gone out with Henry Field Seed Company in 1927 after the crops were in. The brother, Saul Field, was taking excursions out to California. George went out on one of them. He was looking for land of his own. We rented from Dad, you know. He bought this acreage in the Sacramento Valley. Twenty-two and some acres.

"That was agetting just about the time everything went blooey. My brother Lawrence and his wife, Emily, sold out and he got him a Chevy truck. Wasn't nobody of our family out there yet. My brother-in-law, Carl, and my sister, Edna, they decided to take a trip. They had bought them a 1928 Chevy. We had a 1928 Chevy. That was the first touring car with the lights and everything like that. Always before that, we'd had side curtains [transparent fabric windows] on our car.

I remember that 1928 Chevy. It sat north of Grandma's house when, as a displaced preschooler, waiting for Mom and Dad to settle their difficulties, I drove it all over, wrenching the wheel and burring my lips. I remember the smell of moldy leather and rusty metal. I guess I "drove" that car all the way to California and back at least once myself.

Sixteen people made the excursion across the prairie, two cars and a truck, over the Rockies, across the desert, over the Sierras and into the Sacramento Valley. They had no schedule, no deadline, no time they had to be back. Hazel and George both had large, extended families, so there was always someone to take care of the farm. Grandpa was able to get away, once he had planted the crops, because his sister Grandma's aunt, Ella, and her husband, Ollie, checked the livestock and took care of the crops.

For Edna and Carl, Lawrence and Emily, with little kids in tow, it was probably less of a vacation, but it gave them a chance to keep an eye on Hazel, to keep her busy and preoccupied with something other than her troubles.

They took the Lincoln Highway, U.S. Highway 30, along the Platte River. They camped in Cody Park, along the river in North Platte, then they split off onto U.S. 6 to the high sagebush plains of eastern Colorado and into Denver. To a flatlander, the snow on the peaks looked like a line of clouds in the west that would, normally, build and grow into a magnificent thunderstorm. But as they approached, the clouds turned into snow-capped mountains.

By 1900, nearly all the deer were gone from Nebraska. Deer wandered among the wonders of icy giants towering over more trees then Grandma could have imagined.

Grandma could lose herself in all the new kinds of vegetation, flowers that don't grow in Nebraska, thick stands of pines and spruce. She stopped to notice them just as she stopped to notice plants at home and, midwife's granddaughter that she was; she'd have wondered how to use them.

"We camped on the way. We had tents. We had a bed in the car; the kids slept in there. We had Army cots.

"Edna and Carl had a tent. Carl and George and Lawrence, they'd put up the tents and everything and Edna and Emily, they'd take care of the babies. We had a gas stove. We had beef steak and all that kind of stuff—potatoes that we'd fry. We always had potatoes. The kids always said George could fry better potatoes than I could. He would take care of the fried potatoes sometimes. We had a gallon fruit tin for our coffeepot. We poked holes around it and put gravel in it and had a little iron over the top. Emily had canned a whole lot of tomatoes earlier that summer. Cooked them up into tomato butter. We had tomato butter all the way out there. It was good on bread. We always had our bread."

"Hank Meents went with us too. We done the cooking. Every time we'd get together after that, Hank would always say, 'You remember, Hazel, they'd have starved to death if it hadn't been for you and I.'"

"Carl and Edna had Keith and Loren Lee, and on the way out there, she told us she was pregnant. She was kind of crabby. Mary Ann learned to walk on the way out there, Lawrence's Mary Ann. Edna and Emily had those babies to take care of, still in diapers.

"Lawrence's, of course, had the truck and they just built a thing over the back of it and they slept in it. Maybe it was the first camper."

She grins, her first bit of visible mischief since she started the story.

In Utah, the trains, carrying the country's goods from one end of the country to the other, passed them as they trekked west on U.S. Highway 50. She'd always felt a pull from the train that passed west of the house. She'd lift her head and look west when she heard it, maybe remembering when it took her brother away during World War I and brought him back quieter and more serious, maybe remembering the few times she'd taken a train to a new place.

In the desert, Grandma found yet another new plant community, plants with spines and barbs. She didn't mention any blossoms, but the strange shapes and characters of the cacti gave her something to think about, too.

Grandma's description of that trip lifts like a dark cumulonimbus cloud swept by skudding prairie winds. The closer she comes to California, the more she sees, the better she feels, the clearer and more detailed her description.

Sometimes oceans frighten people. You can't see the end of them. Grandma, who grew up under open skies, surrounded by infinite horizons, on the edge of the Great Plains where grasses stretch away in endless undulations, just like the Pacific Ocean, didn't flinch. I remember Mom telling about taking Grandma to see the Grand Canyon for the first time. She said Grandma stood on the rim and gazed across for a few minutes, then said, "Well, ain't that somethin'." I can almost hear her saying the same thing, time after time, as they crossed the western half of the country. She must have thought it many times, too, as she peered into the corollas of strange flowers she'd never seen.

"All of us went out there together. And Lawrence decided to stay. He went on this land of ours. We furnished him money and he built a house on there. Then he bought it, because we come back.

"We weren't out there but two or three weeks. Later we went again and spent a year, but that first trip, I saw the mountains for the first time; I saw the desert for the first time; and I saw the ocean for the first time. I thought it was pretty wonderful. And after that trip, I got all right. Just the change of climate and getting away you can get to brooding on things just around you; what you have to do ever day and ever day and ever day. You get kind of bored, I guess.

"I was taking medicine all that time, but I quit taking that medicine after I come home. I never took any afterwards and I was all right."

She can't remember finding the pin. Maybe it's still caught up somewhere between the floorboards at the edge of the linoleum. Maybe some time when I'm wandering through the front room, I'll spot something shiny. It turns out, though, that you can get along without some parts of yourself that seem essential, although you may have to stop and search for them before you let go.

Grandma would have died without the hospital and the surgery and the strangers who performed it. But her wounded spirit continued to struggle for nearly a decade. We have estrogen therapy now and drugs to treat depression. And those are good things. But it took a family, a large, extended family, watching and caring for Grandma, to bring her back from the abyss of loss.

Today, I fear, with our nuclear families and our scattered lives, we try to substitute drugs for love and there will never be enough.

You know—we've had to imagine the war here, and we have imagined that it was being fought by aging men like ourselves. We had forgotten that wars were fought by babies. When I saw those freshly shaved faces, it was a shock. "My God, my God—"I said to myself, "it's the Children's Crusade." Kurt Vonnegut

My Dad's War

It would be incredibly presumptuous of me to assume I can even imagine the horrors my father faced during World War II. And that's the point, I think, as least for my dad. All the years of silence were supposed to protect me from knowing what he did and what he saw. Maybe I'm breaking faith with him somehow in my desperate attempt to understand his life, but I think we've become too glib about the cost of war. As much as Dad would have liked to shelter those of us who came later, I think we need to know, I need to know. Throughout my life there have been warriors in my life. I'm still trying to understand them. I want to know the silent man I lost before I got to know him and, perhaps, through him, the men I've known.

I can't even reconstruct the facts, since all the most general of his service records burned in a 1973 fire at the National Archives. All I can do is try to fill in the blanks between what I do know. Then I can describe for myself, the bald facts, without embellishment, as my family often does when faced with unimaginable losses.

None of that means I'm helpless to understand the silent, brooding man who died just as I was beginning to realize that parents have lives before parenthood. As I've tried to make sense of what the war cost my father, I've also tried to learn about the man he was before the war. My first clues came during our first and only family vacation nearly fifty years ago when Dad took us to see his sacred places. He revealed more about himself during that trip than all the years when I was growing up in his presence. It just took me decades to begin figuring out what I'd learned.

I can't imagine what that trip meant to my father, nearly thirty years after he'd last seen the redwoods, Lake Tahoe, Lassen Peak and the glaciers. Now I wonder if he suspected that he would never see them again.

We took that trip, on a shoestring, in an old, gray, 1950 Dodge. Money was tight and travel was a real strain on our budget, but somehow Dad and Mom decided we would do it anyway. Like our grandmother more than thirty years before, my sister and I saw mountains and desert for the first time. And we saw the trees. Dad always saw critters before the rest of us, and I remember him pointing out our first deer somewhere in the Colorado Rockies.

I don't remember stopping anywhere on our way until we reached the Truckee River late the second evening. Somewhere along the river, near Lake Tahoe, we stayed in a rustic cabin where we slept to the tune of rushing water and the scent of pine and spruce forests, an absolutely new experience for Jo Ann and me. Next morning, Dad drove us around the lake and I remember the little island with its mysterious stone structure. Dad grumbled then about how over-developed the lake had become. That was 1962. Development has continued apace.

My sister, Jo Ann, has a photo Mom took with Daddy's old Brownie, of Dad and Jo Ann and me, side by side, against the trunk of a giant redwood. I don't know where that was, but I don't think there are redwoods there anymore. In 1962, there was barely enough light in the forest to take a picture and it's pretty dim, but I'll never forget the reverence in my dad's expression and I'll never forget the trees. It was so quiet there, without car engines or people talking, bird songs or animals chattering, that we found ourselves whispering. It seemed that something ancient lived there and I almost expected to hear a pterodactyl scream. I didn't know then that the trees were the ancient presence and it never occurred to me to ask Dad if he felt the same sense of permanence. Maybe that was, for him, what was sacred.

When we reached the Sacramento Valley, Dad drove directly to Uncle Lawrence's place near Red Bluff, where our cousin, Dale and his wife, Marion, were running a dairy with their sons, Dick and David. I had developed a crush on my cousin, Dick, the year before, when I met him at Great-grandma Frank's funeral, so my attention was diverted. But I was sort of interested in all the machinery that sucked milk out of all those cows. We didn't milk cows; we ate them or sold them for somebody else to eat. I remember a trip to hay fields somewhere in the Chico area that seemed far away to me. I grew up on four hundred eighty contiguous acres where nearly everything we needed was within our own borders.

After a few days with Dale and Marion's family, we went into the mountains near Mineral to spend some time with another cousin, Donna Mae Wilson and her family. While we were there, we climbed Lassen Peak. Needless-to-say, flatlander that I am, I was sucking air while my nine-year-old cousin, "Pete," chattered away, asking questions I could barely get the breath to answer. I wasn't about to quit, though. I knew Dad would be disappointed. He walked right behind us and made it to the top, even though he'd recently quit smoking and his weight had ballooned fifty or sixty pounds. I think that, like me, he struggled.

My first clue to the meaning of that climb came in a letter I gained access to more than twenty-five years after Dad's death.

"I was quite a mountain climber once," he wrote. "I don't mean dangerous stuff. Just climbing. I set a record climbing Mt. Lassen (the only active volcano in the U.S.). There's 2 ½

111

miles after the road stops. Went up in 49 minutes . . . . Lassen is only 10,500 ft. I also scaled Mt. Shasta and that was rough. Four started and only three reached the top. It's 15,280 ft., about 10,000 of it above the trail. Started at four in the morning and reached the crest at 2:20 in the afternoon. Completely exhausted. Didn't take so long coming down."[cxi]

After our trip to the mountains, we made a whirlwind tour on the way home. We spent a night with one of my classmates, Bonnie Killough, who had moved to the Portland area with her parents, Mom's and Dad's pinochle buddies, Orville and Yvonne. I've tried to reconstruct our route, but the Interstate highways have so overlaid the old roads, I'm a little lost. I'm not sure how we got there, but after we left the Killough's we drove through a little town named Colburn, Idaho, just north of Sandpoint. Then we drove a few miles into Canada up Idaho One and British Colombia Twenty-one, across on BC Three, then back south on U.S. Ninety-five, just so we could say we'd been there. Didn't need a passport then.

After our little jaunt into a foreign country, we picked up U.S. Highway 2 into Glacier National Park.

"I was a camera fiend at one time," Dad had written. "Those pictures represent some awful chances and awful work."[cxii]

I remember almost nothing about Glacier until I returned there in 1991. It didn't occur to me then that my father had been there before, but now I wonder if I photographed some of the same places he did. I have a photo of Johnson Glacier that I have compared often with current ones on the Internet. The ice sheet is almost gone. I wonder what it looked like in the mid-1930s.

As I read Dad's letters all these years later, I realize I never saw any of his Glacier or Mt. Lassen or Mt. Shasta photos, or any other photos that he snapped, and I'm bereft. They were apparently among the things my mother either gave away or burned in the weeks after Daddy died. Now I know where my passion for nature photography comes from.

I'm not sure when Dad saw the trees for the first time, or when he climbed the mountains. Maybe during the year the family lived in California after Grandma's breakdown in 1928 or '29. Maybe it was after high school graduation when there weren't any jobs.

I have a black and white photo of my dad, standing in front of the same school building in Blue Hill that I attended. It's a junior-year class picture and Dad stands out because of his unruly shock of black hair and the collar of his sweater, which looks like someone used it to lead him to his place in line. It's 1932 and maybe he still has hopes that they'll make some money on the farm before his graduation, so he can go to college.

But there wasn't any money. Grandpa had lost all his deposits in several local banks, during the bank failures after the Stock Market Crash in 1929. Even with their little family of four, they were having trouble supporting themselves. Grandma said they ate a lot of beans from a garden they watered in buckets. At least the well didn't dry up.

Grandma told me that, when Dad finished high school in 1933, he hung on for another year, working on the farm. Once Nina was graduated, though, Dad took off for California. He and his friend, Ralph Vavrika, and his uncle, Joe Colburn, hoped to find work like Grandma and Grandpa had in the late twenties.[cxiii]

She said Dad was hanging out with Uncle Lawrence and his family, doing whatever jobs he could find, when the CCC enlisted it's third set of recruits. He signed up and went into a training camp, where the Army conditioned men for work as part of the cooperative project in which the Labor Department enlisted men, the Army trained them, and other departments like the Forest Service gave them work and supervised projects.[cxiv] I don't know if Ralph signed up or, if he did, whether he ended up working in the same place as Dad. At thirty-five, Uncle Joe was too old to qualify.

As a strapping farm boy, Dad didn't need a whole lot of conditioning like many of the city kids he would work with during the year to come. But he got some training in Army discipline that would seem familiar a few years later. And then he went to work in the forest, Tahoe National Forest, I think.

I can't remember if the "yeti" story came from our vacation when we were in the Tahoe area or from general conversation at the time the abominable snowman started to appear on the evening news. Dad never claimed he'd seen any strange creatures in the woods. He just said that the camp would go to sleep with a store of fifty-gallon oil drums, full of oil, on site and they'd wake up to find those oil drums scattered all over. He didn't know of anything that could lift those things and throw them around like that. That's all he said. We could make of it what we would.

What I make of it all these years later has little to do with a mysterious creature than lived in the woods. It's about my dad's sense of wonder and wellness, living strong and free, having the best time of his life. I'd had just a hint of that wonder for the first time when we all went to California.

My dad died just a year after our trip, so I never had a chance to ask him about his life before me. I can only guess that, after his year in the woods, listening for the thump of oil drums slung by something bigger than he'd ever seen, Dad just drifted. He could have returned to the farm, but like a lot of the kids hitchhiking the Interstate Highways during the 1970s, I think he wanted to see more.

I remember bits and pieces, talk of "riding the rails" and camping along the railroad right of way with hoboes. A phrase from one of his letters startled me into thinking more about Dad's life during the Depression. He said he knew the Rocky

Mountains well and I wondered when he'd had a chance to learn anything about the mountains. But then I realized there are five years between his year in the CCC and his enlistment in the U.S. Army. Apparently he spent a couple or three years of that time bumming around the West. He must have seen Glacier National Park then and I'll bet he spent some time in Rocky Mountain National Park. He probably travelled some of the same roads I have, up over Bear Tooth Pass into Red Lodge, Montana. Maybe he even visited Ollie and Ella Lease up near Glendive, Montana, where there isn't anything but wind. That was another of our stops during that 1962 trip and I vividly remember crossing dry stream beds to get to their ranch, which didn't seem to be near anything.

Grandma explained that Dad eventually returned to the farm and worked part of the time at a Works Progress Administration job. By the end of the decade, the economy had begun to recover and the prairies were beginning to green up as the rains returned. Grandma said Dad had been building up his cow herd and getting ready to settle down on the farm.

By 1940, when the country was gearing up for a possible war, Grandpa was on the local draft board. As a necessary farm worker, Dad would have been exempt, but he didn't want to put his dad in the position of deciding. So he enlisted in the Army in February, 1941, and headed back to California for basic training at Camp Roberts. I have a photo of his platoon lined up in front of the barracks. I even tried to find some of the other guys on the Internet, without success. When Grandma died, though, I found two big boxes of hers and Nina's correspondence. I've sorted through one of them and found four letters from Dad. He wrote to Nina from Camp Roberts that he wasn't optimistic about getting home in a year at the end of his enlistment.

"It seems a cinch," he wrote on May 22, "for us to be forced to kick Adolph around before I get back. If we don't, there is only 280 more days.

"I don't hardly ever go to a show," he complained, "let alone to town. If I don't do something soon I'll probably go nuts. But don't let that bother you. I've shot about 50 different kinds of guns already. Why don't they let me go? It looks like they have about 500,000 other guys asking the same question about 10 times a day. I guess they may all recover.

"I'm going to have a big day tomorrow. We are going to have a preview of a parade . . . Our regular acting corporal is going to be gone tomorrow and as second in command, I have to take over."[cxv]

As I searched for my father, I spent hours with Nina's thirty photo albums and scrapbooks. There I found Dad's drop-dead gorgeous girl, Pauline. At least, when he left, he thought she was his girl. He wrote about her, too.

"I guess Pauline got tired of me giving her heck for not writing, so it looks like that was over with," he wrote. "That's one reason I haven't been writing. I've been pretty blue, but may live."[cxvi]

In the scrapbooks, I found several clippings from Dad's Army years. He finished boot camp on June 18, headed across country to a replacement center in Charleston, South Carolina, and boarded U.S. Army Transport Irwin to Panama. In a letter printed in The Blue Hill Leader, he wrote that he landed in Colon and took "one of the fast little Panama trains" to Camp Paraiso.

"This camp is surely a beautiful place," he wrote. "The grass is all green and there are tropical trees all around. It is situated on the Panama Canal and about a mile inland the jungle begins . . . . This is the rainy season. It clouds up and in a few minutes it is really pouring down. It rains harder here than I ever saw it rain in the States.

"A rain like that would cause a flood in good old Nebraska," he wrote in another letter. "You get so you hardly notice the rain down here. I've seen fellows only about ten steps from the barracks stand there rather than walk over in the dry."[cxvii]

On September 4, he was still thinking of Pauline. He wrote Nina that he'd received some letters, "or rather I didn't get them. The C.Q. didn't know anybody by the name of Colburn and sent them back. I wrote a letter to Pauline but didn't get an answer and wondered if that was it."[cxviii]

It wasn't.

He wrote to his grandparents that he'd just got paid. "When I got through making up stuff that was lost coming down here and buying what the army made me buy . . . I only had $7.25 left . . . . The laundry will be about five dollars. You could do your own but for the sheets and a few other things."[cxix]

He also confirmed what he'd suspected even before he left the States. "I guess Congress passed the bill to extend us eighteen months but nobody in the army has any faith in congress anymore since they broke faith with us once . . . . Everybody thinks we will be in for as long as congress wants us to be in and don't trust their promises any further than you can throw a bull by the tail."[cxx]

If boredom kept him moving during the last half of the thirties, it stalked his days in Panama. The few surviving letters are about scratching sand fleas, losing a few sheckels in a friendly game of craps and counting the days until he could go home. And he wondered if he would ever be good for anything when he got back to the farm, after the enforced idleness of Panama.[cxxi]

But Dad wasn't totally bereft of novelty. Sometime during his stay there, he discovered Panamanian weed. He never told me about smoking marijuana, but someone, probably Mom, passed along his story about getting so high he thought he was going to walk across the canal, something of a feat since he was going to have to walk on water. It probably didn't seem like much of a stroll to Dad, only a couple of football fields, and he'd run that distance over and over again, in football practice. He'd run increments with people hanging on him, playing all but three quarters of every football game during his senior year of high school. And think of the miles he had run on the basketball court playing on a team that made it to state. He'd played center. Hell, he could probably jump the canal.

Evidently some of his buddies tried to dissuade him. They must have thought he was too stoned to swim when he sank, but they had to resort to physical restraint to keep him from stepping in. My imagination fills in the details of my father, swaying a bit as he strides toward the water and a couple of other guys, maybe giggling, hanging on the tail of his khaki shirt. I imagine all of them, in the end, laying on the bank, tripping on a sky full of stars.

Besides smoking dope, something he probably didn't write home about, Dad wrote that he was occupied with trying to get some sleep among "all his little pets. I'm so covered with bites (sand fleas) they will soon starve to death looking for a fresh spot to nibble on."[cxxii]

Sand fleas weren't the only pets he encountered in the Panamanian jungles, he didn't write home about the snakes either. The "bushmaster" belongs to the genus Lachesis, venomous pit-vipers whose name refers to one of the 'Three Fates' in Greek mythology, the one that determined the length of the thread of life.[cxxiii] The snakes were certainly capable of determining the length of a man's life line. Bushmasters are capable of multiple-bite strikes that inject large amounts of venom. Even a baby's bite can kill a man. Before long, the snake's name would be central to my dad's life.

He was still in Panama, maybe smoking some dope, probably shooting some craps and definitely counting the days—there were only a few left—on December 7, 1941. He had signed up for just a year, but the attack on Pearl Harbor blew a hole in any hope he still harbored that he'd get out at the end of his year. When Japanese aircraft ripped into Pearl Harbor, Dad and his buddies were energized. They were ready to kill some Japs.

One letter from Dad, written on December 19, starts, "This sure is a dangerous life. You don't know when you are going to stub your toe or even get a finger cut . . . . There's no use

118

worrying over me because I never heard of anyone dying by just wanting to get into action."[cxxiv]

In a letter to his folks, he asked grandpa about the farm. "What do you intend to do with what was my farming operation?" he asked. "It's pretty darn sure I'm not going to be able to do any good for myself for a while anyway. Do it any way you want to but I wish you'd let me know what you are going to do."[cxxv]

Though his service records are gone, it seems apparent that Dad had to worry about stubbed toes and cut fingers for a while yet. I haven't been able to confirm details of his service, but in one of his letters from Panama he mentioned he was with the Fifth Infantry. That unit went to Europe in 1944, but, during the early days of the war, the Army used men from the Fifth as replacements to bring other units up to strength.[cxxvi]

The Arizona National Guard was one of those pirate units, made up mostly of men from twenty-two native American nations and a large number of Hispanics.[cxxvii] They sailed from New Orleans under secret orders the day after the attack and by January 2, 1942, the 158th regiment had arrived in Panama for jungle training.[cxxviii] They were to guard the essential canal against sabotage. Dad saw combat with the 158th later. His tombstone is engraved with "1758th Service Command Unit" and "Bushmasters" (the158th nickname). I imagine he joined them in Panama, where the new recruits got to know the snakes, too.

By the time they left the Canal Zone, they identified themselves with the snake, acquiring the nickname "Bushmasters" and an insignia depicting a machete wrapped in the body of the snake. Their motto, "Cuidado," was a warning, not just to themselves to watch out for the snakes, but to the enemy to watch out for them.[cxxix] They didn't earn it until later. The action Dad and his fellow Bushmasters craved was still in the future.

The 158th remained in Panama for a year, until January 2, 1943, when the Bushmasters walked up the gangplanks of transports and headed for the Southwest Pacific. Their first duty station was at a race track in Brisbane where they camped out for a couple of months before they shipped to Port Moresby on the island of New Guinea.[cxxx] After a brief stay, they moved on to Milne Bay where "America's only jungle trained unit was mostly used as labor troops involved in unloading ships, building roads and larger camps for even more troops that were to arrive. Battle-ready Bushmasters, who had become very tired of hearing the hated 'Spic and Blanketass Bunch' name by that time, saw these work details as just more abuse," wrote B Company Captain Hal Braun years later.[cxxxi]

A brief item in The Blue Hill Leader noted that "Staff Sergeant Cecil Colburn . . . . spent a furlough with home folks after spending 42 months overseas in the Southwest Pacific. He was among the first troops trained in jungle warfare . . . . He was awarded the coveted Combat Infantry Medal for action at Arawe, New Britain."[cxxxii]

In New Guinea, while the First and Third battalions of the 158th were busy building airstrips and harbor facilities on Kiriwina Island, the Second was providing security at Sixth Army Headquarters on the leeward side of New Guinea—"well dressed, well fed and rested," as Anthony Arthur wrote in his 1987 book, Bushmasters: America's Jungle Warriors of World War II.[cxxxiii]

When a battle at Arawe, to divert Japanese forces from a major landing planned at Cape Gloucester, began on December 15, 1943, the Second was held in reserve until December 20. Then Company G climbed into PT boats and left for Arawe.

Radio transmission was deplorable there, so battalion commander, Lt. Col. Fred Stofft gave G Company commander, Captain Orville Cochran, two passenger pigeons with instructions to let them go if radio communication broke down.

"Just tell me where you are and your losses," he said.

Two days later, with no radio contact, Stofft was waiting at the pigeon coop. He thought it should only take the birds about twelve hours to get there. When they finally appeared, it looked like they had casts on their legs. The "exhausted" birds "tumbled to the ground in front of Stofft," who stripped the "encyclopedic account" of every move made by G Company from their legs.[cxxxiv]

I don't know if Dad was part of G Company (if Joe Mendez's[cxxxv] memory serves him correctly, he was) or if he came later with E or F, but the pigeons lent an aura of goofiness to the action at Arawe that continued into the fighting after they landed. According to an unnamed Yank magazine correspondent, there was a "definite front line" with trenches. The men have "flapjacks for breakfast and hot biscuits at dinner." At night the men put their cots in a ditch so they'll be protected when "washing machine Charlie" makes his nightly strafing run, his engine so out of synch it sounds like it won't make it home. Then a patrol will report that the Japs are "becoming numerous enough to think about getting bodacious" so the soldiers attack beyond the perimeter. And that's where the goofiness ends. "Like fighting Japs anywhere, it's shooting invisible snipers out of trees, digging mole-like machine gunners out of dugouts, seeing your buddies fall all around you and not being able to get the bastard who did it . . . ."[cxxxvi]

What the Yank correspondent left out of his report, Dr. Irving A. Bunkin, a captain in the Army Medical Corps, fills in. Parts of his diary, published in the March/April, 2011, edition of World War II, describe a "fiercely-fought contest at the height of the monsoon season in ferociously hot and humid conditions."

The battle raged for several days with the 112th Cavalry Regimental Combat Team on the front lines before G Company joined them, with "a huge supply of rations . . . and we now have fruit juices of various kinds, dehydrated potatoes, salt, sugar and sausage."

The Yank correspondent didn't mention the nearly-continuous bombing and strafing runs that made landings, at best, interesting. The PT boats had to come in single file, because a reef blocked the harbor, so the troops' exposure to

Japanese Zeros was extended. Once landed, of course, someone had to unload all of those supplies, and of course, G Company got to take part in that exercise.[cxxxvii]

Two marines who became the subjects for an HBO mini-series called simply, "The Pacific," described the drudgery that punctuated the moments of sheer terror.

"We spent a great deal of time in combat carrying this heavy ammunition on our shoulders to places where it was needed – spots often totally inaccessible to all types of vehicles," Eugene Sledge wrote. "This was done under enemy fire, in driving rain, and through knee-deep mud for hours on end. Such activity drove the infantryman, weary from the mental and physical stress of combat, almost to the brink of physical collapse."[cxxxviii]

"You were not fighting every minute," Sidney Phillips said. "The war is actually planned by the officers, but it is fought by the privates and the privates do 99 percent of all the hard work. My recollection of World War II . . . is largely a matter of hard work and hunger and sheer terror at night for short periods of time . . . .You couldn't leave and go home. You were there."[cxxxix]

Even as they were unloading, G Company got to help protect the supplies from "a desperate Jap who brazenly stalks into our area and tries to steal food," Bunkin complained. He wrote that the Japanese had already stolen a lot of the supplies dropped by parachute.[cxl]

Arthur wrote that the Japanese were near starvation and dying from dengue fever. "Under normal conditions, dengue fever would not kill a man; it was like a very bad attack of the 'flu,' requiring long and total bed rest. But the heart of a man stricken with dengue could collapse under the strain of vigorous exercise. Dozens of soldiers lay dead beside the trail, young men whose hearts simply exploded within them."[cxli]

Bunkin wrote that the day after G Company's landing was the worst day he'd experienced. Washing machine Charlie may have been the only bomber to harass the troops at night, but in the daytime, particularly December 21, Japanese planes made repeated bombing and strafing runs.

"The Japanese were continuously harassing us despite our air cover . . . . The bombing planes came down so low over us," Bunkin wrote, "that it was possible to hear the bomb bay doors swinging open just before the release of the bombs."

Apparently, "our flame-throwers arrived" with the Bushmasters and cleared "practically all of the Japanese nests off the ridge, which is about two hundred yards from us [the aid station]."

Of the rain, Bunkin wrote of layering the slit trenches with coconuts and coconut leaves in an attempt to keep the patients dry. He described wedging a stretcher in his trench at night to keep above the water level.

"The land crabs, insects, falling cocoanuts, and an occasional huge rat help disturb what little sleep we do get down in the damp hole in the ground."

He wrote of little pieces of turkey passed out to the men on Christmas Day. "Fancy eating Christmas turkey on New Britain down in a mud hole?"

The uproar of constant bombing and strafing, sniper fire and enemies sneaking into camp led to the most common and most untreatable casualties. "One of my own men suddenly developed an acute hysterical state and lay on the ground in a semi-stuporous condition . . . . This emotional state turned out to be our most serious medical problem, and there was very little that we as doctors could do for it . . ."[cxlii]

Bushmaster Joe Mendez said that the Second Battalion remained on New Britain for three months, always subject to Japanese sniper fire and bombing raids and rain. "It's always monsoon season in New Guinea," he said. [cxliii]

On January 16, the beach was quiet enough to unload half a dozen light tanks from the First Marine Division. They attempted to flush the Japanese from their coral caves. "The tanks would rumble over the coral, poking their guns into the caves and blasting the enemy from their holes," Arthur wrote.[cxliv]

Bushmasters and the 112th would follow. The Japanese response was to hide until the tanks and the first wave of troops passed. Then they shot the last of the American surge in the back. That sort of mopping up continued until March.[cxlv]

"War is very simple," remembered Bill Lansford, a Marine who also fought in the Pacific jungle war. "You get the enemy or he gets you. It's a very simple proposition . . . . Most of the fighting that we did with the Japanese was done at very close quarters. In the jungle, in the bush and all that, you would be fighting maybe like 10 or 15 feet away from the other guy. They were right on top of you and you were right on top of them."[cxlvi]

Given what the soldiers had to do at Arawe, I can't imagine that Dad "coveted" the medal he received for service there, at least not after he saw the action he'd been eager to see. For years, I looked for the Combat Infantry Medal, without realizing I had one right in front of me in Dad's photograph. Once I knew what to look for, I found it pinned below his various campaign ribbons on the pocket flap of his uniform jacket.

Mendez said that, after Arawe, the Second Battalion spent three months at Finschafen, again guarding Sixth Army Headquarters.[cxlvii] From there they moved to Wakde-Sarmi where, on the basis of bad intelligence and rushed planning, the Second Battalion got more of that hand-to-hand.

A Friday, August 31, 1945, feature in the Leader outlined Dad's service record: "Entering the service in February, 1941, he was a staff sergeant in the Infantry. He was stationed for a while in Panama and before the outbreak of the war he went into the Pacific. He served with Regimental Combat Team 158, Bushmasters, with the Sixth Army, participating in the bloody Wakde Sarmi battle. In twenty-one days of the battle, fought when the Allies were struggling desperately in New Guinea to stem the Jap tide, Sergeant Colburn was the only man unscathed in his squad of twelve men. One other man survived but lost a leg."cxlviii

The enormity of those last two sentences sinks in a little deeper every time I read them, and I've read them often.

There are family stories that you pick up by a kind of osmosis. You know these things happened to these family members but you can't begin to remember who told them to you. Sometimes you can confirm (or refute) them by reading old newspapers or other public records. But one of the stories of my father's service in the Army remains unconfirmed or denied. I think it was my mom who told me that he had a squad of convicted felons who had been released to fight on the front lines. She said they sent that squad on a lot of "suicide missions."

Dad seems to have taken it personally when his squad kept getting what he considered hopeless assignments. He'd do his best to stay alive and to keep his men alive, then, when they rejoined the battalion, he was always mad.

He never called men "casualties." They were men. When they got killed they were dead men. And each of their deaths was unacceptable, an individual shock that he took out on superior officers. He'd track down whatever commanding officer he could find, probably Lt. Col. Stofft, and start yelling. That would get him busted to corporal and he'd peel potatoes for a while or mix up revolting powdered eggs.

The next time they had to "get bodacious," they'd try to send his squad with another sergeant, but the cons would sit down, backs against trees, and refuse to fight until Colburn was back in charge. "So what're ya gonna do? Put us in the brig?"

125

"They knew I was going to try to stay alive," Dad remarked once about his squad.

After decades of taking that story as gospel, I wonder if twelve released felons would really have ended up together in a squad. Maybe it was just the "blanketasses and spics" that the Army considered expendable. But it also seems possible, even likely, that no prejudice was intended. These were, after all, jungle-trained warriors and they were sent to take out a threat to Allied victory. It can and has been argued that MacArthur's insistence on plowing ahead to the next battle before the current one was fairly begun led to many unnecessary deaths, and my dad was NOT a MacArthur fan. But MacArthur's risks seem to have been equal opportunities.

Actually, Wakde Island was already in Allied hands when the 158th landed. They had to capture Japanese airfields on the mainland because they constituted a threat to the newly-"liberated" airfield on Wakde Island. Their difficulty lay in the fact that military intelligence had vastly underestimated the numbers of enemy available to defend the area. The Japanese had been there since the 1930s, digging into caves that permeated the mountainous spine of New Guinea. Although the beaches looked like a tropical paradise, about a hundred yards inland, "the malarial ooze of swamp and the tangling clutch of jungle" harbored diseases that claimed "soldiers who survived death by bayonet, bullet and shrapnel."[cxlix]

During the last weeks of May, the Bushmasters attempted to take Lone Tree Hill, which overlooked a narrow defile through which troops had to pass in order to get to Sarmi and the airfields. As they probed the area, again and again, they had to retreat under withering fire.[cl] They became concentrated in several positions on the beach, which Japanese soldiers infiltrated, dressed in captured GI uniforms, carrying American weapons, and "even standing in the chow line for a good hot meal." The Indians were often the first to notice "strangers in their midst."[cli]

"One of the few units capable of beating the Japanese at what they had made their own game, the jungle, was the 158th. Yet Krueger's plan of attack kept them bottled up along the coast, leaving the enemy free to roam the jungle and swamps of the interior at will," wrote Arthur.[clii]

With the Bushmasters so confined, the Japanese could attack from inland to drive them into the sea. On May 30, they attempted just that. Beginning with a terrifying racket that included the "screech of a single-strand violin, flatulent bugle calls, [and an] amplified recording of "The Rose of San Antone," the Japanese attacked in a slow, methodical movement into American positions. They disabled all but one tank and overran or neutralized all the machine-gun positions. Throughout a night of terror, the Bushmasters held on.[cliii]

When May 31 finally dawned, Japanese dead lay both inside and outside the Bushmasters' perimeter, mixed with dead and wounded Americans. The Bushmasters counted fifty enemy dead and they thought many more had been carried away. The Americans had sustained only twelve dead and ten wounded.[cliv]

When the 6th Division finally relieved the outnumbered 158th, on June 14, the Bushmasters moved on. Altogether, by the time the Sixth finished the mission, "the fighting near Sarmi cost U.S. Army units approximately 2,100 battle casualties," according to a U.S. Army Center of Military History brochure on World War II in New Guinea.[clv]

By July 2, 1944, the Bushmasters landed at Noemfoor.[clvi] One of the infantryman, Glenn Shankle, wrote about that landings, "The 158th RCT landed at Lingayen Gulf aboard APD's (Army Personnel Destroyers). We offloaded by nets over the side onto landing craft which circled and hit the beach collectively. To our relief, there [was] only light artillery fire, but we were greeted by civilians to the point that they were a hazard both to us and to themselves. We quickley [sic] moved inland to the north/south railroad and proceeded north. The rail bridges were blown so we waded rivers toward Damortis."[clvii]

Preceded by "intense naval bombardment, the attack on the fifteen-by-twelve-mile island encountered virtually no opposition. In fact, the first "resistance" they encountered was about forty Japanese who "ran out of a cave" and milled around as if they were lost.[clviii]

My dad never talked with regular people about those caves, only other soldiers who had seen things, like his cousin, Keith. Keith had helped liberate the concentration camps in Germany. He could talk to Keith. He told his cousin that his platoon had stormed a cave once, looking for a Japanese stronghold. He said that the men opened machine gun fire even as the Japanese nurses, the cave's only occupants, yanked up their skirts to prove they were women. I'll never know if Daddy fired. He can't tell me and Keith doesn't know or won't say. I don't think it matters.

Once the Second Battalion set up Headquarters, they encountered some resistance, including mortar fire. The 147th Field Artillery helped "take out" the mortar emplacements without American loss of life.

When the Americans took the Japanese vegetable gardens, though, they were in for a fight, a fight which they won easily.[clix] The lack of supplies, exacerbated by the Bushmasters' raid on their gardens, had the Japanese soldiers' back to the wall, as the Americans would learn more than a month later Second Battalion morning reports indicated that G Company had encountered a patrol and killed five or six men.

At 1630, a patrol from the 503rd Paratroops reported, "Our two bodies that could not be recovered last night were found completely cannibalized. Also four Jap bodies on stretchers had been cannibalized."[clx]

That was not the first or the last time American troops found evidence of cannibalism. It was just the first time it was recognized. Bushmasters had found bodies before with "portions of flesh" cut away, it just took a while to realize the Japanese were eating that flesh.[clxi]

The realization of the desperation to which their enemy had been driven must have been cause for celebration for most American troops, but I wonder if it also excited some pity among them. I wonder how it affected my father.

During his year in Tahoe National Forest, he undoubtedly visited the site where the Donner Party wintered in 1846-47. Some of them resorted to eating those who had died from starvation and sickness, too. Our national response to that episode has been horror and pity for those doomed emigrants. I imagine my dad's reaction to the story was similar.

Starving Japanese soldiers were among the things my dad never talked about, so I don't know how he felt about finding their emaciated bodies. I don't know if he could find any pity for men who had killed and maimed and tortured his buddies. I do know that, when he spoke of the war at all, he spoke of his gut consciousness of the mothers and sisters and wives in Japan, holding their soldiers safe in their minds, like his mother admitted to holding him. Maybe that's why he didn't kill the enemy he met face-to-face in the jungle between skirmishes.

Once, he said, he'd left his foxhole to relieve himself and found himself face to face with a Japanese soldier, also wandering unprotected with similar intentions. Neither raised his rifle. And, years later, late at night when he'd had a lot to drink, I was sometimes able to eavesdrop. Sometimes, he talked about the torture and tried to reconcile the sisters and wives and mothers with the creatures who could turn a brave man to a screaming thing.

I know, too, that my dad didn't consider himself all that special, just a regular grunt who endured what was unendurable and struggled to hold onto his humanity in inhuman circumstances. He didn't have a chest full of medals, just four—a Good Conduct Medal, an American Defense Medal, an Asiatic-Pacific Campaign Medal and an Army Achievement Medal with two bronze leaf clusters. I know that he didn't give a tinker's damn about those medals and I imagine he suffered from what they now call survivor's guilt, in addition to what we now call post-traumatic stress syndrome.

He nearly shot his own father one afternoon when an old cow wouldn't go in. Beyond control, he raced into the house and grabbed the shotgun. His father didn't know where Cecil had gone when he walked across between the cow and the house, easing her toward the corral gate. He didn't know he'd walked across the muzzle of that loaded shotgun, aimed at the cow, but in that moment aimed at his heart. Only my mother knew because she saw it happen, stood helpless as she saw Dad take aim, then suddenly raise the muzzle skyward and carry the gun back into the house. I think Dad did a lot of that kind of thing the first year or two as he adjusted his reflexes for civilian life. He probably was not alone.

That he could even remember his sacred places is testimony to the quiet way he remained a sensitive human being, capable of human emotions like love and joy. I only wish I'd understood more when he was still alive.

Photos

I recently visited an exhibit of artifacts from Pompeii and was taken by mosaics with pieces so tiny I can't even imagine setting them in place. Among the oldest of these photos are some in which the emulsion has broken down and become checkered. Some were printed from scratched tintypes. I've done some repairs, but decided to leave them alone. Like the mosaics, they bear the patina of the centuries.

It's hard to think of the place where I grew up as a watershed. Rain is sporadic and people from one river system are always trying to steal water from another. But the place I inherited has a sweet well that hasn't failed since 1926, although I had to redrill a couple of years ago because the old, iron well pipe simply collapsed. The Rev. Thomas Jefferson Smith (Smythe), my great-great-great grandfather, brought his family from Scotland in 1853 and ultimately settled in Nebraska. In Scotland he'd been a Presbyterian parson, but I don't know if he held services in America.

Catherine Hendricks Smith (seated, right) survived a sister and a brother, as well as a son. She's pictured here with her daughter, Florence Nightingale Smith Claybaugh (standing left), her granddaughter Irene Claybaugh Jensen and her great-grandson, Velet Jensen, on her lap.

Thomas Jefferson Smith, Catherine's husband, left Scotland with his parents and siblings when he as six years old. After serving in the Civil War, he staked a claim next door to his dad. When Catherine spotted him at a camp meeting, she decided to marry him. He made up his mind later. We have no photos of Philip Thomas Hunt, the Smiths' neighbor and a family friend for five generations.

William James Carpenter in his "borryed coat" before he left Ohio with his three brothers for the frontier in Nebraska. He soon had a job as Philip Hunt's hired man.

Frank Aurelia Smith Carpenter and her husband, Will, lived with Philip Hunt until Frank gave birth the fourth time. Then Philip decided that was too many kids and he moved in with his nephew who lived close by.

Will's grandfather, Henry, soon joined him at Philip's house. And then came four kids, Hazel Izetta (standing left), Earl Wilferd, who later became a member of Nebraska's first Unicameral (standing right), Edna Marie (seated left) and Lawrence Finley. Two more arrived after Philip left, Norma Catharine and Mahlon Monroe.

The whole Carpenter Family: Back row left to right: Naomi, Mahlon, Lawrence, Hazel; front row left to right: Earl, William, Frank and Edna.

William James' parents, William and Sarah Ann Bivens Carpenter, soon followed him to Nebraska. They're pictured here, years later, with a grandson, Elora Lease. Sarah's brother, Johnny came from Dailyville, Ohio, in 1912 after the deaths of his and Sarah's parents. He'd been hunting in Arkansas with his friend, George Colburn.

Hazel met George at her grandparents' house when George arrived during a spring blizzard after hunting with her Uncle Johnny Bivens during the winter of 1911-1912. He took a job that spring working for her father and he lived with the family, just as Will had lived with his employer, Philip Hunt.

Of all the family photos I've looked at, William Merle Colburn's face just breaks my heart. All the years of worry, of watching his children verging on malnutrition, of trying to make a living in Appalachia Ohio, with the odds stacked up against him, show up on his face. His daughter, Eva May, followed her brother, George, to Nebraska a couple of years after he settled here, and William uprooted the rest of the family a few years later, but by then he was "all played out."

I think the woman on the left is Eva, the woman in the middle might be Frank's Eva, and the little girl is Frank and Eva's daughter Edna. Grandma Frank's on the right. This is the cabin where the Colburn clan started out in Ohio. After they left, the new owners nailed clapboards over the siding.

As my family moved from one location to another, they got acquainted quickly and exchanged resources and labor with their neighbors.

And when Grandma crashed, just before the Stock Market, the whole family found a way to help her find her way out of her depression. They took a trip in their 1928 Chevy Touring Cars. Lawrence moved to California that summer.

Only a few years after they returned from California, the dust started to blow. They didn't take many pictures, just kept their heads down and worked. This photo of Great-Grandpa Will's place is the only photo of the dust that has survived.

By the time my dad (third from right, front row) graduated from high school, the banks had all closed and the money saved for college was gone with the wind.

When Dad joined the Army, Nina lost her whole peer group. The two had always gone dancing together and when he left, so did most of the young men in the community. I added it up once and found that the equivalent of twelve years' graduating males had joined the military by the end of World War II. Nina's sanity-fix was to support the war effort. Here she's gathered used tires.

By the time he got back from the Pacific, Dad was a master sergeant with three years overseas service, four campaign ribbons, a combat infantry badge and malaria-- maybe Blackwater fever, an especially virulent strain of malaria. He served his last few months in Colorado Springs as an MP and wasted no time finding a wife to bring home.

Dad brought his city bride, a singer with the big bands, home to this little square house with the ruins of the previous owners' home out back and 350 tiny trees the only shelter from the wind. They had no electricity for another six years so she had to wash on a washboard and read by kerosene lantern.

The first winter was nothing but wind and white with a few naked cottonwoods for protection. Mom said she "died a thousand deaths of loneliness."

142

My mother's stage name was Bobbi Bowen. But after nearly starving between jobs in some eastern city, she joined the WAAFs and ended up in Colorado Springs where, one enchanted evening, she met my father and ended up in the middle of the prairie.

From the moment we were born, Nina was there to make sure the portraits got taken. She also shot endless photos of us with her, with the dogs, with the livestock and dressed up in her gowns. (Jo Ann is on the left top and bottom.)

She took me out in the snow and photographed me with Brockie.

Sometimes Jo Ann and I were allowed to use Aunt Nina's rowboat around the farm ponds. One time, Nina and her boyfriend took us and the boat to Harlan Reservoir. For this photo, Nina took the camera, Jo Ann took the oars and I just laid back.

Not only did Nina dress us up in her gowns and take endless pictures of us, she also liked to be photographed herself. (I'm on the left, Jo Ann right, Nina bottom and with me on the ferris wheel.)

Until I was fourteen years old, aside from grandparents and my Aunt Nina, this is all the family I thought I had. Sometimes when things got weird, I wondered if I had a sister hidden away in an insane asylum somewhere and I wondered where some of the memories my mom wouldn't talk about might have come from, but I gave up on getting answers until Nina intervened.

Nina dragged out this picture of me and this little kid she said I called Junior. I have no idea how she got her hands on it or where I got a name, but there it was, playing into those old memories from Chicago. I didn't remember that Mom and Dad had split up and that Mom had taken me away with her.

Nina had kept in touch for a while and she had a picture of herself with Linda in Omaha, I believe, and another photo of this girl she called my half sister. Trouble was, I didn't even think of what a half sister might be. I just thought I'd had a friend so close she seemed like a sister. But, like a lot of other things, I couldn't remember.

Grandma was ninety-eight when it occurred to me that I ought to be recording the stories she'd been telling me ever since I could remember. So this book started with her stories, strong stories that recalled ordinary heroes who took whatever came and lived their lives. And she awakened in me a curiosity about the lives of generations whose blood flow in my veins.

"There is one front and one battle where everyone in the United States--every man, woman, and child--is in action, and will be privileged to remain in action throughout this war. That front is right here at home, in our daily lives, and in our daily tasks."--Franklin Delano Roosevelt

The War Back Home

December 7, 1941. Cloudy and cold. Still. Grandpa George checked the cows and fed the hogs. At dinnertime, Grandma Hazel heard him come in on the porch and shed his coat, gloves, and boots. He came through the screen and then the back door and into the kitchen. Grandma stood at the cob-burning kitchen range, moved into the front room for the winter. When he came through the swinging door into the front room, Grandpa stepped to the stove and dipped some water from the reservoir, poured it into a basin, and washed up. Then he reached for the radio to catch the noon weather and market reports. It crackled, snapping with an announcer's urgency.

"Mom," George said sharply to his wife.

Absently wiping her hands on her apron, she turned from the stove, sizzling pork chops set aside on the reservoir.

"This morning at six o'clock, the Japanese attacked Pearl Harbor." It was President Roosevelt's voice. "Casualties into the hundreds," he said.

Hazel knew what it meant; she knew exactly what it meant. She had just gotten a letter from Dad. He had the hours counted until he could come home. Hours. But he wouldn't be home any time soon.

"Jack Arterburn," she said. "Didn't Clara tell me Jack was at Pearl Harbor?"

George nodded miserably. It was the beginning of more than three years waiting and worrying, not just for their own son, but for the sons of neighbors and friends. The whole community seemed to hold its breath. But that afternoon, the wait was just beginning.

George and Hazel both sat silent, the pork chops forgotten, grease congealing in the heavy iron skillet. They listened to reports of damage and casualties at Pearl, struggling to hear details through the maddening crackle of static. George fiddled with the dials, wondering where Cecil might be right then. Probably Panama. They surely couldn't have moved them yet. Occasionally, they'd look out the six-foot window to the east, as if to see the fires and billows of smoke.

"It struck us as a horrible thing; Cecil was in Panama, and we was just pretty sure that . . . He had been counting the days. He even had the hours marked out . . . We never heard . . . We was pretty sure he was gonna be over there in the Pacific somewhere . . . "

They listened until George stirred himself to do chores again. Then Hazel restarted her heart, rewarmed the chops and called her daughter, Nina.[clxii]

152

Throughout 1941, The Blue Hill Leader had been full of war preparations. The home folks had been preparing themselves, too. Six months before the attack, Grandma Hazel gave a lesson on "Food for Defense and Canning" to the Helping Hands Club.[clxiii] The cost of the coming war had already started to become clear when the paper reported Bernhard Venhaus's death in a "submarine disaster."[clxiv] Although the family had moved to Nuckolls County more than a decade before, local people remembered them and felt the loss as one of theirs.

The Leader ran recruitment information and listed the boys who signed up for the draft. There was information about providing food for the war effort. War department articles exhorted civilians to remember the sacrifices they would have to make, while noting that few of their sons would be exempt from the draft even if they were necessary farm workers.[clxv]

When youngsters reported for the draft, they got their names in the paper and when they wrote home, the Leader ran their letters. That's how everyone knew that Marvin Buschow was in Pago Pago, an island nobody had heard of, situated halfway around the world, with the 7th Marine Defense Battalion.[clxvi] Everybody knew Marvin; they knew what he looked like. He was a friend and neighbor. In fact, his family had been one of three to settle Blue Hill.[clxvii] They had run dairies in the vicinity for decades.[clxviii]

By December, Blue Hill had about fifty young men in military uniform. Many of them were recent inductees in basic training, officer candidate school, or training in a specialty. Some, like Dad, had completed training and were stationed around the world. Some were already on the new front lines in the Pacific.

Without warning at about 0800 hours on December 7, the first of those overseas soldiers, sailors and airmen faced death raining from the skies out of Japanese fighters, bombers, and torpedo planes. Bit by bit in the weeks that followed, the damages came out in radio and newspaper reports. The Japanese sank or damaged three cruisers, three destroyers, and anti-aircraft training ship, one minelayer, and one hundred eighty-eight aircraft.[clxix]

The families of five boys from Blue Hill waited in dread as they learned that more than twenty-four hundred Americans had died and over twelve hundred had sustained wounds there.[clxx]

According to the Leader, Ted Wratten and Burdette Armstrong served at Scofield Barracks in Honolulu and George Miller served on the SS Indianapolis. Meredith Bennet's folks weren't sure where he was, but they thought Hawaii.[clxxi] Within a few very long weeks after the Japanese attack, the home folks began to hear from their soldiers and sailors. The first news wasn't good. The December 12 issue noted that Henry Beitler, Grandma Hazel's distant cousin by marriage, had been wounded during the first day of the war,[clxxii] bringing the terror right into the Colburn living room. And, of course, there was that neighbor boy, Jack Arterburn, to worry about.

Grandma and Grandpa counted Jack's parents among their closest friends. The Arterburns had owned the north half of their section since 1890, long before they moved into the neighborhood.[clxxiii] Weighing in at about three hundred fifty pounds,[clxxiv] still added brawn to neighborhood harvest crews when I was a kid and he'd have provided much-needed muscle amid the smoke and fire at Pearl.

The Japanese attack included more islands than those of Hawaii and Blue Hill had native sons much closer to the Imperial homeland. With only five hours' warning after the attack on Pearl, Marines on Wake Island scurried to prepare for an immediate attack. It came as Japanese planes dropped out of the clouds, bombing and strafing. For fifteen days the Marines held out with supplies and equipment lost or damaged and dwindling numbers of men surviving unhurt. On December 23, Japanese troops

154

overran the island. Of the four-hundred forty-nine Marines who manned the island's defenses, forty-nine died.[clxxv] On January 2, 1942, the Leader announced the news everyone had been dreading. The first of Blue Hill's sons, Reinhold Krueger, numbered among the dead at Wake Island.[clxxvi]

The Krueger family had lived in the Blue Hill area since the 1880s. Reinhold's great-grandfather had organized the Trinity Lutheran congregation. My dad graduated with two Kruegers and his sister with one. Three Kruegers graduated with me and two with my sister. Blue Hill High School graduated at least one member of the family nearly every year in between. Reinhold had left many to mourn and many to fear for own their family members still in harm's way.

As the community grieved this first loss, others' letters, one by one, appeared in the paper. George Miller's appeared on January 9, full of bravado. He had been in the thick of action at Hickam Field, Hawaii, during the attack.

"I didn't mind the bombing of Pearl Harbor very much . . . I am OK. We are all pledged to pay back the score 100 to 1 . . ."[clxxvii] he wrote.

By February 27, Burdette Armstrong had written that he was okay. Marvin Buschow wrote from American Samoa that he was fine.

As more news arrived from the far side of the world, home folks learned that MacArthur had had nine hours to prepare for Japanese attack on the Philippines, but that the Far East Air Force had lost fully half of its planes the first day of the war. Japanese landings followed the next day and continued, with air strikes on island after island, until the main attack on December 22.[clxxviii] Byron Wagoner's family could only follow the progress of Japanese forces through censored news reports. They learned nothing about their son until late February or early March when they heard that he had been seriously injured. He'd been returned to combat, but was missing and believed to be in Japanese hands.

While the Wagoners waited, a letter from Dad, dated December 11, reached Nebraska. "Well I guess we are off," he wrote. "I don't know how long it will last but do know how it will end. If the people back home back us up, we will take 'em. So far this war is a lot of hard work and not much sleep . . . . We can take all that cheerfully because we know we're here for a cause . . . We have to take gas masks everywhere we go . . . sleep in our clothes and have arms and ammunition at hand always . . . . We have to move out in the morning."

George and Hazel had heard about gas attacks from her brother, Earl, after World War I. Even the mention of gas masks filled them with horror, as it did many other parents reading dad's letter in the Leader.

Perhaps the most devastating news was no news at all. As other parents received letters from their sons, the Harrison family waited. Months passed and they heard nothing from pharmacist mate second class, Edward Douglas Harrison. They'd had word at Christmas. And then nothing. No letter. No notice from the War Department. Like Anna Swope two centuries before, they had no letters, no word, only worry.[clxxix]

Unlike the case in America's more recent wars, the home folks could do more than tie yellow ribbons on trees and go shopping. Already on January 9, Ella Bock announced new Farm Defense Plans for 1942. She reviewed the Food for Freedom Program launched the previous year, which was to produce "food for our own people, for all the countries resisting aggression and for large reserves of food to strengthen Democracy's stand at the Peace Conference . . ."[clxxx]

As Blue Hill's Honor Roll of boys in service grew to a full column in July, their families were sending anything they could and recycling everything that might help end the war. On a personal level, families did their best to send their sons, husbands, or brothers anything they asked for. Blue Hill's librarian, Judy Grandstaff, told how that had worked for her family. When her dad, Leon, wrote home requesting a variety of "pocketbooks," his wife, Elaine, wondered what he would do with a bunch of purses, but with no email or phone connections, she couldn't ask. Since he was in Germany by then, she guessed he could trade them to the fräuleins for food items or sewing services if his uniform were damaged. So she gathered together every kind of purse she could think of, even a few coin purses, and sent them off.[clxxxi] She said Leon's disappointment when he opened his box from home and, instead of paperback books, he found women's purses, remained a family joke for decades.

I remember when I was in high school, I drove an old 1950 Dodge. The tires were nearly bald, so my stepdad gave me a big spinner wrench. I changed at least one tire a week and I got pretty good at it. What I didn't realize was that folks were still getting over the years when tires were unavailable at any price and even when you could get them, you tried to get a few more miles out of the old ones. The boys needed that rubber for the war effort, and among Nina's photo albums is a picture of her next to a pile of salvaged tires waiting to go to the factories that made war machines.

Week after week, the paper was chock full of the war effort. Even the serialized fiction had titles like "She was in Love with a Spy." When Fred Peisiger received his commission as a second lieutenant, the Leader ran the announcement. When George F. Krueger joined the Navy and went to San Diego, his progress appeared in the Leader. On April 10, it published a clip-out War Ration Book Application. On May 15, it announced a Pearl Harbor Theme for the annual Blue Hill High School Junior-Senior

Banquet. On the 29th Homecoming was called off until after the war.[clxxxii] I noticed my eyes were wet when I read that bit, thinking about all the families split to sunder on that traditional celebration and remembering the parades and dances, carnival rides and plain good feeling of Homecoming after it resumed. It must have been deathly quiet on Main Street during that week in June.

On June 12, the Leader noted that a contract had been let for an ammunition depot near Hastings, just twenty miles away.[clxxxiii]

The Germans had brought war to American shipping lanes with submarine strikes on tankers and freighters in the Caribbean Sea and the Gulf of Mexico.[clxxxiv] That's where Harold Wegman saw action in the summer. On July 3, the paper revealed that he (and the ship he served on) survived three torpedo hits before making an unscheduled landing on Mexico's coast.[clxxxv]

After sustaining enormous losses at Pearl Harbor and the far eastern Pacific, the U.S. Navy managed to regroup and meet the enemy in the Coral Sea along the east coast of Australia. Allied Australian and American cruisers, along with a Navy carrier task force, fought the Japanese to a draw between May 2 and 8. Then on June 4, on learning of a planned Japanese attack, the Navy sent three aircraft carriers to stop them at Midway Island. Amid the smoke and fire of the sinking U.S.S. Lexington, the Navy garnered its first, costly victory in the Pacific[clxxxvi] and some Navy personnel got much-needed leave time. On July 17th Meredith Bennet returned stateside after participating in both battles aboard the U.S.S. Yorktown.[clxxxvii]

Some of the items about soldiers and sailors involved boys home on leave, but most apparently didn't get back once they'd gone. Between news about Blue Hill's soldiers and sailors are items about War Bonds, a USO drive, Victory Canner, Victory Cooking Sisters, Victory Gardens, recruitment of women to fill manufacturing jobs vacated by men signing up for the military, and even a Fat Salvage Campaign.

After the attack on Pearl Harbor, most of the news in the Blue Hill paper had focused on the Pacific because the first battles occurred there and local soldiers, sailors and airmen already served there. When the U.S. entered the war, though, much of our effort went into supporting our European Allies. The first American forces arrived in Great Britain January 26, 1942. In April, German bombing raids set England's cathedral cities ablaze and American pilots helped defend the British Isles.[clxxxviii] Not without cost. On August 21, the paper announced that Sergeant Marvin Koepke had been killed in an airplane crash over Montgomeryshire, England. He was "the first local man to lose his life with the United States forces in England."[clxxxix]

Hometown folks could look nowhere in the world where their sons and a few daughters could find safety. The high seas, the land, the skies were all filled with danger and death. Some days it set Grandma frantic with worry; other days someone else might need comfort. By September 11 another Blue Hill boy, Louis Cramer, had gone missing at sea.[cxc] The paper didn't explain the circumstances, so we don't know if his ship sank or even what ocean it sailed.

On American soil, training and preparation served up its own perils. On October 30, the town learned that Raymond Austin McCoy had died in the line of duty at Portsmouth, Virginia.[cxci] Again, there were no details.

Just after Thanksgiving, on November 27, a state blackout was announced[cxcii] and I think of all those yard lights out in the country like little lighthouses—and then I remember rural electrification didn't get to my county until almost a decade later. The only beacons on the plains were the towns. Then they were extinguished. Even though it was a practice run that only lasted a few nights, it must have seemed eerie not to see the lights of Hastings across the fields. It wouldn't have taken much then to make the entire middle of the continent disappear at night.

Before long, the censors got to work and the letters arrived in Nebraska, words and phrases blacked out, vacant rectangles cut from the paper. By that time, Grandma was sure Dad had already left Panama, but it appears that he stayed there for about a year with the Fifth Division and then with Bushmasters. Though the family didn't know where he was, they knew he was alive at least—a week or a month before they got the letter.

Because the censors removed any hint of troop locations from military letters home, Grandma spoke, for the rest of her life, about Dad's three-and-a-half years in active combat and so it probably seemed to her and Grandpa. After all, he'd written, in his December 11 letter, that he was "moving out" the next morning. They assumed that he was somewhere on some island in that big ocean they'd seen one time, as it raced onto the beaches near San Francisco, or maybe hopping from one island to another as Grandma and Nina saw often in the newsreels at the local theater.

Sometimes when troops moved, their supplies got lost or delayed. On December 11 the Leader ran Lt. Donald Martin's letter in which he wrote that he'd landed in North Africa short of rations. At least there were people there with food and he'd traded his shirt for food. That week the paper also announced Ensign Vane Meredith Bennett's letters of commendation for heroism aboard the aircraft carrier U.S.S.Yorktown in the Coral Sea Battle.[cxciii] A week later, Wade Knudson, member of the crew of "airplane carrier Hornet sunk in the South Pacific on October 26," arrived home on leave.[cxciv] Knutson had seen some of the same action as Bennett, since the U.S.S. Hornet had also participated in the Battle for Midway Island, along with the Yorktown and the Lexington.

On January 1, 1943, Fred Novak, Blue Hill's music teacher, enlisted. There must have been a rash of New Year's resolutions because a good post-war friend of my father, Emil Wagoner, whom I remember as the local bar-keep, also enlisted on January 1. He was the last of four brothers to sign up. That same week the paper announced Emil's brother, Byron, was definitely a prisoner of the Japanese.[cxcv] His other two brothers, Marlin and Marion were already in service[cxcvi] and I can't imagine his mother's terror, waiting like Grandma and Grandpa and my aunt Nina, watching terrifying newsreels and holding her breath between letters.

Emil made it back to become a local wag who dispensed wisdom gleaned from national and international newspapers to which he subscribed and from every book in the Blue Hill Library—as well as thousands of his own volumes.[cxcvii] It seemed his service time gave him an unquenchable thirst to know what went on around the world.

Two weeks after Emil's enlistment, the paper gave scant details of the tanker apparently sunk by a German U-boat. Harold Wegman, whose ship had survived torpedo blasts in the Gulf, was lost at sea as a result of that disaster.[cxcviii]

"In January, 1943, the Allied forces and the Japanese forces facing each other on New Guinea were like two battered heavyweights," wrote Army General Gordon R. Sullivan, decades later. "Infantrymen carrying sixty pounds of weapons, equipment, and pack staggered along in temperatures reaching the mid-90s with humidity levels to match [facing] a determined Japanese foe on a battleground riddled with disease . . ."[cxcix]

Those are the conditions that drove Lorrin Kral during his few weeks in New Guinea. On February 12, townspeople learned that he had been killed in action there.[cc]

A month later Bennett received an air medal for a raid over Wake Island, as the Allies began to take back territory overrun by the Japanese.[cci] On April 16, Don Martin had been promoted to Captain and injured in action, still in North Africa. His injury was not disabling or disfiguring.[ccii] Captain Martin received a Silver Star to go with his Purple Heart for action in North Africa.[cciii]

On April 23, Dad wrote back about his post in New Guinea, and he was actually there by then. "We . . . still have seen none of our little yellow friends. Not even a Jap Zero has bothered us . . . . I haven't read a paper or heard any news since we arrived [at Milne Bay, I think]. You seem farther from the war the closer you get to the front in a lot of ways. I'd like to get some news. It's really fertile ground for rumors . . . Our main concern over here is the Japs, but I'd like to know how the Germans and Russians are coming out . . . .[cciv]

"This is a wild and rugged country. I would like to have pictures of it. The man who called the South Pacific Isles romantic certainly didn't have reference to this country. The natives, or Fuzzy-Wuzzies, like the Yanks and seem real friendly. They sure hate the Japs. They are a rough, wild-looking outfit and are great workers. I've heard that there are some in Jap-occupied areas that still practice cannibalism. They can eat all the Japs they can get and more power to them!"[ccv]

Reading that letter in the local paper, I wonder, again, how Dad's attitude toward cannibalism might have changed when he encountered it first-hand later in the war. And I consider, once again, how that kind of information would affect a mother, my grandmother, waiting at home.

"Once . . . it was six or eight weeks that we didn't hear from him," she said. That was," Grandma paused and I waited, and waited, wondering if she'd lost her train of thought. "That was bad," she whispered. "There was never a moment he wasn't in my mind. It was pretty fearsome to know he was over there and maybe getting shot at. I must have put it in my letters . . . One time he wrote, `Mom, don't worry about me. No Jap's got my name on his bullet. I'm coming home.'"[ccvi]

The Harrison family had no such letter. They had nothing for a year and a half. But finally, they learned that their son, Ed, was alive but a prisoner of the Japanese.[ccvii] I imagine the people closest to him were finally able to breathe, although they probably took pretty shallow breaths. Grandma talked once about the war-time breath-holding that kept her awake at night.

"Well, I thought about it an awful lot, and I thought maybe he can will himself so they won't get him . . . I just can't describe it how you do think about those things . . . Of what could happen . . . I didn't sleep very good."[ccviii]

Perhaps the nights she didn't sleep were those days when her son slogged through the jungle, trying to see snipers before they saw him. Perhaps the days when she worked, distracted, were the nights he lay awake in the jungle, listening to the screams of other soldiers who'd been captured. Maybe they were the nights that he slept, exhausted, to find, when he woke, that the soldier in the next hammock dripped blood from his slit throat. Some kind of matter awareness may have carried across those thousands of miles, joining their consciousness in some way. Maybe those nights he couldn't stay awake, she protected his sleep. Mercifully, people in Blue Hill didn't know yet about the torture and the way the Japanese soldiers infiltrated U.S. encampments. Mostly, they never knew because the men who did almost never talked about it.

On May 14, the home folks were back in the news. An article entitled "Pork Production for War Purposes Full Time Job at Colburn Place" featured my grandparents' war efforts. The article enumerated over one hundred hogs that

163

Grandpa had raised during the previous two years and some three hundred seven hogs of all sizes he had on hand, including one hundred fifty-two pigs from nineteen sows, "which is a nice average." Grandpa was farming six hundred eighty acres of land, five hundred acres of that in crop land, putting up silage for cattle feed, including eleven dairy cows.[ccix]

"All of this represents a lot of long hours of hard work, most of which is done by the Colburn family. Mrs. Colburn is a very efficient farm hand and it is also her job to milk those cows and take care of the milk, besides tending a flock of about one hundred fifty hens and starting some little chickens. Their daughter, Nina, carries on most of the responsibilities in the house, besides being a very efficient seamstress, and no small demonstration of this is the array of things she has made from print feed sacks in which concentrate for livestock comes to the farm."[ccx]

Immersing herself in work probably gave Nina some relief from the lack of fun and of people to enjoy. All the dances she and Dad had attended together had mostly disappeared and the boys she danced with had gone as well, and so was her beloved brother. The feed sacks were a resource that wasn't rationed and that she could recycle while still making something lovely as the war kept grinding ahead.

By June 4, the Honor Roll of men in service had nearly reached two columns.[ccxi] At the end of the war, I counted one hundred eighty nine names on that list. When I look at that list, I realize I went to school with many of those men's children or nephews and nieces. Some of them were my teachers. Some of them, like Jack Arterburn and Ray Echternach remained family friends and some even shared harvest work with us. Some of them, like Woodson Bentz, who had been a tank mechanic and who opened a farm implement dealership and repair shop with his brother, became the merchants with whom we did business. The

Bentz brothers probably sold Grandpa the toy tractors I wheeled from him when we went to town.

As I try to imagine what their absence meant to my home town, I remember that my graduating class consisted of thirty-one students and my son's class was about the same size. I also know that Dad's and Nina's classes were similar, so I did the math. Assuming half were males, I'm a little startled to realize that Blue Hill's Honor Roll represents the equivalent of twelve years' graduating senior males.

When I close my eyes, I can remember Blue Hill's Main Street just a few years after the war, with Johnny's Café on the south side, Karsting's Feed and Seed, Higgin's Store with its brick arches forming a shaded alcove and the new Sterling Theater, where people could forget their fears for an hour or so—after the news reels. Now, I think the most important features on Main Street might have been the benches in front of the stores.

The women could gather on those benches and exchange news about their husbands or sons, brothers or nephews. And they did. The men, of course, gathered in the tavern to play cards and discuss the same things, some of them with frightening insights from their own service time. When I was a little kid, they were all still worrying about their warriors' attempts to adjust to civilian life. They didn't call it PTSD then but many of the soldiers were "shell-shocked," a term that seems to encompass both post traumatic stress and injuries from concussions and other brain injuries.

By the middle of 1943, a sprinkling of men had come home with honorable discharges. Charles Boom was the first. At the same time, though, the Army was organizing a Nebraska Unit of the Women's Auxiliary Army Corps to be used in stateside specialties so more male soldiers could be released for "active duty."ccxii

August 20 brought good news and bad news. Byron Wagoner, a Sergeant in Military Prison Camp No. 1, was in "poor health, but under treatment and improving." Pfc. Andrews G. Arends, with coast defense at Fort Huse in the Philippeans, was also a prisoner, but "uninjured and in good health." Marlin C. Luhn, who had been aboard a sub-chaser in the Pacific, was still in Lincoln, his condition unchanged. He had been hospitalized for eighteen months. His right side was completely paralyzed. No details were given, except he was trying to stay optimistic.[ccxiii]

Others had survived basically unhurt, but still in harm's way. William Nass served part of his military hitch in a prisoner-of-war camp in Germany, unhurt and with buddies who had also been captured.

Max Waterbury survived a transport crash in Burma where he had to parachute into the jungle. "My chute opened OK," he wrote when he got to safety. "and when I hit the ground I landed on the side of the mountain and sprained my left ankle . . . the natives came around us . . ." Although these natives were head hunters, "they treated us swell . . ." After the Air Force parachuted supplies and medical personnel to them, the transport crew walked to safety. "We walked one hundred thirty-eight miles over the mountains and I don't care to climb any more mountains."[ccxiv]

Even the soldiers, sailors and airmen serving in the states were at risk, as Lt. Max Foy died in a plane crash somewhere in the western U.S. and Sgt. Ben F. Schmidt died in April of burns he sustained in an accident at Concord Air Field in California.[ccxv]

Southeast of Hastings, the pressure to provide ammunition to the armed forces must have caused manufacturers to cut corners or maybe the workers made mistakes. On April 7, 1944, between one and two o'clock in the morning, an explosion at the Ammunition Depot gave Blue Hillers something else to worry about. The explosion resulted in the death of three workers with twelve unaccounted for and at least thirty-five injured. "Many people of Blue Hill work in the plant, most of them on the daylight shift," the Leader reported.[ccxvi] In coming weeks, it announced no Blue Hill deaths at the plant.

Again on Friday, September 22, though, "This community was shaken shortly after nine o'clock Friday morning when a blast at the Hastings naval ordnance plant took three lives and injured fifty-six persons. The dead were servicemen." No Blue Hill deaths or injuries were listed this time, either."[ccxvii]

To recap, the Leader published the following: ". . . the blast . . . was the second in six months and the third this year. A blast last April 6 claimed eight lives and on January 7, three seamen were killed in an explosion."[ccxviii]

The plant hasn't stopped posing a threat to the community. It is now a superfund site.

When I talked to Grandma later about the war years, she spoke of always waking with the knowledge that her son was in mortal danger. It seemed as though, for the three years he served during the war, she was divided. Part of her mind always strayed to its vigil in the Pacific. I try to imagine three years of somnambulance.

"I tried to will him to be all right, like if I would concentrate on him hard enough the way he was, he would stay that way."[ccxix]

I wonder what power a mother's will has over her child's fate. Why the soldier next to him? Why not Cecil? If my son were in trouble, across the street or down the block, could I help him, I wonder. Can a woman really will her son safe? Can her thoughts traverse thousands of miles— or even a couple hundred yards?

Hazel said, "Of the bunch he went to New Guinea with, he was the only one. Some of them might have been wounded and brought back before that but he was the only one that really come back."[ccxx]

"I hadn't seen him for four years," Hazel said. "I don't know just exactly how much more than that it was."[ccxxi]

He came back with malaria that kept him huddled behind the cook stove in the dining room, all through his furlough. His mother didn't know if he had nightmares. He didn't "prowl around" at night.[ccxxii] But a pheasant breaking out of cover would flatten him on his belly.[ccxxiii] He befriended everybody equally, the county attorney and the town drunk. It didn't matter. They were all alive and so was he. Sometimes he drank too much and once in a great while he would talk about that which is unspeakable. Then he'd have another beer.

"There couldn't nobody help him," Hazel said. "He had to help himself. He always—things bothered him."[ccxxiv]

On August 24, the paper announced that a bomb disposal squad was moving from Europe to the Pacific. Another item told vets where to get the pamphlet that would explain their benefits. A major focus of this issue was reconversion.[ccxxv]

"With World War II finished, and with the nation's great armament production due to be slashed, interest mounted in the government's program for switching industry back to a peacetime basis and providing high employment."[ccxxvi]

On August 30, the closing of the ration office and an explanation of the GI Bill of Rights appeared in the Leader.[ccxxvii] Finally, people would be able to get sugar and coffee and tires. The soldiers would get some education. My dad took night classes in agriculture for a while, to catch up with the latest research.

By the end of 1945, the Leader had listed twenty-four killed in action and five who were still missing. Another of Grandma's cousins, Robert Beitler, was dead. Two prisoners, Harlan Wenzinger, captured by the Germans, and Ed Harrington, a Japanese prisoner, had not yet been accounted for. So for some, the wait continued.[ccxxviii]

The report on September 29, 1944, of Arthur Schulz's death appears to have been greatly exaggerated, because he appeared again on May 4, 1945, as a German POW and June 15, as he arrived home.[ccxxix] Some who left Blue Hill to serve during World War II settled in the towns nearest bases where they served. Some of them never returned. Some never quite settled down in Blue Hill or elsewhere. Some died halfway around the world. In time, the losses added up, but at first the survivors needed to celebrate.

In the first euphoric days at war's end, Dad was elected commander of the Blue Hill American Legion and Dalvin Krueger vice commander. Dad appointed Mom membership chairwoman. By late September, the Legion had taken over the Blue Hill Opera House and begun renovations.[ccxxx]

Homecoming in 1946 must have been a lollapalooza. The boys who were coming home had arrived and begun to settle in. The farms had enough workers, especially since many, including the Colburn farm, had mechanized, retiring the horses and replacing them with tractors. Main Street business was thriving. Mom and Dad bought the first new car in Webster County and the Leader predicted that washing machines and ironers would soon become available,[ccxxxi] although not on the farms. Electricity was yet to arrive in the country.

But those benches remained on Main Street for more than a decade and the women gathered there to talk and wonder about their mens' silence. The men gathered in the tavern and played cards and drank beer and talked. But there were silent places they didn't touch. No one asked and, mostly, the vets didn't volunteer, except with each other.

And the scars began to heal.

Blue moon, you saw me standing alone/without a dream in my heart, without a love of my own. Blue moon, you knew just what I was there for/you heard me saying a prayer for/someone I really could care for/And then there suddenly appeared before me, the only one my arms will ever hold . . .-- Richard Rogers and Lorenz Hart

Bobbi Bowen

Blue Moon. That was my mother's theme song. And therein lies the rub. Lacking any examples of stable, ordinary love, my mother succumbed to the highly romanticized love-at-first-sight of ballads and fairy tales.

My father knew better. He'd grown up with a woman who had married the homeliest man she ever saw, with that homely man, and with their love that only grew as their years together passed. He knew the grace of his grandparents' love, an old love that always stayed young. But he succumbed to the exuberance of life, of still being alive after seeing the men around him die.

When my dad wrote to his sister about Mom, "I guess she knows what a farm is, but wouldn't swear to it,"[ccxxxii] he didn't have a clue how important that lack of understanding would be. My Mom had become accustomed to a lot of glamour and really didn't seem to realize how "skin deep" it was.

171

My mother grew up in what a Brazilian journalist friend of mine calls quick time, that is, time without history. In quick time, people become separated from the land, which is ancient, and from the generations with their wisdom of old loves and stable communities.

But it wasn't just the old country mouse/city mouse split that made the difference. An ambitious doctor's experiment drove the last wedge into my parents' union.

When my mother, Bobbi Bowen, met Dad, her memory of jobs she didn't get because she wouldn't "put out," was very fresh. She clearly remembered wandering the streets of a city far from home, when one singing gig ended and she didn't have another job. When she talked about that time, even many years later, it was obvious she had been terrified of starving to death. Even more terrifying, I think, she believed nobody would know or care.

She hadn't forgotten, either, the gentle man who gave her a job when she hadn't eaten for three days, with no strings attached. He even gave her a meal before she went to work.

"It was all I could do to eat like a lady instead of a wolf," she'd said. ccxxxiii

My mother's real name was Ella Mae, after her maternal grandmother. She came from adesperate broken home. She says she never knew why her parents' families fragmented, but she suspected May Ford's marriage to a previously-divorced Protestant Welshman, Paul David Bowen, tore the fabric of the Irish Catholic Ford family. Mom said she only met one of her mother's sisters and then only a couple of times. Mom didn't know her father's family either, and she rarely saw her half-brothers,

172

because they lived with their mother, and I've learned almost nothing about them.

My mother's family had only itself—one man, one woman, one child—a stripped-down nuclear family—to meet its own needs for comfort and support. These three people tried and failed to provide companionship and succor to each other during devastating times. And, finally, mom's parents divorced when she was quite small.

Once my mother talked them into getting back together, she told me.

"That was the worst mistake I ever made in my life," she said. "They fought and they yelled. They were just miserable."

She wouldn't talk about her own misery.

In the 1930s, when money came in fits and starts, economic necessity sometimes drove Mom's parents back together, but their relationship was never quiet and it never lasted any longer than the temporary necessity. It provided the only pattern my mother had for stitching together a marriage and a family.

When her parents lived separately, mom shuttled between them. She rode the bus from Akron to Cleveland when school got out every spring, to live with her dad. Before school started again each fall, she climbed aboard the bus and moved back in with her mom. She was never able to believe that both parents wanted her. Instead she thought that they shuffled her back and forth because neither wanted her. She never had grandparents to cherish her. She never had the days I had on Grandma's kitchen floor, playing with pans and spoons and listening to the chatter of two women canning fruit or dressing chickens. She never squinched the dust between her toes when she stopped to examine an animal track on the way up the steep hill to Grandma's house. She had no sisters or brothers to help her strain tadpoles out of muddy pools with a rusty flour sifter.

One spring, before she left for her dad's, there was a polio outbreak in Akron. They had closed the neighborhood swimming pool to contain the spread of a disease that crippled thousands every year, especially kids. Mom loved to swim, so she climbed the fence and went swimming anyway. Soon she began developing water blisters under her arms. The blisters would break, the fluid would run down her sides, and she would form new blisters. When her mother, Mae, took her to a doctor, she learned that her body had been successfully fighting off polio.

When she was a teen, a stranger grabbed her on her way home from school and tried to drag her into his car, but my mom was an athlete who spent her summers swimming in Lake Erie. She fought him off and ran home. She never told her mom.

During the Depression, Mom saw her dad, a respected chef and restaurateur, doing pick and shovel work with the Works Progress Administration. When her mother couldn't get her usual work waiting tables, or when the tips wouldn't stretch, she scrubbed floors. And when mom realized she could make money with her voice, she sang for her supper.

As soon as she finished tenth grade at fifteen, she went to the nightclubs and the bars. While other girls her age attended high school classes, she slept. While they slept, she sang and fended off passes from other women's husbands. She worked in Michigan and Ohio and along the Eastern seaboard, singing with the big bands, always opening with her theme song, Blue Moon.

That's how she ended up alone, broke and hungry in a city she couldn't (or wouldn't) remember. She said that one singing gig had ended and she didn't have another to go to. She didn't even have bus fare to get home. So she kept pounding the streets, looking for a nightclub that needed a female vocalist and wondering if anyone would miss her if she died there.

She longed for a life free of the need that had driven her into the nightclubs and she decided that, if she lived through this starving time, she would marry money, enough money to buy the security and stability she'd never had. She looked for men who wore carefully shined shoes because she figured that men who had the money for little extravagances—like regular visits to the shoeshine boys— must be well-heeled.

Given her rough, lonely existence those years, she must have thought her chances might come up on the same rare night as a "blue moon."

Mom was a feminist, but she expected responsibilities to go with the rights she demanded. Until she died in 2005, she said that rights and responsibilities are part of the same fabric, rights the warp, responsibility the woof. If men must answer to a draft board, she thought that women should, too. The guaranteed regular meals probably made her decision easier, although her career was beginning to take off in 1944 when she enlisted in the Women's Air Force. Days after she joined up, she finally got the break she'd waited for—an audition for a radio show of her own. But by then, Uncle Sam had dibs on all her engagements for the next two years, and by the spring of 1945, she had an engagement in Colorado Springs as a radio technician.

Even in the Army, she kept singing, spurred by hope. Even though she'd missed her big chance, she thought perhaps she could go back after the war if she kept in good voice. In Colorado Springs, she had made friends quickly. The enchanted evening when she met my dad, she'd been tending bar and singing for some of her new friends in their nightclub.

Cecil Colburn was not one of those men who kept his shoes shined, Mom said. But he did get her attention. When I asked her how they'd met, she still seemed under the influence of the musical "South Pacific." As she described it, I imagine a dim room filled with blue smoke. Some small group plays big band music. I can hear my mother's rich alto mingling with sax and clarinet or maybe a trumpet and trombone in her theme song. Dad leans one elbow back on the bar as Mom leaves the stage and scurries behind the bar between sets.

"He just came back there and he grabbed me and kissed me," she said. "I thought I ought to slap him, but I was afraid he was one of those shell-shocked veterans and he might hit me back."

"What'd you do that for?" she asked.

"Seemed like the thing to do," he said, shrugging.

He beamed down at her, a spark of gold glinting in his smile as she waited in confusion for him to release her. She thought him a ruffian. Perhaps she was right. He'd only been back from New Guinea for a few months. He hadn't had time yet to slip into any veneer of civilization. He never did entirely.

Yet he was handsome, tall enough to stand out in a room full of men, and dark, with an unruly shock of black hair over his forehead and a mouthful of strong white teeth, a sliver of gold in the front. He stood more than six feet with shoulders so wide and hips so narrow he could never buy suits, just jackets and pants of different sizes.

"We tried to buy a suit one time," Mom said. "The tailor would have had to overlap the back pockets to make the pants fit."

Shortly after they met, Dad wrote home to the folks, "I think I've met the girl I'm going to marry," he wrote. When they asked what she's like, he wrote back, "She's stacked."[ccxxxiv]

My dad had to convince my mom that enthusiasm, not boorishness, had prompted his kiss. Perhaps, like the unrestrained sailor in Times Square on V-J Day, bending a woman back over his arm, Dad celebrated the very fact of his life. Perhaps he felt he had to live for the ten men in his squad of twelve who didn't survive, and the one who came back without a leg. That would take a lot of living, and Dad was already twenty-nine.

Grandma Hazel told me about his first letter. Dad told his parents that Bobbi, Ella Mae, had come from Ohio just like his father and his grandfather, but from the cities. She'd never even visited a farm. He didn't write until later that he planned to marry a WAF, but then, he was the only member of the family who had a problem with military women.[ccxxxv] A pissed off soldier had told him one time, aboard the ship coming back from New Guinea, that he would marry one and Dad had knocked the guy out cold. But there he was dating one.

"I thought the WACs was all right," Grandma Hazel told me. "It didn't bother any of us. Josephine Zimmerman was in the WACs and Wilma Schultz. We just thought it was awful fast."[ccxxxvi]

I'm not sure my mother ever knew why she went out with my dad. He certainly wasn't the rich dude she'd set her heart on. But she did go out with him and, six weeks later, they were married. I can't even imagine what my parents knew about each other in six weeks. Dad never once talked with me about it. By the time he died, I was still too young to ask. Mom said she'd recognized Mr. Right immediately and predicted for me that some magical day, I would meet my Mr. Right, too. I'm sixty-five now and I'm still waiting. Maybe it's because I don't believe. I don't know what Mr. Right looks like. Mom said she didn't either, but she knew him when she saw him. My eyesight's not 20/20, though, and I'm not sure I'll recognize him if I see him. It would be nice if he'd wear a yellow ribbon.

I'm sure Dad didn't realize how important it was that mom was a city girl. I'm sure he didn't realize that their lives together would have to survive a clash between two cultures, two entirely different ways of living. My father's life had always been a thread in the whole fabric of his community. He knew his extended family. He knew the neighbors who shared the work and the merchants who bought the produce. My mother's life, too, represented a thread in her community's fabric, but hers was the pulled thread.

Mom taught me to sew and one of the first things she taught me was to "pull a thread." That one, individual thread, carefully and patiently extracted, provides a baseline for mapping out the pattern of a garment that fits smoothly and comfortably. Mom's city-based, nuclear family, even while it held together, existed as one of many fragments, no longer obviously part of a whole, integrated community. Maybe their pulled fragment provided a pattern for someone, but it gave them no structure. Mom told me once that it's pretty easy to be dreadfully lonely in a room full of people. I suppose if you represent the gap, the absent thread, it's easy to ignore you.

I doubt that Dad understood how much of himself remained separate when he couldn't share what he read like he had with his mother and sister. I doubt my mother realized when she married him that my father's idea of a night's entertainment involved descending into the plot of a good book. She'd had the glamour, peeking from the kitchen as a little girl, of the up-scale restaurants where her parents had worked and the clubs and bars where she'd worked.

Transplanted from bright lights and noise, suddenly she had only a twinkling, light years away, and whispering prairie grasses.

I've known both my parents, sort of, and I've tried to guess what drew them together. I think Dad's first letter home describes the first attraction. They were both handsome. My father's rose garden tells me a great deal about why beauty, including physical beauty, might have had supreme importance to him right then. I've asked myself how a man comes back to life after he's spent three and a half years hiding behind trees and in holes in the ground, slept next to men pouring blood from throats slit in the night and listened to the tortured screams of captured comrades. My father planted a weeping willow tree on the High Plains and watered it every night when he came home dirty and tired from the fields. He planted hybrid tea roses with names like "Peace" and "Crimson Glory" for his wife and tended them like his life depended upon it. Maybe it did.

My parents recognized more in each other than physical beauty, of course. Although my mother never seemed to see it in herself, I think my father recognized her intellect, her vibrant curiosity, but I'm not sure he realized how differently the two of them used their minds. Mom, for her own part, had learned very quickly that farmers aren't stupid oafs as she'd always believed.

179

"I found out that some of them even had college degrees!" she said once, looking back at her move to farm country.

"Your mom was a better mechanic than your dad," Grandma said. "He had two left feet when it came to doing things. First time he had to harness the horses, he tried to put the collar on upside down. His dad was fuming!"ccxxxvii

I remember my father sweating and swearing over an old Allis Chalmers round baler. He would tinker and poke at it, take things apart and put them back together as though he hoped he'd accidentally alter something and the baler would magically work. But it didn't and eventually he would realize he was beaten again and he'd stomp into the house for help. If Dad hadn't thought he should do the repair, because he was the man, they might have made complimentary opposites. But I think Mom's ability to fix things Dad could only fumble at embarrassed him.

I know Mom didn't realize how Dad relied on her good, common sense. She didn't know about the pattern his grandparents and parents had followed. Both men depended on their wives to help them make decisions— about equipment, about livestock and about crops. Dad followed that same pattern, always consulting her about major decisions. But I think she thought he was patronizing her. She knew that soldiers had relied on Dad's memory to settle bets She knew that, if he said the New York Yankees won the 1933 World Series ten to eight, the loser paid off, no questions asked. If he said that the moon rotated as it revolved, the loser paid. If he said he didn't know how many toes a fruit bat had on each foot, every man kept his own money and looked for another bet to make. Mom admitted to being in awe of that kind of memory, overwhelmed by it. She placed too little value on her own ability to determine how things worked and too much on his grasp of abstractions—trivia really.

180

Their reading habits were polar opposites. He read novels. When she read, she read how-tos. My sister still has the book she used to learn how to crochet. Each of us has a pineapple pattern bedspread and an oak leaf table cover that represent hundreds of Mom's lonely hours. She said she felt swallowed up by the power of my father's genius. She told me, almost guiltily, that she never signed her checks "Mrs. Cecil Colburn," but instead signed "Ella Mae Colburn."[ccxxxviii] Signing her own name provided her a scrap of herself to salvage. It seems that Bobbi died when she married.

I asked once if she'd given up too much to marry my father.

"I had no choice," she said.

"Of course you did."

"No. I asked your father to be my agent, but he didn't want to do that, so I came here."

She wasn't even open to the possibility that marrying my father was a choice.

Instead of the ivy-covered cottage Mom often sang about, though, Dad brought her, pretty much unprepared, to his parents' home where the wind whistled through the screens during silent summer nights when stars seemed to rest on the shoulders of the prairie.

"I never met her until after they was married," Grandma Hazel recalled. "I guess we kind of took to each other right away. Cecil got his discharge first and he come home. She came afterwards and then she went on home for a week or two to tell her mom.

"All that summer, they was there with us. We waited until she come to see what she would say about moving that other house down there. We let her decide—her and him together, I suppose—where they wanted the house. Then we got them out there working right away.

"We'd already bought the Britten place. I think George wrote to Cecil and asked him what he thought about it and Cecil said it was a good deal. We bought the north quarter, Butch's place, for $1,600, ten dollars an acre, when Cecil was in Panama. It had that house on it. We'd bought the Britten place while Cecil was in the Army, too. We paid $2,400. They dug a basement down there and walled it up and set that house down there. They didn't have the house finished when they moved in."ccxxxix

My mother couldn't wait for her own home. She said she almost died of embarrassment the night the bed fell down. "The house was absolutely quiet," she said, "and the bed just collapsed. I must have been red clear to my ears next morning because everybody had to know what we were doing to make that bed fall down. I put off coming downstairs as long as I could."

In a few weeks, they moved into their own stark little square of a house with a steep hip roof, at the foot of Hazel and George's hill. She had no running water and kerosene lanterns provided the only light.

"The electricity was the thing," Grandma said. "That was something that just about . . . I think she filled the chamber pot full before she took it out to the outhouse. Boy, that was the best day of her life when that electricity come along [so they could have a flush toilet]."ccxl

Rural Electrification Administration day must have been a great one for me, too. My only memory from before kindergarten is of wading through snow up to my hips to go to the outhouse. That must have been the blizzard of

'49. Mom waded those drifts, too—more often than I did because she had to empty the chamber pot.

It's become increasingly apparent to me that, once the bonds are formed and intimacy achieved, the realization descends that we're still foreign to one another. I suppose it was her parents' pattern Mom followed soon after they moved into their own house when she fought with Daddy. She told me about one fight. She couldn't remember what it was about, but she remembered throwing a glass at my dad. That must have been a shock for my father who had never seen his parents fight. He'd never even heard a heated argument. It must have shocked a man whose grandparents were still lovers.

Before he could recover, he slapped his wife, open-handed, and said, (probably roared,) "Don't you ever do that again!"

Mom said she got on the phone and called Grandma, told her Dad had hit her. Grandma came right away and got my dad's face between her hands, slapping him on each cheek in rhythm and told him to "never do that again."

Neither one of them ever did that again. But mom never really did fight fair.

Still, I have to love Grandma's stories about my mother. I love how game she was—how bright and willing to laugh at her own mistakes.

"Whenever there was a cow having a calf, she was out there watching to see how it was done. My dad [my great-grandfather, Will] got the shock of his life when Ella Mae come out there. We always called on Dad whenever there was something wrong with the stock, and she was right there helping. When they castrated the pigs and

183

everything else, she wanted to see everything. Cecil tried to get Ella Mae out of there, but she wouldn't go.

"Dad didn't think women should see those things. I don't know what he thought we did when we had our babies. When he was breeding horses, he even built a tall fence so the women and kids couldn't see what was going on. And then there was Ella Mae—but he got so he didn't think anything about it.

"She'd try anything. She turned out better as a farm wife than a lot of the girls that was raised on the farm, because she was right there trying to learn everything.

"She'd ask some of the darnedest questions," Hazel recalled. "She thought you had to have a rooster before a hen could lay. She tried to wring a chicken's neck once, but they got away from her. I think when she had to butcher chickens by herself, she took a butcher knife and chopped off their heads.

"At first, she thought Cecil was crazy. As soon as they decided where to put the house, he planted trees— hundreds of trees. He hauled buckets of water to them every day. You see, it was a little late in the year to transplant trees. He'd get off the tractor in the evening and bucket water to them trees. Ella Mae, she thought trees would just grow. She came from Ohio, where they couldn't get rid of the trees."[ccxli]

Mom had other reasons to wonder if she'd married a lunatic. She was right when she guessed that Daddy was a shell-shocked veteran. By the time I became aware of them, Dad's occasional explosions mostly occurred when we worked livestock. But Mom and my cousin, Bud, pieced together a picture of my Dad's first Fourth of July that remained with them both for fifty years.

Apparently, somebody thought it would be funny to light firecrackers under Colburn and watch him jump, but the fireworks backfired when Dad grabbed a man by the throat and almost choked him to death. Mom said she heard that it took four healthy farm boys to pull him off.

Bud was just a little kid then. He was with them that day and he says that Dad came storming into the store where he and Mom were grocery shopping, demanding that they go home "right now." Dad took the wheel and they roared out of town with Bud clinging to the seat and Mom saying soothing things that neither can remember—until Dad finally calmed down.

Mom has always said she was afraid to leave me alone in a room with him when I was toddling around, because I might pull myself up to the couch when he was asleep and he might hurt me before he could completely wake up. When I remember my father, I remember that we always tiptoed around him, even years later. We never woke him suddenly if he dozed off on the couch. We anticipated with dread the days we had to work livestock because Dad, swearing and shouting, seemed as out of control as the skittery critters that scattered in response to his craziness.

My mother has said of my father that he was a gentle, patient lover. But she has also said that he was never very "demonstrative." I only remember seeing my parents hug once. I have the sense that, aside from their first, spontaneous kiss and maybe the six weeks of their courtship, Dad hardly ever expressed spontaneous affection. Grandma said that was the Scotch in him.

"I died a thousand deaths of loneliness," my mother said.

Mom's music may have given her some respite from the quiet of the prairie, "lonely quiet," she's said. She told me that there was never a moment when some melody didn't pour through her head. She sang constantly as she went about her chores and I never think of her without a song.

185

With her knitting and crocheting and whatever scraps of attention she would coerce from Daddy, Mom hung in there through the first winter with its inevitable trips to the outhouse -- if only to empty the chamber pot. By spring, 1946, she knew she was pregnant and when I was born, the fabric of their marriage ripped apart.

"Ella Mae had an awful lot of trouble. She was scared to death. She would go uptown and talk to—I can't remember who she was running around with then. They told her all about childbirth. Cecil always said they scared her to death."[ccxlii]

Mom talked about months of morning sickness—all day and all night. The sight of food, even the smell of it made her vomit.

"Your father was afraid I'd starve to death," she said. "One time, he made me some mashed potatoes. I thought I could eat that. He brought it to me and I threw up."

"She had trouble anyway," said Hazel. "Right away they decided she wasn't big enough to have a child. She took a whole lot of treatments. She told me they took a thing and went in there and tried to stretch her.

"I went to town to telephone her mom, finally. But she didn't have any money. We sent her money. She was here for a while and then she went back. I think it helped to have her here.

"They didn't have no car. We had a white Chevy and they kept it down there at night. George was working at Soil Conservation Service then and I was stuck at home when they went to the hospital, and I couldn't hear and I couldn't hear from them. They was up there for two or three days. I finally called Luther Echternach and he come down and got me and took me up there. By the time I got there, you was here. It was so long."[ccxliii]

In fact, my mother was in hard labor for seventy-two hours. Mom had begged the doctor for relief, but he waited and waited, to see if his "treatments" had worked. This was not my grandmother's birthing room. This was not a neighbor assisting a neighbor. This was a man serving his own ends. But finally, Dr. Webber went into surgery.

As Dad paced, one of the nurses raced through the door on some errand and Dad got a glimpse of his wife on the table with her belly sliced open. He vomited.

When it was all over, the doctor told him we were both alive, but he didn't expect me to be much more than a vegetable.

Without the caesarean section the doctor finally performed, my mother and I would both have died. And I got lucky; I actually came out of my mom's suffering with a functioning brain. But I have to wonder if a neighbor would have risked my life, my very ability to function as a human being, on a theory.

To my father, the long ordeal must have seemed like a return to New Guinea with its helplessness, fear and guilt. Again, he remained uninjured while those around him suffered. As Mom sweat and begged, he remained as unable to give her relief as he'd been unable to save the men in his command. And when it was all over, when the doctor told him I'd likely be nothing but a vegetable, it had all been for nothing. I've always understood that my daddy didn't celebrate my birth, he grieved it—at least at the time. For my own part, I'm pretty ticked off that a man who called himself a doctor would risk my mother's life, and my health, maybe even my life, for an experiment.

Dad told me once that I'd looked pretty bad. He said he took one look at me and said, "Have faith and it'll turn out all right." But he didn't have much faith. He went out and got rip-roaring, stumbling, passing-out drunk that night. Dad and Jumbo Van Boening. No one ever told me who was with them, but some woman claimed later that she and Dad had had sex. She filed a paternity suit. Dad had no idea. He'd blacked out, so he made a settlement. Mom stewed on that, gritting her teeth and enduring the isolation. Finally, she left. She took me with her at first and we landed in Chicago with her mother.

"It meant my whole life. Everything. For a while, I felt like everything was gone. But I knowed I had to stand up for Nina," Hazel said. "She was having her trouble then, too, you know."[ccxliv]

Taking Care of Business

In April, 1955, Grandpa George knew he was going to die. Unlike most of us, he knew how he would die and he had a pretty good idea of when. So, with the limited time he had left, he took care of business, which wasn't new for Grandpa. Maybe that was because of his hardscrabble childhood.

Coming home from the hospital, he leaned heavily in the door frame. He shuffled over the threshold, that same scarred block of wood he'd stepped over for almost thirty years coming from the fields. Grandma Hazel hovered while he worked his way, leaning on the oak dining chairs one by one, into the back bedroom to lie down.

In the first few days after he received the doctor's verdict, he worked with his lawyer, Ralph Baird. He and Ralph devised a will that gave Hazel income from the six hundred forty acres they'd accumulated. After her death, the land would be divided equally between their two living children, Cecil and Nina. Then, sure he'd taken care of everyone, Grandpa George went on about the business of living as long as he could.

"He was agetting so weak by the time he got out of the hospital, he couldn't walk around too much," Hazel said.

He couldn't even go outside to escape my piano practice.

Oblivious, I just kept pounding the keys. I'd been taking piano lessons and, since we didn't have a piano at home, I practiced every day at Grandma's and Grandpa's house. I'd made it all the way to the second grade method book, though my method was very slow and not too methodical.

As I plunked away during those six months, Grandpa deteriorated until he could no longer get out of bed without help. The family decided my piano lessons would have to wait. When Grandpa got wind of it, he put his foot down and it was a pretty determined foot for a dying man.

The lessons and the practice would continue.

At nine years old, I really didn't recognize Grandpa's rapid deterioration or understand why he didn't go outside to work anymore. I'd been around when he was building Grandma's fence. I lived on a farm. There were a lot of fences and I didn't realize this one was special.

In March and early April of 1955, during the evenings after the day's farm work was done, Grandpa built a fence around the yard. It seemed to him as he worked alone, always tired, always slow, that it took forever. He set new gate posts, hung gates, drove line posts and stretched up strands of woven wire. He hung a ten-foot gate by the garden for the little Ford Ferguson to disk the ground every spring. He hung two small gates for access to the front doors and another back gate for Hazel to go out to the fruit orchard, the chicken yards and the brooder house to feed the baby chicks in spring. Each gate pushed open from the inside, so no errant livestock could shove in from outside. Each closed automatically by means of a chain, a pulley and some old piece of iron for a weight.

The back gate pushed open from the inside, like the rest, but since Grandma couldn't push in from the outside either, Grandpa made the back gate wider than the gateposts, allowing the edge to stick out far enough for Hazel to lever it open with her elbow, leaving her hands free for the apron full of eggs or apples or cherries that she often brought back to the house.

Grandma wasn't there to see him hang that last gate. For more than two years, she'd lived with her mom and dad five days a week, taking care of her father after his stroke. She only got home on weekends when her brother took over. She didn't know George was sick. Grandpa thought she had her hands full so he didn't tell her about the indigestion and fatigue, symptoms of the same disease that occurs in conjunction with the sassafras Grandpa harvested and probably used as medicine in Ohio.

Grandpa remained silent because his wife didn't need anything more to worry about and, Lord knows, Hazel could worry about things that would never happen!

His daughter, Nina, knew he was sick, though, and she quit her factory job in Hastings to come home and take care of her dad. She really didn't tell Hazel how much she worried about her dad, although she "gave her the devil" for being gone so much.

"He'd never let on to me that he was feeling so bad," Hazel said. "Food didn't agree with him. He'd doctored with Doc Kamm for quite a while when I was gone and got some medicine, but he couldn't get well."

Grandpa figured he just needed to wait it out. They'd all survived the flu in 1918 and this didn't feel anywhere near that bad. The doctor couldn't find anything, so he must be all right. He thought maybe sixty was getting old enough to feel his age. In April, with Hazel home for good after her father's death, he went to see Doc Kamm again.

A few weeks later, after exploratory surgery, Grandpa learned he had cancer and that it had metastasized.

"You see, cancer was in his liver and it had spread all over," Grandma Hazel said. "They told him he could take radiation treatments, but they didn't think it would do him any good. They explained to him what it might do. He says to me, 'Mom, there's no sense in going to all that expense and maybe suffering from it. I'll just take it as it comes. I know I'm not going to get well. I'll live as long as I can.'"

Grandma and Nina fixed up a couch on the south porch that was all windows on the east and south. "He spent most of the time out there and he had more company. They was always acoming. Prettinear everybody in town come out to see him, short visits, because he couldn't take too much. Elmer Echternach come to me one time wondering if George could drink a beer. When I said it was against doctor's orders, he brought out a whole gallon of ice cream."

I've thought about Grandpa's last days from time to time and I gained some appreciation for what my piano practice must have been like many years later when my daughter took piano lessons. I remember once standing in the kitchen preparing a meal and hearing her play the same phrase about twenty times—wrong every time. I walked out into the yard for a while to get a break from it. I thought that at least Grandpa didn't have to endure my drum practice. That came years later.

I told Grandma about my belated epiphany, but she stopped me mid-story. He enjoyed it, she said firmly and she left no doubt that he really did.

I've thought about that possibility a lot since and somewhere in the deepest recesses of my imagination is an image of my fingers flying over the keys in smooth, legato passages that soothed my dying grandfather's soul. Now when I hear Beethoven or Chopin or Brahms, I imagine us in a kind of soaring dance —him dying and me just starting life.

I remember reality. There were no smooth, legato passages. I was slow, hunting for notes, arranging fingers where they didn't want to go. My timing was abysmal and I found I could sustain notes that need to be held by stepping on the right pedal, so my music became a cacophony of notes played over each other.

He enjoyed it?

I've tried to come to his perspective and the best I can do is to believe my rough pounding was evidence to him of life going on with all its roughness and messiness. Maybe my persistence in reaching again and again for that right note helped him to feel confident that we'd all do all right, even without him. Maybe that's why only I sensed his presence when Grandma was dying forty-two years later.

"He talked," Grandma said. "We talked more, I think, than we had for years. He'd say, 'Don't worry, Mom, we'll be all right.'

"He was very patient when he was sick. Before, he'd always – anything had to be done, he wanted it done right now. He was impatient with Cecil quite a bit when he was growing up. I think he was. Cecil wasn't a person that really watched his dad. Some kids would have been out awatching his dad more. He wasn't like that. He was more of a daydreamer. First time he went to harness the horses, he put the collar on wrong side up and George just about had a fit. He never yelled. No, he never did. Nina said, 'You know, I always knowed when my dad was mad. All I had to do was look at his eyes.'

"When he got sick, he was patient. He wasn't wanting you to do this and wanting you to do that. As long as he could, he waited on himself. He would read."

Grandpa fought to the death for every ounce of life he could salvage. He was still fighting in the west bedroom when a storm whipped up from the southwest. The old cedar tossed and twisted in the yard as the wind screamed around the corners of the house. The women flew from window to window, peering out between the trees, looking for a funnel. Then the wind stopped dead and they hurried into the bedroom. The sky boiled with greens and purples and indigos. They didn't see the funnel lick down out of the clouds like a black tongue that grew and grew until it was lapping up leaves and branches and shingles.

"It took the basement door off," Hazel said, "took it down over the garage, took that one south window in the living room out, while he was in bed in the next room. Nina and I, when it come, we tried to get him as far over as we could next to the bearing wall. We was both in the bedroom trying to shield him a little. We couldn't do nothing. Course it was just gone like that.

"It was apouring down rain. We had a bunch of old doors outside. I went and got one of them doors and nailed it on the outside over that window. I got it on there before it got too much in the house. Seems like it wasn't quite coming from that direction. If it had been coming from the south we'da been drowned. It was kind of late in the evening."

In the dark pause of Grandma's telling, I remember that she would have been fifty-nine that fall and that those windows are sixty-six inches tall. I can see her running out in the rain, slipping and sliding in the muddy yard, water streaming down her face and down her back. Her shirtwaist dress is plastered to her skin. She wrestles a solid wood door from a neat stack in the old shop.

Outside again, wind whips against her, slamming the door against her shins, carrying her a few steps backward—north and mostly east toward the barn and the windbreak. And as she gradually turns the door edge-on to the wind and struggles back to the other side of the house, Nina stands guard over her father, getting more blankets, covering him, protecting him.

Grandma fights and wins against the wind and when the door finally slams against the side of the house, she holds it with her hip. As she grabs the hammer from her deep apron pocket, where it's been banging against her thighs, and fishes a nail from another pocket, Nina begins mopping at the wet floor that borders the blue living room carpet. As Hazel pounds a nail and then another and another, through that door and into the side of the house, Nina jerks all the towels from the bathroom cabinet and sops water out of the carpet. And finally the wind stills and the women have the living room all dried out and they're all still alive.

My grandfather lies in the bedroom, dozing maybe, maybe remembering the feel of changing air pressure in that house and the roar of the tornado and the feel of those two women's warm bodies shielding him from the storm. He must have known then as never before that there was nothing more he could ever do to protect them from anything—no more than he could protect them from that storm. I wonder if he felt any regrets in those moments, any realization of how much we all still needed his steady good sense and his ordinary insistence on doing right.

He must have sorrowed over the things he and Hazel never got to do, even as he celebrated what they'd done, how they'd lived the life they'd planned – free and independent, helping people who needed help, making and keeping friends who helped them as well.

I remember, too, that Grandma once told me they'd been planning for retirement before Grandpa got sick. They'd planned to see some places they'd never been, maybe go up into Canada and see where their old family friend, Philip Hunt, had come from. Maybe they'd go back to California and spend some time with Hazel's brothers and sisters and their children or go to see Grandpa's family in Ohio. With all those plans gone, I can imagine Grandpa saying, "Now Mom, when this is over, you take Nina and you go to those places, just like we planned." And I can imagine her agreeing that yes, she would go, and wondering what she could possibly get out of it without him.

"I done everything I could for him. I fixed something he could eat. I give him his baths. I took him to the bathroom and I done all that kind of thing. Well, I almost had to carry him. You know, I've thought about it a good many times. I never had to clean up after him. Never. He always had control of that.

"He itched. I stood up half the night for several nights and just rubbed his back. It itched so bad. And then it got his feet."

Doc Kamm didn't know the reason Grandpa itched, but it was persistent and maddening. Kamm recommended a series of shots to Grandpa more comfortable and asked if anybody could give the shots so he wouldn't have to travel to the farm every day. My mother, Ella Mae, was there then and she'd been vaccinating hogs. She thought she could do it, so she did.

196

I learned many years later that the deep itching that tortured my grandfather resulted from the same blockage of the bile draining system as the jaundice that turned his eyes yellow. It is common in end stage liver cancer.[ccxlv]

By my ninth birthday, Grandpa was too weak to get out of bed, except to go to the bathroom with Grandma's help. They got a commode for the bedroom.

On my sister's fourth birthday, October 18, Grandma almost had to carry him.

"'Course he never was very heavy," she said. "I don't think he ever weighed over one hundred forty-five. And he got so he didn't hardly weigh anything."

They took Jo Ann to the bedroom and stood her on a chair so he could see her new birthday outfit, a red cowboy hat with a fringed red-and-white western skirt and blouse.

"Well, Jo Ann," he said, "my little cowboy."

He was exhausted by then. She couldn't stand still. There was a moment of suspended animation, then she was off the chair and out the door on about the business of living.

That was the last time either Jo Ann or I saw our grandfather. As Grandma reminded me of that moment, some recess of my memory brought back Grandpa's soft, gentle voice, weakened by disease, saying his last goodbye to my little sister, as a caress. I hadn't remembered his voice for years. I remembered his face, wasted and skeletal, but quiet, as calm as if he planned something ordinary, like a Sunday checking fence on the little Ford tractor with fencing pliers, a coffee can of staples, a roll of barbed wire and a wire stretcher in a wagon trailing behind.

His sister once chewed him about not going to church and he said checking fence was his church. I imagine him

in the pasture listening to the rhythm of the tractor engine
and the jingle of the staples and tools bouncing in the
wagon bed. I took out his last hedge post in 1992,
remembering that it had been there for three
generations—the last of a carload he'd bought when they
moved to the place. I think of him digging the hole that
post sat in for seventy years, semi-conscious of cool
morning air, a gentle wind singing in the fence wires, the
metallic clank of a windmill somewhere over the hill, and
the smooth, legato call of a meadow lark. I can still see the
pattern he laid on the land.

"Just a day or two before he passed away, he said to
me – Uncle Harry had just come back from Missouri and
Aunt Myrtle was a nurse, you know – he said, 'Do you
suppose you could get Aunt Myrtle to come and help you?
It's getting too much for you.' I didn't even have a chance to
ask.

"He was asuffering right at the last. He was suffering
heart pains. We called the doctor out. I called for my
brother. Earl come. I remember George saying, 'Doc, let's
get it over with.' That's just the way he said it. Doc gave
him a shot. It quieted him down. Nina and I and Cecil and
Ella Mae was there.

"He knowed he was dying. The last thing he did, I was
aholding his hand. He squeezed my hand. He was gone."

"It is a riddle, wrapped in a mystery, inside an enigma; but perhaps there is a key."ccxlvi -- Winston Churchill

Faith

To me, my Aunt Nina, Dad's sister, has always been a riddle. What made her so different may the times when we visited her at Engleside, an inpatient mental hospital near Hastings, where she was receiving electroshock therapy. At about nine or ten, I felt uneasy with the antiseptic smells and the institutional green walls. Our footsteps echoed on the tiles where most of the patients' steps whispered. Some of the voices drone on and on. Occasionally there was a shout. My family's silence concerning this place and what Nina was doing there only added to the unease and I confess that, when I learned about her private detective's license years later, it only added to my discomfort. What on earth would a woman living in Blue Hill, Nebraska, detect?

The most memorable thing about Aunt Nina is her photo albums. She was an amateur photographer, not a great photographer, but a prolific one. The quality of the photos didn't matter because her pictures had only one purpose—to record her family. She took pictures of Grandpa on the tractor and Grandma with a bundle of apples cradled in her apron. She shot Daddy with his tennis racket and Mom posed on the fender of the car. She

199

photographed me on my sled and Jo Ann with the dogs. She even took pictures of all the farm equipment lined up for auction like defeated soldiers.

Besides her own photos, she gathered all the old portraits and snapshots into some thirty photo albums I have scattered around my living room. In those albums are grandparents and greats and great-greats. There are aunts and uncles and cousins, babies and old women. She had prints made from the old tintypes and daguerreotypes. She had multiple copies made so the rest of us could know what our ancestors looked like. She was recording a very particular history that had enormous meaning for her.

After she died, in addition to all the photos, we found the private detective's license and a dental mold tucked away in her cedar hope chest, along with a letter from Eleanor Roosevelt. I was really young when Nina earned the license and acquired the dental mold and the letter, and I was away from home part of that time, so I didn't witness any of what happened. What follows is Nina's story as I've pieced it together.

Grandma said Nina was a tomboy. She said she climbed "on top of everything" including the platform of a twenty-two foot windmill with the blades running. Grandma had to hope Nina wouldn't be caught by the spinning blades before she could run out to stop them.[ccxlvii]

". . . she didn't know how to get down. I knowed I didn't dare yell at her. I had to climb up there and get her down . . . She didn't go up there again, believe me. I tanned her pants for her. We believed in spanking kids in them days."

Like me, Nina wandered the home place, inspecting everything. She brought whatever she found into the house, even a "big worm" . . . a garter snake. She climbed trees and looked into birds' nests. With her girlfriends, she rode a cow and got brushed off. She lay on her back in the grass, listening to bug whispers and watching clouds blow by.

The year she and Dad went to school in California, Nina played basketball and went out for track. She was painfully shy and sports allowed her to get acquainted. She made some good friends there and she certainly didn't want to leave when the banks closed and the family lost all its deposits. Grandma said that there were a lot of boys that kidded around with her, both in California and back in Blue Hill, but she never seemed to have any interest in them.

During the summer, that year in California, the family picked fruit and olives. When the time came for prune plums, though, Nina backed out. Unlike most tomboys, it seems, Nina had an aversion to getting her hands dirty. I guess I got that from her. I used to enjoy maintaining my car, but I couldn't get through an oil change without washing my hands at least once. I can't explain it in my character any more than I can in my aunt's.

"You had to have someone to knock them off on the ground. Well, Cecil knocked. Nina picked one day. . . she told her Aunt Emily, 'I'll look after the kids [her younger cousins] and you can go.'"

Apparently, Emily was glad to get away and Nina didn't have to get her hands sticky, with "them old mushy plums," although I'll never know why that bugged her— only that sticky hands make me crazy, too. Grandma thought Nina kind of regretted her offer after a couple of days, though. Lawrence and Emily already had five children for her to take care of, ranging in age from one to seven years, but she'd given her word and she kept it.

When they were in high school, together with their friends Dad and Nina went to a lot of dances. Small orchestras played even in small towns on the prairie during the early thirties and they took advantage of those shows. One of their friends told me that Nina was so concerned about her appearance that she insisted that the car windows be kept closed, even in the blistering heat of summer, to keep the wind from mussing her crimped waves.

"She would spread her skirts over the top of ours, to keep them from getting wrinkled," Aggie Britten told me years later.

That vanity shows up among the pictures in the photo albums. I find pin-up photos of Nina in swimsuits and dance dresses. She recruited Grandma to take those pictures for her and she pasted them into the albums as well.

Nina, herself, told the story of going with her friend, Gladys Magner, and her family to the State Fair. They spent the night in Lincoln and on the second day, the girls still had a little spending money in their pockets. They wanted to know what people peep at during a "peep show." So they spent the last of their money to go to the show. Nina said she got an eyeful, but what she remembered best was that the family decided to stay until much later than planned. She was out of money, so breakfast was her only meal until they got home very late that night. She wasn't about to ask for a loan.

She rode to school in an old Chevy with her brother at the wheel until he graduated in 1933. About two weeks before school started the next fall, it occurred to her parents that she didn't know how to drive, so Grandpa took her out for a driving lesson. When he got back to the house, he said, "She's going to board in town. She almost run off the culvert."

"We just never thought to teach her," Grandma said. "She couldn't handle the gearshift; not in that little time anyway."

The change of plans cost more than the cheap gas she and Dad had used getting them to school the year before. Grandma and Grandpa paid for it with produce.

"That last year Nina went to school, we milked cows . . . . We'd bring a can of cream to town and a crate of eggs, twelve dozen. Take them to the store and pay her board, $2.50 a week. She came [to town] on Monday . . . and we came and got her on Friday."

After graduation in May, 1934, she was at home and away a lot and she went dancing when she could. Right after she graduated, Dad went to California with his friend, Ralph Vavricka and Uncle Joe Colburn, so she ran around with the Toepfer kids.

Nina's aunt, Edna, Grandma Hazel's sister, and her Uncle Carl Meents lived about a mile east of the Colburn place. Like Grandpa George, Carl was a hard-working farmer. Edna had married at a more advanced age than her older sister. She was very shy because of a stroke she'd survived when she was sixteen. Though it was hardly noticeable, she had a facial tic that seemed to make her self-conscious. Because of the stroke, she lost some school and she never finished high school. She and Carl were getting along okay on a rented farm. Though they had survived some drought years, the dust storms had not yet begun. Like many farmers in those days, Carl would come to the house for the noon meal, then take a quick nap on the couch. Edna used to gripe at him for folding his hands on his chest when he slept. It looked like he was laid out for burial, she said, and it gave her the creeps.

Her creepy feeling turned out to be prophetic. On May 30, 1934, shortly after Nina's graduation, Carl died from a ruptured appendix. Nina moved in with her aunt while

Edna gathered herself up and soldiered on with four stair-step children ranging in age from eighteen months to nine years. The Meents family suggested that Edna apply for welfare, and she did.

"Lady come out and looked at her," Grandma said. "She thought Edna could economize a little bit by wearing cotton stockings instead of nylon. Edna said, 'I wish I'da pulled up my dress and showed her the rest of them. They was all ragged.' Soured Edna on it right away. But I think she got $12 one month and that was the end of it.

That's when the family took over. Edna had five brothers and sisters, all with families of their own. Grandma Hazel and Grandpa George taught her to drive (Nina, too). She had a 1928 Chevy, just like theirs. At harvest time, the family harvested her crops for her. At about that time, her brother, Uncle Earl, moved into town because his wife, Ollie, and her mother had both been blinded by diabetes. He and Ollie moved in with the Reeves so he could take care of both women. They had the telephone "central" in Guide Rock, where they connected calls for all their neighbors. When Earl and Ollie moved, Great-grandpa Will and Great-grandma Frank moved to Earl's place, leaving their farm place for Edna. There she had a house, a chicken house, room for a garden, a barn and some pasture for a milk cow and a few meat animals. She sold cream and eggs and an occasional calf. Grandpa Will and Uncle Earl farmed the two places, but when Edna's boys got old enough, Earl hired them to farm his place.

"Whenever we wanted to get something, we'd get something we knowed she needed," Grandma said. "It was a duty, but we wanted to do it."

Meanwhile, as the family gathered its resources to take care of its own, Nina was needed in other family transitions. Her family "positions" took her into very different households on very different occasions. In a

204

couple of weeks, Uncle John and Aunt Nina Colburn, Grandpa's brother and sister-in-law needed her to help out after the birth of their first child, Billy, June 16. I only met Uncle John a few times, but I remember him as being unusually quiet and very tentative. He seemed painfully shy and his wife, though I knew her even less, seemed much more confident. The challenge of moving almost instantly from a grieving household to celebrating must have been wrenching, especially since she returned to Edna's when John and Nina were done with her.

This was work a lot of young women had done for generations; the same kind of help Eva May had provided for Grandma when my dad was born. They would live with the family for a few days or a couple of weeks and take care of household chores so the new mother could stay in bed and get acquainted with her new baby. They didn't earn much, but it helped supplement their families' income.

In March, 1936, Nina was helping her Aunt Laura Hiatt after the death of her baby, Eunice Ann, when the first of the dust storms roared in. At least this time she had months rather than hours to prepare to help her pretty, timid aunt grieve her terrible loss.

Grandma and Grandpa were out visiting one night when Nina was at the Hiatt's.

"It was a nice evening and we went over to Jack Meents' to play cards. All at once the wind come up and it went to howling, and it snowed a little. It was just awful bad. We all had to stay all night. We couldn't get our cars started.

"When I got home, the bed was black. The curtains was just hanging full of dirt. It just come right through the windows . . . they was shut, but everything was just hanging with dirt. The floor was all covered and the table was all black. It took me quite a while to get it cleaned up . . . about that time another one would come. We'd wet a sheet and hang it over the windows. That would catch it . . . It didn't get in your beds and you could breathe.

"Little children. It was bad for them. They had to do a lot of things for little kids . . ."

Nina's services were especially valuable during and after those storms. They would hang damp sheets over the cribs so babies could breathe. During the times she was at home, Nina helped her mother battle the dust. Grandma said the house smelled like dust most of the time.

"It was a mess. Nina and I cleaned up after one storm. We was cleaning in the dining room. See, whatever direction it would come, that room would catch it. We finally was playing tic tac toe in the dust on the floor. It was bad."

Like her mother, Nina served as a caregiver, starting with her own family—cousins and aunts and uncles. Then she worked at the county poor farm; she tried something different for a while, serving as the central telephone operator in Inavale. But soon, she was back to care giving, with a job in Hastings at Sunnyside, an "old people's home," where she stayed until she was ordered to give enemas. That wasn't in her job description and she wasn't about to do it. She could lift people and make beds and she had procedures of her own for cleaning up people's messes without messing her hands, but enemas—no way! So she returned to the home place until she found something else.

Dad returned to the farm after working a while with the Civilian Conservation Corps in the Sierras and then knocking around the Rocky Mountains. With the beginning of World War II in Europe, farm prices had improved and he had started his own cow herd as well as taking a share of the farm work. But in February, 1941, he joined the Army and left for boot camp. Nina, scared and bereft,

206

returned to the home place where she could worry with her mom and dad.

"She come home . . . you couldn't hardly get any help. George was aworking away [with the Soil Conservation Service] part time. We was pretty much in the hog business then. Carrying water from the windmill out to that west lot, that was my job. We had a barrel with a hog waterer on it. That was my job, to keep that barrel full. On hot days, I carried millions of buckets . . . We made a shade for them hogs, then put straw on top of it. When it got real hot, we'd carry water out there and throw it on that straw. Nina helped me do that . . . . She cultivated corn with four head of horses."

"She didn't work in the fields too much but she wanted a new dress for the Fourth of July one year. Her dad said, 'Think you can run the cultivator? If you go out there and cultivate that field of corn, we'll see you get that new dress.' It was dotted Swiss and it had two tiers on it. She went to a dance somewhere with that Toepfer kid and somebody stepped on the lower ruffle. Tore it off. She had to come home with it pinned up. I think she finally give it to your mom and she made you a dress and Jo Ann a dress out of it."

The war "was pretty bad for Nina. Her and Cecil was awful close. It broke her up quite a bit. She always was doing something."

There were always cockleburs and sunflowers to cut. Maybe she even felt some sense of connection with her brother as he hacked his way through the jungles half a world away. There was rubber and leather and metal to recycle and she might help bring him back sooner if she helped keep the war effort supplied.

She turned to music during those years. Grandma says she took piano lessons. She and Dad had taken them when they were kids, Nina practicing faithfully while Dad learned to play by ear. Nina kept dancing—with younger "kids that wasn't in the Army." Grandma and Nina watched a lot of "picture shows" during the war years, trying to glean anything they could about the war from the newsreels.

"I don't think she worked out any during that time. Except she might have worked for Bertha Thomas when some of the kids was born . . . two of her boys."

And finally, Cecil was home, April, 1945. He'd been gone four and a half years. Nina must have been dancing a jig along the fence rows. But he came back a changed man. Not only had he come back with malaria than kept him huddled, shivering, behind the cook stove in a bundle of quilts, he was also quiet and "broody," the mischief gone. After about a month, the Army took him back for medical treatment and debriefing. Next time he came home, he was married to a stranger.

"It was hard on Nina. It was really hard on Nina. It took her longer to accept it than it did any of the rest of us. She had waited for your father to get back."

Grandma said that Mom and Dad sometimes took Nina dancing with them, but she must have felt like a fifth wheel hanging around with a newly married couple who had only known each other for a few weeks. Perhaps Nina was struggling to accept the facts when she insisted that Mom and Dad have a wedding portrait taken. The photo was part of recording her family, although that hadn't become an avocation yet.

Later, she "got a kick" out of telling the story of my parents' wedding.

"One of them had sent their clothes out to the cleaners and they didn't come back," Grandma said. "They had to borrow a suit from someplace else to get married in their uniforms. When the service was going on, a dog ran through the chapel and upset the flowers . . . They never got their pictures taken until they came back . . . Later years, Nina enjoyed telling that story."

So Aunt Nina moved into the post-war years without a dance partner. With Dad back on the farm to take over his share of the work, she got a job in Hastings working at the Naval Ammunition Depot, a forty-eight-thousand-acre facility that provided forty percent of munitions used by the U.S. Navy from the time it went on-line in 1943 until the end of World War II. So, near the end of the war, Nina became part of the stable work force that had drawn the Navy to Nebraska. She remained there for ten years, until the end of World War II and through the Korean War, doing work she didn't or couldn't discuss.

In her moving ahead without Dad to run around with, she allowed herself to get involved with a Navy dentist assigned to the depot. Her new dance partner was apparently separated from his wife and Nina fell pretty hard, according to my mother. And then he just disappeared. Nina must have been frantic. What could have happened and why didn't he tell her? Even when he dropped out of sight, she believed in him.

That's when she earned her private detective's license.

With love and with hope in her heart, she sought him all over the country. She had to know what had happened. Perhaps she'd done something to hurt him. Perhaps something awful had happened to him and he felt he couldn't come to her. She followed even the most unlikely clues to find him, even writing to former First Lady

Eleanor Roosevelt. I assume she used a pseudonym because Roosevelt sent a polite response to Miss G.

"I wish I could help you with your problem," she wrote, "but I'm sorry to say I do not know any dentists in your community. With many regrets and my good wishes for the New Year. Very sincerely yours, Eleanor Roosevelt." ccxlviii

At last she located a man with his name in a suburb of Chicago. By the time she found him, Mom and I were in Chicago with Grandma May. Nina asked Mom to go with her to visit this man and to learn her fate. Reluctantly, because she knew something of seduction and the men who prey on vulnerable women, my mother agreed to accompany her sister-in-law. When they arrived at the address they walked up the front walk and knocked on the door. Mom said that a woman answered and a man was coming down the stairs behind her. Without a moment's hesitation, Nina said, "I'm sorry, I've got the wrong address." She walked away, got in the car, and came back to Nebraska. She told Mom she'd found the wrong man— obviously she had.

She didn't look any more.

Nina kept her job and kept on keeping on. She may have had a friend to share her grief, but as far as the family was concerned, they just didn't seem to know much about it . . . or they weren't talking. Grandma may have known a lot more than she ever said. Now that I know about Aunt Eva, I know there were times she just didn't talk.

Before long, though, the family needed her again. After her father had a series of strokes, Grandma began spending five days a week helping her own mother, Frank, care for Grandpa Will Carpenter. Nina quit her job and came home to keep house for her dad.

After Great-Grandpa Will's death, Grandpa George had his surgery and learned that he had terminal cancer. When Nina heard the news, she gave up. It was just too much to bear. While he was still in the hospital, she found an old pistol Dad had brought back from the Pacific and she tried to shoot herself. The pistol didn't work, or maybe the cartridges were damaged or didn't fit. Grandma couldn't remember why it didn't work. She was just relieved. The family talked Nina out of killing herself. After all, Grandpa would need her help.

After that, Grandma said, Nina just refused to accept that Grandpa was going to die. She thought he ought to have the radiation treatments that he had already rejected. When he became so weak he couldn't get to the table for meals, she asked the doctor if he wouldn't be better off in the hospital.

"Nina, he's getting better care here with your mother and you looking after him than he would get in the hospital and he's contented here," Grandma quoted.

"Before Grandpa died, she was getting kind of . . . things wasn't going right for her," Granma said. She imagined things. Just kind of withdrawed into herself."

Until the very end, Nina thought there was something more that could be done for Grandpa. She was in the room with him when he died. Along with Grandma, Dad, Mom and Uncle Earl, she heard his last words, saw the fire leave his eyes. And it made her crazy.

"I don't know," Grandma said. "She just insisted they hadn't buried him, thought they'd taken him to the University. I just don't have any idea why she got that notion."

Grandma never said it, but my mom told me Nina even accused her mother of poisoning Grandpa. Eventually, she began to accuse her Uncle Earl of "doing things." Earl had helped out when Grandpa was sick and he was there to help and support his sister and niece when he died. Earl arranged the funeral, as he had for several other family members. In her confusion, Nina blamed Earl. And the doctor. Finally, they decided she had to get treatment.

She refused to go, even as an outpatient. And so, literally, the guys in white coats came to get her. Again, she physically refused to go. Grandma called my dad and he came to talk to Nina, told her she needed help, that the people at Engleside had helped him out of a rough spot. If Dad had asked her to jump out of an airplane without a parachute, she'd have jumped. So she went quietly.

Dad tended to believe in science, but I don't know that he realized how limited knowledge of the human brain was at that time. Sometimes I wonder, if Dad had known what they were going to do to her, would he have been so persuasive?

I imagine people in white coats dragging Nina down institutional green hallways to the shock therapy room and them practically carrying her back to her own room. I imagine her sitting across from a psychiatrist answering questions and trying to determine what she had to say in order to stop the treatments. Nina was not dumb. In less than three months, she had it figured out.

"I don't think they were a bit of good," Grandma said. "She just gradually talked to people there and one thing and another. They thought she was cured, sent her home. I guess she made up her mind she had to come out of it herself. She went right to work. Nina was a workaholic around the place."

212

Until she was too sick to go out, Nina climbed trees and trimmed out dead branches. She chopped sunflowers and cockleburs and pulled weeds. Before she declared war on them, my sister and I often had to repair bike tires damaged by puncture vine. But after she got back from Engleside, she pulled all the vines and burned them. Every summer for about three years, she pulled vines, until she had eradicated them from the home place.

Every morning, she dusted all the furniture and dust mopped all the floors. In fact, the floors were always so well shined, they were almost dangerous and we occasionally slipped on them. She even dusted the top of the refrigerator where nobody thinks to look.

Dad and Mom tried to get her to go to dances with them and I guess she went once or twice but "she'd kind of lost out with the kids." Apparently, there weren't any singles her age around anymore, but finally, Mom and Grandma took her to a square dance in Hastings.

"She wanted to go. She'd been hearing about it on radio or TV. Well, she hadn't been there very long till Ralph come over and asked her to dance. And, you know, it wasn't only just about . . . I think there was a dance someplace else about the middle of next week. Here he come on our doorstep. And he was there for thirty years."

My dad taught me to two-step, but Nina taught me to dance. I remember seeing her dressed up in silk flowers and ruffled organdies or square dance dresses, excited as a child, going out to a dance with Ralph. It was some time during the Ralph years that she bought the book. I still have it. *Arthur Murray's How to Become a Good Dancer.* Murray wrote a chapter on "How to Prepare for Partnership Dancing While Practicing Alone." And we practiced alone together. I can remember the rhythms from records she bought to go with the book. We tried the fox

213

trot, using Murray's "Magic Step," the waltz, the cha-cha, the samba, the meringue and the tango. I remember feeling pretty ridiculous following Murray's advice to "raise your arms in typical dancing position as you practice alone," and I have an enduring image of Nina and I balancing on our toes, with our arms held up, trotting around Grandma's front room, because "a flat-footed, firm stance belongs on the golf course, not on the dance floor."[ccxlix]

Ralph hung around those years, even after the square dance club disbanded. He brought his guitar and sang to Nina and I remember he held each phrase in a clenched grin that turned it into a tight hum. They took a lot of road trips, with Grandma along as chaperone. Nina insisted. Once, they took Nina's rowboat down to the Republican River and Ralph rowed her from Red Cloud to Guide Rock. He asked her to marry him many times and she refused just as many times.

Grandma told me that Nina had said, "If I say 'yes,' he'd run like the dickens."

It turned out that Ralph and Nina had a great deal in common, not the least of which was their mutual history of in-patient, electro-shock therapy at Engleside. In my mind they were a pair of strange ducks who didn't seem to have a connection to the rest of the world. Maybe that's what kept them at least relatively sane.

Those were the years when Nina gathered up the old photos, wrote names and dates on the back when she knew them and placed them in the albums. The techniques she learned to find her dentist must have come in handy because, when she turned to genealogy, she found people Grandma had only heard about. Investigation must have fascinated her because she spent hours with books and microfilm and, when she had enough information to make them count, she made two trips to Washington, D. C. to visit the national archives. Because of her, we all know

214

about Uncle Jasper who served in the Civil War. We know about T.J. Smith who came from Scotland with his family when he was sixteen, at the cost of his sisters' lives and his mother's sanity. We know what T.J. looked like and how Aunt Ollie wore her hair.

Nina never again accused anybody of body snatching, but she never did give up her ability to deny the facts when they hit her in the face. When my father died, she seemed to understand he was gone and to believe his remains were right where they were supposed to be. But when my mother married Benjamin Eugene "Speck" Copley, about a year later, she chose to believe they were living in sin—all the more annoying because they were living in her brother's house. Once in a while, I'd catch a flash of fanaticism in her eyes, but she didn't let it show very often or for very long. She became a religious fanatic during that time and pounded us all with Bible readings. In the seventies, she bought fresh, new Bibles for every one of us, Jo Ann and I and my two children.

One day, when Speck wasn't running himself quite as ragged as usual taking care of the five women that were part of the package when he married Mom, she got him cornered and started lecturing. I think she'd accepted him as Mom's husband by then, but wanted him to know what was in the Bible. I wasn't there, but Sean, my oldest, will never forget the day because he spent it waiting for the fireworks.

Dad grabbed one of Grandma's bent-backed chairs, turned it backwards, sat and leaned on the back and said, "Nina, what would you have me do?"

She quoted Bible verse at him and he responded with a verse of his own. She quoted and he quoted back. Sean says that went on for hours. That Bible duel got, not only Sean's attention, it made Grandma a nervous wreck. And it got Nina's attention. Although she didn't stop lecturing the

215

rest of us, she'd learned that Speck already knew his Bible, maybe better than she did.

Sometime later that decade, she started dragging her left foot. Grandma suspected a light stroke and wanted Nina to see a doctor, but Nina had seen all the doctors she wanted to see. Dentists were okay and she obsessed about her teeth, but no doctors. Eventually, she lost control of her left leg, but that didn't keep her from her self-assigned chores. She simply dragged one of the bent-backed chairs outside with her and leaned on it while she chopped sunflowers and musk thistles. She tied a bag around her wrist and made sure to get all the musk thistle blooms in the bag for burning. The last time she chopped weeds, my brother-in-law found her tangled up in a barbed-wire fence, unable to get through or to back out. He had no idea how long she'd been stuck there, but she'd obviously been suspended, unable to stand or sit, for a long time.

This time, the family forced the issue and my mother and grandmother dragged her off to a specialist in Omaha who diagnosed Lou Gehrig's disease, ALS amyotrophic-lateral sclerosis and gave her a year to live. She didn't believe him. She never believed him, even as she lost the use of her right leg and her hands and when she couldn't hold her head up any more. She refused to believe him when Grandma was practically worn out, caring for her at home.

Grandma was in her eighties by then. She was too short and Nina too tall for Grandma to lift her into a wheel chair. So Grandma used one of those all purpose, bent-backed chairs. She'd lift Nina into the chair and drag her backwards across the front room where they spent their days, over the original threshold of that old house, through the long kitchen and into the bathroom. She'd lift her onto the toilet and when she was done, Grandma lifted her back onto the chair and dragged her back over that yellow pine threshold, two inches higher than the kitchen floor. I've never encountered wood harder than old yellow pine. When we cut the furnace ducts, we didn't really cut them, we burned them with a circular saw. But Grandma and Nina managed to wear the middle of that threshold down to the lower level of the kitchen floor.

When the muscle spasms began, Nina refused to believe, as her legs jerked uncontrollably keeping her, and Grandma, awake—sometimes all night. Nina said it was just her legs trying to dance and she often dreamed of dancing, moving smoothly to rhythms she heard in her dreams. Nina still didn't believe when Grandma gave up and got her a room in the local nursing home.

We all settled in to visiting Nina there, sitting on the floor to talk with her because she couldn't lift her head and she refused to wear the collar that might help. For twenty years, we helped Nina celebrate her last birthday, her last Easter, her last Thanksgiving and her last Christmas. And somehow she believed until the very end that she would walk again. Perhaps she even believed that she'd win back the thing she loved most—dancing.

Though she chose not to believe in her disease, she believed in families—in her family. Whenever one of us visited, her first and last questions were about the family, how the kids were doing, if they were happy. She cherished letters and cards from cousins in California, Idaho and Kansas. Nina believed in little girls and she knew how to make them—at least this one—feel like little princesses. I reminded her, near the end, of the times she dressed me up and took my picture, told her how she'd made me feel like a princess. "Well you are," she said. And I felt like a princess yet again, a graying, middle-aged princess.

During those last days I once asked her why she hadn't married Ralph. She gave me the same answer she'd given Grandma. Then she mumbled something else. "I've only loved one man in my life," she said. "I could never love another."

There was a time when I thought Nina's affair, if that's what it was, was unbearably romantic, especially because it was so mysterious. But, except for the years I've been married, I've engaged, along with many other single adults, in a peculiar courtship ritual I call hit-and-run romance. Now that I've been smacked down a time or two by this hit-and-run ritual, like a rabbit, full of vinegar, running across the road, forced suddenly to duck and dodge the whining wheels of a truck, I feel differently. Nina wasn't about to tell me how it was for her and it was just too private to ask.

She talked about the land. She always wanted to make sure it was still there. The Home Place never stopped being her home, even when she couldn't get there. Grandma thinks it kept her alive for twenty years. Nina had decided never to believe in death, never to believe in disability and never to believe in doctors—just family and that four hundred eighty acres of land.

She was sick for a long time and her body died an inch at a time, but her mind refused defeat. In her own way, Nina managed to defeat the disease that held her prisoner. She simply denied its existence. Even after more than twenty years of increasing helplessness and the isolation that comes from being unable to get around, she thought life still worth the effort. Until the very last day of her life, she continued to give orders to revive her at all costs.

"Some life!" I think.

But Nina didn't see it that way. Nina lived for nearly twenty years of misery on nothing but hope and denial. Somehow she thought that life was worth living. Even for a crazy woman, that's a lot of hope.

The human understanding is like a false mirror, which, receiving rays irregularly, distorts and discolors the nature of things by mingling its own nature with it. -- Francis Bacon

The Girls in the Madhouse

Once, years ago, I stood at the vanity in the powder room at work next to my friend, Michele. As we washed our hands and checked our hair, I happened to look up at Michele in the mirror. I stopped and stared a moment, then looked directly at Michele and back at her image in the mirror. They were the same yet drastically different— like twins with opposite personalities. The mirror personality was somehow sinister. I felt I'd peeked through a portal into another dimension.

I grew up knowing my family had a secret. I found it unnerving, every time I asked about a fragment, like a badly-faded photograph from a past I couldn't quite remember, that my mother would always say, "Some things are best forgotten."ᶜᶜˡ I'd conjured some family predisposition to incurable madness and someone locked up somewhere in an asylum. I even dreamed, night after night, of some ghastly thing swinging through the trees

219

that Daddy had planted to protect us. In my dream it always carried Daddy away.

I didn't confine my questions to my mother, but my whole family evaded them. I heard about all the trouble I gave my mother fighting my way out of her body, but nothing more about that night. Sometimes it felt like that looking-glass step into another universe that I couldn't quite see, just scraps like the shifting pieces of design in a kaleidoscope. I had early memories of somebody my mother called Uncle Something; some little boy I placed in Chicago; a monstrous teddy bear that appeared on my Grandma's sun porch; and a fearful, dark, noisy journey I associated with a train.

Mom said none of those things existed. They must have been dreams. It felt like I'd lived my whole life with ghosts and you can't hold a ghost accountable—but accountable for what?

I grew up with a dad and a mom, the same ones I'd always had, as far as I knew. I spent a lot of time with my dad's sister, Nina, and my grandma and grandpa. I thought they'd always been there, too. I was sure my proud grandfather is no looking glass memory. When I was little, he'd carried me around the streets of Blue Hill and when we passed the implement dealership, I'd begged for toy tractors just like Grandpa's. I always came home with something. Dolls? What can you do with dolls? I had some. Really beautiful ones. They just weren't interesting. My little sister, Jo Ann, was born just after I started kindergarten. Now there was a doll!! And when she got big enough, we had cats and dogs to play with; trees to climb; creeks to wade; and a pond with a rowboat. But we weren't allowed to use it by ourselves.

I remember very few times when I had my father to myself, but I remember being quite small and chasing grasshoppers with him. We baited hooks with our catch and caught a few bullheads. I remember Grandpa's west pasture that time and the sun and the clacking sound of the grasshoppers along the edge of the pond. I remember a slimy, flopping fish or two with whiskers, but no reflective scales.

Nina took endless photographs of Jo Ann and me, some of them in the rowboat. Of course, there were the portraits—the conventional toddler pictures in ruffled pinafores my mother made for us. In one my hair hung in long Shirley Temple curls my mother had wound around her fingers. In Nina's outdoor pictures with cats and dogs, we wore flour-sack playsuits stitched on the Singer. In one series, I stood beside Nina's doll collection, carefully displayed on the limbs of the lightning-smashed cedar in the yard. Jo Ann didn't appear in those. I'm not sure she'd been born then.

In front of her round, beveled mirror, Nina dressed me up in her ruffled organdy gowns, pinned silk flowers that smelled of cedar in my hair, hung jewelry around my neck and on my wrists and posed me on the piano bench for hours. I swept down the grandma's steep and narrow staircase, carrying yards of skirts that threatened to trip me on every step. I changed dresses and flowers and jewelry in Nina's sunny south bedroom upstairs and swept those stairs over and over again. Nina and I spent whole afternoons absorbed in making me into a grand dame, one afternoon here and another there during long, hot summers when the trees had all been trimmed, the sunflowers cut, the creeks waded and all the new books read. Nina made me feel elegant, positively regal. My sister would say "stuck up," if she commented at all, but mostly Jo Ann just stayed out of the way. Nina had taken dressed-up pictures of her, too, but Jo Ann considered dressing up a particularly perverse sort of torture.

When the photographs came back from the lab, Nina carefully penciled in names and dates and placed them in photo albums. One summer afternoon, when I was fourteen, the secrets unraveled when Nina and I got out the photo albums. We looked at them in Grandma's blue living room, sitting on that same piano bench. Dad was working in the fields that afternoon, Mom was canning something. I suppose Jo Ann was outside avoiding a possible "photo shoot."

I began to see photos I didn't remember. I recognized myself sometimes in unfamiliar places and I thought those photos must have been taken when Mom and I visited Grandma Mae in Chicago when I was three. I think I remember a photo of two little kids facing each other, one with Shirley Temple curls. I can't find that picture in the photo albums now. No one else remembers it. I didn't recognize the little girl on the next page, either. I glanced at Nina.

"Your half-sister, Linda."[ccli]

My half-sister, Linda. I didn't remember having any little friends before I started school and suddenly there's one so close she's like a sister. I wondered how and where I met her and how I could have forgotten. But somehow I didn't ask. I wondered where she'd gone, but I didn't ask that either. Maybe I was afraid. Yet it kept nagging me as we looked at the other photos, the ones I knew about. I thought maybe I did have a little sister, raging somewhere against steel doors or padded walls. The half part eluded me at the time. I didn't even stop to think what a half-sister might be. We didn't have many blended families back then.

That evening, Daddy was lying on the couch, reading, with his foot over the back. Mom was crocheting and Jo Ann was outside playing with the dog. I went into the bathroom to do something new with my hair. I kept thinking about the picture and when Mom stepped in behind me, I mentioned it. Aunt Nina thought we were such good friends, she called her my half-sister, I said, and

I don't even remember her. I asked Mom if she could remember who it was.

She didn't say anything then. She just left the room. I continued primping in front of the bathroom mirror, knowing she'd heard me. Her silence felt evasive, like little things I'd encountered before from my parents' past—my past—things I just couldn't put my finger on. "What the heck was that?" I wondered as I curled a strand of hair over my ear. Maybe I do have a sister in a madhouse, I thought idly. The secrets had just come to seem normal.

I was still primping when she came back a few minutes later and closed the door, making the hair on the back of my neck stand up. I was certain I'd just jumped through the looking glass. As she talked, I guessed that she'd gone to consult with Daddy. She told me, in skeletal detail, about the divorce. Dad had remarried, and had a daughter with his second wife. Then Margo had left him and he and Mom had remarried each other. As she talked, I thought that I had to know my sister. I asked where she was. Mom didn't know. I didn't know if I believed her. If she could keep her divorce a secret for my whole life, why not my sister's location?

When I walked out into the living room, too stunned to really think, my father's eyes were wet. He said nothing, just looked up from the book he held. I walked awkwardly across the living room toward my bedroom. I thought I should say something to Daddy, but I didn't know what. I wanted to say, "It's okay. This is not a big deal." Maybe he needed to say something, too. Neither of us spoke. I suppose I broke eye contact first. Daddy wouldn't have. He'd have left himself open and vulnerable to whatever pain I chose to inflict, any accusation I wanted to make. But he didn't help me either, and we lost that one moment when we could have really reached each other. We might have opened the conversation I craved, a running dialogue about what we believed, about how we wanted to live, about what had value to us. We never had another chance.

Mom's revelation was anti-climactic for me. I'd lived so long with the dark feeling of secrecy, the truth seemed too simple, almost commonplace. I thought I really needed to find Linda. She was part of the family, after all, but no one would give me any hints. Nina, after opening the worm can, kept mum, so I had no place to start. And then days passed and then weeks and months . . . I thought of Linda often, but did nothing about finding her.

Years later, I learned from my mother why Nina clammed up. Right after she told me about Linda, while I was sitting in my room sorting it out, Mom went looking for Nina. She caught up with her in Grandpa's orchard. She must have been livid when she got there, because, after an initial, tentative "hello," Nina turned and started to walk away.

"Wait a minute," Mom said, "I want to talk to you."

Nina kept walking. Mom caught up with her, spun her around and slapped her face. Then she had her say. I don't know what Mom said, but she took control of anything I might have learned about my sister and my own past. Then she turned and walked away herself.

Again, two very different ways of thinking had collided and my mother had spiced it up with a little violence. Mother felt that Nina had meddled in private business between man and wife, but Nina believed she'd been engaged in family business. She'd tried to keep the family in touch. From the beginning, she'd taken the forbidden pictures out to the fields so my father would at least know what his daughter looked like. When she got letters, she took them out for him to read. She believed that secrets can only hurt families.

Apparently, Mom had had too much family openness. In the Bowen family, all the conflicts had been open and painful, sometimes violent. She may have even hoped that, if she ignored it, it would go away. I remember her using that very phrase when she talked about physical pain. And ignoring it had seemed to work for her. The whole thing had disappeared for ten years.

Mom won, of course, but so did Nina. Nina never mentioned her niece—baptized Nina Linda—again, at least not in my presence. But the cat was loose and Mom had to tell me about my sister. She told me nothing about why or how it all happened. "Some things are best forgotten," she repeated.

I'd been there when it all happened, but I was an infant and a toddler and, with Mom's help, I forgot what little I knew. Here's what I managed to piece together before everybody who could tell me died.

The night I was born, after all the trauma and the waiting and the devastating prognosis, Daddy went out and got drunk with Jumbo Van Boening. He took care of Dad that night, took him home to sleep it off. Then there was the paternity suit. Years later, when they were talking about my birth night, Jumbo heard about the lawsuit.

"Well, hell," he said. "I wish you'd asked me. There's no way Cecil could have gotten that woman pregnant. The only time he was alone with her, he was unconscious!"[cclii]

"I knew he hadn't slept with that woman," my mother told me, "but I just felt overwhelmed, like I didn't know who I was any more. That gave me an excuse when I [couldn't take it anymore]. I'd been laying in that hospital . . . and . . . he was out partying."

I asked my grandma how it was for Daddy when Mom left, how it all happened.

"Cecil come up there one morning and told me she'd left," Grandma said. "She took the car and you and he was a wreck. Absolutely a wreck. I was almost afraid to leave him alone. First he couldn't . . . settle down to anything.

"Finally we got him to take some counseling. That's how he met Margo. The psychiatrist give him one of them lonely-hearts papers. Told him he should write to someone.

"They wrote back and forth for awhile. They didn't even know each other."[ccliii]

Apparently, I was still in Chicago with Mom when Dad went to Tennessee to meet Margo. He spent a few days there with her and in August of 1949, they went to Georgia and got married. Margo said they honeymooned in the Smokey Mountains. Dad wove some bushes or saplings into a living lean-to for them where they could rest in its shelter. After three days in the hills, they picked up Margo's three boys and headed for Nebraska.

"You were in Chicago with your mother then," Margo told me. "Ella Mae would call Bill—I called him Bill so I wasn't calling him by the same name your mother did—and put you on the phone. You would be crying for your Daddy."[ccliv]

"Your mom brought you back . . . about Christmas time," Grandma told me, "and she told me that she intended to stay. But [Cecil] told her that he'd already married Margo. It was a blow to her, but she left you with me and went back to Chicago."

Grandma said I stayed with Dad and Margo a little while, but we "someway didn't get along." So I lived with Grandma. Still it didn't work out for Dad and Margo. For Margo, the final indignity came when she began hearing her husband crying in the night when he thought she was asleep. She decided she couldn't live any longer with the ghost of another woman, and she asked that my father take her back home to Tennessee.

"By then I was pregnant," Margo said, "and I asked that he wait to divorce me until after the baby was born."

From here, there are at least three versions of the story and the timing just doesn't work out in any of them. Dad was dead by the time I started getting answers to my questions, so I couldn't ask for his version.

After he left Margo in Tennessee, he went to Chicago to get Mom and me. We were coming home. Dad had bought me a brass-and-silver-plated dresser set. He brought it with him to Chicago, tucked in its blue satin-lined case, under his arm, like a ransom he paid for the return of his family.

"But when he got there," Margo said, "Ella Mae was having a party. She told him she was already married to Joe. So Bill called me and told me to get Nettie, my sister, to come with me . . . and meet him in Chicago. So Nettie and I got on the bus and went to Chicago. When we got there, he'd been drunk and he was a mess. He had a turtle in the bathtub. We drove back to Chattanooga and got the boys and went to Nebraska."

Mom wasn't married then. I don't know if she said she was to make Dad jealous or if Margo was mistaken. I do remember once I asked her about her engagement ring. She admitted that Daddy didn't buy it for her. Someone else had given it to her and she said she was embarrassed that she hadn't returned it. I wonder if that someone else was "Uncle Somebody." I asked Mom but she didn't remember anybody I called "Uncle." I asked why we didn't go home then.

"He was wild," Mom explained. "I was ready to go back, but when he came, he was so wild, he scared me . . ."

Dad ended up with Margo again, back at the farm, but it didn't last. I made another mirror leap when I heard Margo's story. Her timing didn't fit with anything I heard from Mom and Grandma.

"You went back to your mother's and she was calling and you were crying and Bill was crying," Margo said.

Sometime early in 1950 she left again, carrying Cecil Colburn's child. She gave birth to Linda Faye Colburn on May 4, 1950, in Chattanooga, Tennessee. She baptized her daughter Nina Linda in the Catholic Church. Margo seemed to have a strange thing about names.

In the stories I've been told, it seems like years must have passed, but Dad and Margo were only married a few months. I don't know how long Mom and I were in Chicago, perhaps that was longer than I imagine. When I look into my silver-and-brass-plated mirror, I see an image of my mother and father and Margo during the time when got it. Like my unsettling glance at my friend, my image of them seems distorted. That's how my family has always seemed to me. What I could see seemed normal but I always glimpsed a mirror image, a sinister shadow just outside my peripheral vision.

Linda wasn't the only secret that inhabited our house. Dad only spoke to a cousin and a neighbor, both veterans like him, about what happened in New Guinea. Perhaps those were the dark secrets that shadowed my family. Maybe it was madness, just not the kind where they lock you up. It was the kind of madness where you wander around trying to find a place of safety, all the time stumbling against someone else's danger zones.

I don't think my parents and my stepmom were the only ones who skipped courtship after the war. I'm

228

reminded of an old German horticulturist I used to know who said that, if you want something to produce you should hurt it. He was referring to plants, but I wonder how many families started on the spur of the moment because people had realized how fragile life is. My mother often said that the men who fought the war weren't its only victims. I'm still looking at the legacy of my father's war in the faces of women and children who lived with the survivors.

When my mother and father reconciled, it was on my mother's terms. Daddy was never to see his second-born daughter, or to have contact with her mother, and I was never to know my parents had been divorced. The knowledge would destroy me, she said. Here I am, though, undestroyed. Linda, on the other hand, has suffered a lifetime of hurt.

In my family, secrets had become normal. Each of us lived in our own world. Our separate, secret lives isolated all of us from each other—and that felt normal, too, and familiar. But there was one more secret I wouldn't learn until my sisters and I, and our children, were all that was left of the family.

Oh yes, let them begin the beguine, make them play!/'Till the stars that were there before return above you,/'Till you whisper to me once more, "Darling, I love you!"/And we suddenly know, what heaven we're in,/When they begin the beguine! -- Cole Porter

The Turtle in the Bathtub

I keep coming back to the turtle and my father sitting in a car on a busy street in a city he could barely stand, with only a frustrated turtle for company. It was hardly the tropical paradise evoked by Begin the Beguine, his favorite of the songs Mom sang.

When Margo mentioned the turtle, it had seemed incongruous. Turtles just don't belong in cities and even less in hotel bathtubs. Yet I recognized my father in that incongruity. He often brought wild critters in to be nursed or just observed. Raccoons and 'possums occasionally lived in our playhouse and he was always complicit in our attempts to save an orphaned baby rabbit. So I think about how my father must have identified with the turtle carrying all its baggage on its back. In his search for peace, harmony and the love and safety of a family, Dad must have felt all the same futility as the animal, trying and failing to scale the sheer white cliffs surrounding it.

231

What's even more incongruous to me is my parents' struggle to understand one another. I was only three when they finally got back together so I've had to reconstruct everything. Mom offered hints from time to time, but I grew up on my dad's turf and it's difficult to really understand her complete displacement. When she talked about losing herself, not knowing herself anymore, that was meaningless to me until I read one of my father's letters to Margo. He complained about taking "a trip to the city every year and sometimes twice. Those night club pioneers—Cleveland, Akron and Chicago."[cclv]

Right then, I remembered that that's what Mom knew. My dad lived about a half-mile from his parents. Mom was hundreds of miles from hers who lived in those cities. Dad saw his high school friends every time he went to town. Mom never saw hers. Dad was still farming with his dad. Mom had been on her own for eight years when they met, making her own decisions, responsible for her own living. And then she was married, expected by cultural mores of the time, values she believed in herself, to defer to her husband. She'd wanted someone to take care of her. She couldn't understand, herself, why she was so ungrateful.[cclvi]

Mom mentioned the silence as a constant enemy and that too has been hard for me to process, since I crave it. But as I've tried to picture my mother's life before dad, I see excitement and noise. In the nightclubs where she worked, she heard the band and her own voice amplified. In the background she heard the clink of glasses, voices murmuring, sometimes arguing, clatter and chatter from the bar, maybe even a car horn from outside. Off work, she would hear engine noises, footsteps, shouts, an occasional siren, the clatter and clank of people moving goods, sounds that never stopped. On the farm, she might hear a meadowlark, the wind moving around the fence corners, cattle at the tank out back, and maybe a tractor in the distance. For nerves adjusted to turmoil, the quiet seemed very empty.

As if that weren't enough, Mom had to make peace somehow with months of a kind of mechanical rape, as her obstetrician tried to force her pelvis wider, from the inside. And that might have been the oppressive silence that did her in, because she never told my dad. Grandma was the only person she ever told about the horror that lasted throughout her pregnancy.

Then, for the second time in her life, she had to wonder if she would survive when I was born. After all the hours of pleading for the caesarian section, she finally emerged from the pain, alive, with a baby. She expected a reward for all that suffering. She expected a baby she could cuddle. But, she said, I wouldn't cuddle. I have some explanations for that, mostly that she unwittingly denied me her embrace. But what matters is that Mom still felt alone and outside of herself.

And finally, after all the turmoil with the perjured paternity suit, the wind still blew across the fencerows and the nights were still silent and Mom was a lost soul. She cut and ran.

My father seemed insensitive to the change in Mom's life her marriage to him represented. When she couldn't take it anymore, he didn't try to accommodate her very different life style. Instead, he went off into his own search for himself. And his psychiatrist's idea of help was to pretend that all women are interchangeable and if the first one didn't work out, just go find another one.[cclvii]

I never heard even pieces of my Dad's story from him, only from the two women who loved and abandoned him. I'm reduced to reconstructing Dad's struggle from the stories of those women and my grandmother, who was there when the others were gone, and pieces of letters Margo shared with me almost forty years after Dad wrote them. But I have an idea of how it must have been for him. I grew up in his country with his people.

Dad was puzzled by Mom's unease with her pregnancy. Grandma said he talked to her about it. She provided the only real hope of understanding. Although she'd tried to hide it, he remembered the year he and Nina had come home from school, day after day, to see she'd been crying. Maybe she had some understanding she could give him.

One morning when he arrived at the house, he sat her down in the cool, cavernous front room and asked for help. Sitting in the straight-backed chairs at the dining table, she told him to be patient; Mom was scared of the caesarian, which she certainly was. But Grandma can keep a secret and she evidently kept Mom's. Maybe they were both afraid that he would blow up and hurt or kill the doctor. The result was that Dad had no chance to comfort his wife, or even insist on finding another doctor. Perhaps he wouldn't have intervened. He may have thought that doctors know what they're doing. Mom apparently did, although on some level, she must have suspected she was being abused.

Given the prognosis for me, and my mother's suffering, my birth couldn't have been much of a relief for Dad. But he would have gone back to work, it was almost harvest time, and tried to return to some kind of normal. In those days, a caesarian would have left Mom at less than full strength for some time, so Dad would have helped out with me and maybe some work around the house. Grandma was close by, too.

My mother was pretty good at playing the martyr and, when she found out Dad had been drinking while she was lying in the hospital, still in pain, she must have treated him to her long-suffering, raised-eyebrow sigh—often. She

234

was still pretty self-righteous even after he'd died. So Dad's guilt and shame had to be palpable when his so-called one-night stand came forward. It would probably have been more intense if he'd known what Mom had endured.

But . . . they seemed to have gotten beyond it.

Then one day she was gone and the craziness began, with its near-suicidal depression, the visits to Engleside, and the letters to a woman he'd never met.[cclviii]

By the time Dad picked up the turtle, he must have been beside himself. Two failed marriages, a child he adored and feared for with one wife, and three stepsons, boys he'd become attached to with a second wife he'd learned to love in the months they'd had together.

This was not the way life worked. He knew how it was supposed to work. As he went on with his work, cutting hay with the red Farmall, he couldn't help remembering his parents' tranquil marriage and wondering if he were capable of forming such a union. He wondered, again, what was wrong with him even as he tried to put self-doubt aside and live on doing what had to be done—and hope. He'd done it before; he could do it this time as well. But he knew he'd lost his sense of fun somewhere in New Guinea. He knew he sometimes scared people just by looking at them.

The trip to Chattanooga with Margo and the boys was undoubtedly a mechanical blur of guilt and lost sleep with Margo silently weeping in the seat beside him and the boys silent, for once, in the back seat. He'd have probably stopped a couple of times along the way, silently unloading suitcases into a hotel room, then loading them up again, so his family, about to be his former family, could rest. But I've seen my father's mind wind up over much less important events, moving cows for example. Though I never saw him explode, a blow-up often seemed imminent. I'm sure he hadn't slept since Margo asked him to take her home. It surprises me that he managed at all. But, I remind myself, he'd managed the war.

After goodbyes in Chattanooga that he thought would be forever, Dad headed north on U. S. Highway 41. As he tore his sleepless way out of Chattanooga, he couldn't remember when he'd had a good night's sleep. When he passed the base of Lookout Mountain, he guessed he'd slept pretty well during his honeymoon there with Margo. For just a few moments, he allowed himself to remember how they'd lived the dream he'd dreamed by letter.

"On our honeymoon . . . we'll go to the Great Smokey Mountains and . . . [wander] hand in hand beneath the towering peaks through the soft quiet lanes under the stately oaks and maples . . . [and] capture those precious moments that will live forever . . . as a guard against ever becoming too downhearted to think that small problems and difficulties are insurmountable . . . . There I will take you in my arms and cure that feeling of lonesomeness forever by giving you what you need too much. Just an awful lot of lovin'."cclix

He'd done just as he'd promised. Well, he guessed that forever turned out a little shorter than he'd expected. Who knew she wouldn't be able to stand him either.

He followed the Tennessee River for a few miles. Maybe that's where he picked up the turtle. Some kind of living presence must have comforted him in some way.

Then he climbed onto the Cumberland Plateau, riveted on the road, never noticing the laboring car engine. Driving through dense forest on corkscrew roads, struggling up

236

steep slopes and blasting down, he tested his reflexes with sudden switchbacks and other traffic. I once drove roads like those in Arkansas and managed to get off the highway as it passed through some little town. But Dad had been over that stretch of road and was at home with the trees and mountains and whatever critters might cross the highway, looking for love or just another waterhole.

He probably tried to keep his mind blank, but he couldn't help going over what had got him in the mess he was in. He'd written to Margo about his terrible uncertainty after Mom left and about visiting the psychiatrist who had assured him there was nothing wrong with him, he'd just fallen too hard for the wrong woman. "If he hadn't said that, "I'd never have had the courage to try again,"[cclx] Dad wrote.

Maybe the shrink had been mistaken. Maybe Cecil Colburn was the problem. How could he have chosen two "wrong women?" He must have wondered if trying again had been such a good idea after all. If life had been complicated before he started over, it was a mess after and he'd caused enough misery to last a lifetime.

With a beer between his legs, a six-pack on the seat beside him, and with every nerve strung tight, humming like high wires in a prairie wind, he blasted up the belly of the continent. He watched the sun set to his left as he crossed the Ohio into Indiana and headed into farm country.

Perhaps he remembered the letters he and Margo had exchanged. She'd sent him her poetry and he'd been thrilled. In the evenings, he'd tuned the radio to a station that played Larry King waltzes, lit a kerosene lamp, and sat alone in the little, square house, with its steep hip roof, that Grandma and Grandpa had moved from the north quarter for him and his bride who had left him. He'd read Margo's letters with hope in his heart.

"Lassie, sharing your poetry with me is so sweet. I could worship you forever for your romanticism. Don't ever lose it, please. I don't worry about what to say and can just be myself." cclxi

He'd thought sometimes that she could read his mind long distance. Maybe he should turn around and go back, try to persuade her, beg her, to stay with him. But he kept driving north, ripping his way toward the cities. Little towns and cities didn't look all that different than they did in Nebraska, except they were much closer together. So were the farm places with their yard lights announcing their presence like dozens of lighthouses.

Dad thought about his own family farm and how Mom just couldn't get comfortable there. After the painful breakup, Dad had tried to anticipate conflicts—probably based on Mom's complaints. He'd warned Margo before they ever met. She'd asked for brochures about Nebraska and he used the opportunity to describe the country as fully as he could.

"Lassie . . . I hope I don't discourage you, but it's a flat country with rolling hills. It's treeless except what man has planted. The wind blows hard and it's cold in the winter and hot in the summer. If you don't have it in you, it would be a hard, lonely country. I make no apologies for it, for it's my home.

"It is lonely on a cold winter night and there's no sound as forlorn as the howl of a coyote. A pack of coyotes yelping as they chase a rabbit makes the goose flesh raise on anyone. There are rivers close but they are the wide, flat, shallow, dirty plains rivers." cclxii

He also explained what Mom couldn't seem to understand—maybe Margo would. "Maybe the country itself is a challenge to me, for if we are going to continue to feed this country, the soil must be saved. I have convinced my dad and we are setting the example. We are putting a lot of farm ground back to grass and . . . planting trees for they help control the wind."cclxiii

He'd taken the opportunity to write about his trees. Mom never understood them. "My pride in my trees is because it's hard to start them. I carried water for two years after work and on Sundays before I had the pump fixed to water them. There was about 350 trees and now they are big enough to take care of themselves."cclxiv

In the evening after work, Dad could stand in the front yard, pouring the two five-gallon buckets of water he'd brought from the cattle tank on the feed of his weeping willow tree. The willow, a graceful presence in the middle of the circular driveway, never sustained itself. Dad watered it every night, every summer, until the day he died. Then it died.

After Margo, he hurried through towns, stopping only when he had to get gas and a sandwich. The car radio kept him company as he approached the cities, Gary and Hammond, Indiana, and Chicago. He could see the glow of city lights, like the northern lights, above the horizon. As the static got quieter, he could hear those soothing waltzes he needed.

"I like music very much," he'd written to Margo. "I guess that got me in trouble because the ex-wife could really sing! She was big time before she joined the WACs. She used to sing my all-time favorite, 'Begin the Beguine.'"cclxv

Radio crooning, he neared Chicago, adjusting to city traffic and noise. He tried to think of a dream he could offer his former wife, but nothing he dreamed about seems dreamy to my mom. He didn't like bright lights and big parties and smoke-filled rooms. He seemed baffled by my mother's big city sophistication. His struggle to dream a dream he could share kept bringing him back to Margo. In his letters, he's pronounced himself thrilled by Margo's "old-fashioned" values.

"The modern girl don't believe in them. Who knows better than I; they would seem very silly to them. Don't you dare get modern!"[cclxvi] he warned.

Yet he was driving toward Chicago, still trying to find values his former wife could share. He could barely contain his anxiety. He was not in a party mood but when he arrived at Mom's apartment, she was having a party. When she opened the door, smoke and noise poured out into the hall. Shocked to see him, she said she was married, to buy time to think, she said later.

Dad exploded, lashing out at Mom and everyone else he could see. I imagine a struggle in the next few moments that must have frightened Mom and everyone around her.[cclxvii] Dad didn't have quite the adrenalin rush of his first July 4th, but he remained frighteningly volatile for the rest of his life. For one thing, he was big, six foot two. Although he didn't weigh much, one sixty or so, his strength showed up in broad shoulders and deep chest. His eyes made clear, "Don't mess with me." It took several partygoers, men who must have sobered up very quickly, to push my father back out into the hall and keep him there long enough to collect himself.

In the end, Dad found himself with a door and a husband between him and his former wife. Frantic, he must have stumbled back to the car where he sat with the turtle on a busy street, finished the six-pack he'd been nursing for twelve hours and wept.

When he finally roused himself, he found a liquor store and a hotel. He found a pay phone—always a public place to talk—and called Margo. Thinking anything he'd ever hoped for with my Mom was over, he asked her come get him. Shouting to be heard, he said he was just not up to making the drive, alone, again. She agreed.

240

Then he slammed out of the phone booth and went to his room with the turtle under his arm, it legs and head drawn into its shell. Closed into his generic space, he lay propped against the pillows and permitted himself to go back to his dreams with Margo, while he drank himself calm.

"Share your dreams with me, will you?" he'd written sometime in June, in the lonely little house at the bottom of the hill, in the glow of kerosene. "I mean those wonderful impractical ones as well as the others. It's so hard to be practical all the time when it can be so very nice to let pure sentiment take over. I'll bet we could build some beautiful dreams together. Don't you? Don't you hate to be practical all the time? I do, but have never had a chance to indulge in sentiment very much in my whole life."cclxviii

Like Nina, for him the most important dream was about family. He closed out the sound of my voice and my mom's voice that ran through his head whenever he let us in and wrote, "I don't think it's possible to get tired of honest affection. I'd sure like to try a few years to find out with you. I'd also bet a dozen roses against the chance of ducking you in a snowdrift on a cold winter day that you would weaken first."cclxix

He and Margo had had only a few months together to live their dreams, before she gave up. Now, with everything settled, they could hope for more. "Our farm is completely mechanized," Dad had written in the months before they'd met. "It's not hard work, just driving a tractor . . . There's not very much to do in the winter,"cclxx and they were heading into the winter.

When I think about that winter, I'm still haunted by a single line from one of my father's letters. As he wrote about companionship, respect and marriage, he wrote, "Margo, no secrets, so I'll talk about sex . . . I never rushed my ex-wife until she wanted it and it was hard, sometimes once a month."cclxxi

241

That one line makes clear that Mom and Dad never got back the intimacy they'd enjoyed before me. Once more, I realize the enormity of the damage the doctor did to my family. My mother's doctor had betrayed her trust and my dad had no way to understand. Not only had Dr. Webber made sex into a painful, humiliating, memory of abuse, Mom was terrified of another pregnancy. She told me once that she had used the rhythm method of birth control. But apparently she was so scared, she eliminated almost every day of her cycle. I wonder if the doctor helped her out with that, too.

Margo and Dad had no such hang-ups between them. They could aspire, without fear, to a big family and lots of winter nights making it. Still, they weren't able to make it happen. Margo told me that she completely gave up when she began hearing my dad crying at night when he thought she was asleep. Sleeping in my Dad's house did not lend itself to deep slumber. Even all these years later, I sleep with an awareness of everything around me and startle at the slightest change in sound.

Margo and Dad had a tiny bedroom in the back of the house. The boys bunked in an even smaller space across the living room. Margo had no chance to miss the crying, as much a Dad tried to be silent. The house was too small, the silence too great, except maybe on windy nights.

By the time Margo gave up the second time, Dad knew that Mom had not married Joe Marsala, although it had been a near thing. Mom and Joe had planned their wedding for just a couple of days after Dad's explosive visit.^{cclxxii}

What he did not know was what Mom had been doing in Chicago while they were separated. I can only guess that she started by trying to revive her interrupted career. By then, the big bands were giving way to rock and roll, though, and Mom had been away for six years—a long time in the entertainment business. Her mom couldn't support her; she and Joe could barely support themselves. That may have been when she tried to reconcile with Dad, driving back from Chicago, hoping for a sweet Christmas and many more to come, hoping she could adjust; this time, that she could make Cecil understand her need for more than silent days on the plains.

When it turned out that Dad was married, she went back to Chicago and got a factory job, leaving me with Grandma, assuming I would live with Dad and his new wife.

During that winter, though, Margo says that I was back in Chicago with Mom and that Mom would call and put me on the phone and that I would be "crying for my daddy."[cclxxiii] Dad was crying too. It was just too much for Margo. Again, she left.

I think Mom must have done the driving the second time, bringing me and the car back home. I remember that reunion, sort of. I remember a large teddy bear, a panda, with a red bow around its neck. I remember a lot of hugs I didn't know how to take. I remember sitting with the panda on Grandma's sun porch. I don't remember Mom and Dad. They must have slipped off to their own little house at the base of the hill to get to know each other again. From there on they "fought happily ever after," as my Dad said. They struggled, but they managed to make it work.

From the time I was old enough to talk with Mom about her relationship with my father, long after his death—I heard that Dad was not "demonstrative." Mom said she "died a thousand deaths of loneliness."[cclxxiv] I remember seeing my parents hug only once, so that was easy to believe. Even now, touching and hugging are uncomfortable for me. I never questioned Mom's assertion that I pushed her away—until I read Dad's letters to

Margo. Now I feel like I'm in that bathtub with that turtle, clawing away at the slick white sides.

Over and over in his letters to Margo, Dad wrote about touching and holding hands, snuggling and holding her in his arms. So why couldn't he touch my mother in the same way? And why is to so awkward for me to hug my children or to accept a hug from a friend?

The letters have left me questioning who I am and how I got this way. Mom always called me "standoffish," but now I wonder how inevitable that might have been; how much a self-fulfilling prophecy.

I have a lot of theories. Perhaps, when you're terrified of pregnancy and the sexual intimacy that leads to it, you become terrified of any kind of intimacy that might make it hard to resist. Maybe Mom was the one who resisted intimacy.

I have discovered in my own life that, if I deny or suppress one powerful emotion, I can't feel or express any others. I couldn't ask my dad about it, but perhaps the grief he denied for the daughter he never saw affected his ability to respond to the rest of us.

Dad's letters to Margo also led me back to the unending conflict I had with my mother. We were often at odds, though in fear of abandonment, I suppose, I mostly kept my opposition under wraps. Grandma said once she could always tell when Mom and I had fought. I would come in the back door and pound on the piano. I asked her once why I could never satisfy my mom. She'd tell me to do one thing, then be pissed that I hadn't done the opposite.

"I think your mom was jealous of you,"cclxxv Grandma replied.

244

I didn't notice at the time that Grandma used the word jealous, not envious. I assumed that Mom was "jealous" because I'd earned the college degree she had only wished for, even though she had been the one who made sure I had the means to get it. It made my life much easier than hers had been.

There's another interpretation I hadn't seen, though. Dad's letters are full of comments about his "charming infant," his "pin-up girl, Faith Ann," the "smartest kid he ever saw."[cclxxvi]

So now I wonder, if you leave your husband, then disrupt his new marriage by putting his crying daughter on the phone, can you be sure, when you get back together, whether he wanted you or that daughter?

And I never had the courage to ask my mother, but I suspect that she never stopped being that twenty-something woman with the empty belly and the empty pocketbook, pounding the pavement because her life depended on it. For her, it was all about control, trying to control everything so she could feel secure. But trying to control people only drives them away. The consequence is a family unable to connect and a generation lacking the capacity for intimacy.

Troll sat alone on his seat of stone,/And munched and mumbled a bare old bone;/ For many a year he had gnawed it near,/For meat was hard to come by.---J.R.R. Tolkien

Gnawing Old Bones

One night in fall of 1988, I awoke about three in the morning to that windless still when the coyotes have finished their evening hunt and the dog sleeps dreamless on the porch. The shotgun was still in its little alcove just a step away from my bed.

Something seemed to hover in that room where my grandfather had died thirty-three years before, but the thing that woke me wasn't human or even animal. I felt it almost like an out-of-body experience. I could see myself but I wasn't quite inside myself.

I rolled onto my stomach and looked out the tall window at the head of my bed into Grandpa's orchard. I looked over the propane tank a few steps outside the house and saw only what I knew was there, dwarf apple and cherry trees and a sturdy apricot tree, volunteered from a seed Grandma had thrown out.

Satisfied that nothing lurked in the orchard, I listened to the house, to the cavernous front room with its one eye looking out over the hill and to the living room that opened into my bedroom. Not even a breeze stirred the rumpled

247

cedar in the yard beyond the two tall windows. I listened for mice rustling in the kitchen on the other side of the house, but nothing moved there. I heard nothing in the bathroom where a rat had once come through holes made for the plumbing and nibbled on my hair when I was sleeping. Nothing stirred upstairs.

My head felt light and signals my brain sent didn't seem to get to my body. Silence shrouded my nerve endings and when I sat, my body moved, but my head seemed to lag. My vision was just weird. I could see, but I felt like I was looking through a tube. I never dreamed of flipping a switch. I knew this house.

I leaned on furniture and walls as I floundered into the bathroom. Then, guessing what ailed me, I recrossed the bedroom and eased into the living room where I turned the thermostat to the bottom end and began moving up. Fifteen steep, narrow steps; the first was bare, cracked, and needing repair; the fifth had a loose carpet seam. I couldn't seem to stay focused on danger. Instead, I pictured Daddy and his sister, my Aunt Nina, slender and young in their last years of high school, creeping up those same steps, whispering and giggling about a dance and about how, for once, their Mom was asleep. And I imagined "Mom," my grandmother, lying in her bedroom, listening as her children came home safe.

Thinking about my own kids, I checked on my youngest, Ben, sleeping in his crib upstairs. Then I moved to my grown sons' empty bedroom, my father's old east bedroom, and went back to sleep, secure in the knowledge that all the air leaks in the upper floor, leaks that allowed fingers of prairie wind to stir curtains and send drafts scuttling across the floors, would keep us safe from the carbon monoxide downstairs.

As I drifted off, I remembered that once Grandma had told me she'd noticed a yellow streak down the side of the house, below the east bedroom window. When she'd thought about it, she'd realized that my dad had been whizzing through the screen at night rather than going to the outhouse. When she told him to quit that, he kind of ducked his head and half grinned—and quit.[cclxxvii] I dozed off wondering if my sons had ever dampened the screens rather than running downstairs to the bathroom.

Next morning, strange things continued in my head, dizziness that wasn't exactly dizzy and vision that would shear off sometimes, like light through a prism. My skull still felt too full.

I lit the wood stove and shut down the furnace entirely.

After breakfast, I called a doctor and a furnace repairman. The furnace guy removed a sparrow's nest from the stack through my bedroom and installed a screen to stop the birds. The doctor prescribed Dramamine. It didn't help much.

When I finished at the doctor's office, I went to the lumber yard and picked up patching plaster. I had decided to move upstairs, into my father's old bedroom, most recently occupied by two of my sons. The two boys, step-brothers, not only looked different—Jason taller and heavier, Chuck thin and not fully developed yet—they thought very differently as well. The two disliked each other almost from the moment they met and we never convinced them otherwise. The big shelf units that divided the room existed to keep the peace.

That afternoon, I slid the shelves down the stairs and stacked them on the entry porch where they could hold tools like fence testers, staples, flashlights, and pliers. Then I began patching the nicks adolescent boys make in fifty-year-old plaster. The plaster on the brick chimney didn't want to stick, but satisfied at last, I began to paint my father's old bedroom a soft, sunny yellow that seemed to complement the airy room.

It had been several months since I'd tucked my purse under one arm and my little boy under the other and fled to a women's shelter. That spring night, May 13, my husband had come home stomping, grabbed the high-powered rifle, growled something about the neighbor, and left. I had tried to eat some of the meal I'd prepared and I choked. I'd stalked the house, then sat on the couch with Ben on my lap for a few minutes. Then I called the county sheriff, jumped in the car, and ran. I had always thought my husband was all bark, and I tried to continue thinking that, but I couldn't.

I had refused to return until my husband was gone . . . way gone. He'd never frightened me before even though he'd often threatened. He wasn't a large man and he'd suffered heart valve deformity as a result of a childhood infection with rheumatic fever. I felt I could hold my own, until he got out the gun. That changed everything.

When I refused to go near him, he got a friend to take him to an alcohol treatment center and checked himself in. I went home. Next day, he checked himself out. I refused to pick him up and prepared to run again. But he got another ride and went to his parents' home, four hours away. I was still afraid he'd come back some night to get even. He'd been making threats for months.

When I started painting, I was an emotional disaster and that's when the writing began to appear. As I painted the west wall, light from the east window revealed something that I hadn't seen when I started. There were initials I couldn't quite read and "95." I thought maybe some faded ink had reacted with the moisture in the paint, and I tried to figure out what 95 meant. It was a welcome diversion; something else to think about.

250

I thought of my kids' and step kids' graduation dates and birthdays. None fit, but I wasn't alarmed. Yet. These were kids' scrawls. I sat on the third step of the ladder I'd been using and thought about Dad. Did 95 mean anything to him?

I imagined my dad as a boy in that bedroom, looking out over those same hills in the evenings after he'd cut sunflowers and cockleburs. He must have thought about the Grand Pawnee earth lodges that once stood on the banks of the Republican River, out of sight over the hills. Like me, he must have imagined ghost figures, perhaps the faint outline of a man with a feather in his hair or of a woman in fringed buckskin.

Like his mother's family, Dad read voraciously and I pictured him in that bedroom, looking up from a book and day dreaming himself anyplace in the world. I still had his copy of Teddy Roosevelt's book, Roping Lions in Grand Canyon, and imagining my dad reading on his bed up under the eaves helped me calm myself.

But, looking back at the wall, I knew '95 had nothing to do with him.

I thought briefly about the Arnolds, builders of the house.[cclxxviii] I suspected that Oscar and his brothers had used that bedroom. Maybe '95 meant 1895. But, for heaven's sake, the bedroom had been plastered and painted since they left in the eighteen-nineties.

Still puzzled, I went back to my painting and finished up the first coat. Sure enough, it would need a second.

As I worked on tightening up the windows in that bedroom, it seemed like the lights were always on somewhere, even when I knew I'd turned them off. I'd go to bed and see the glow of a light somewhere in the house. At least, when I got up and turned them off, they stayed off for the rest of the night. After getting up several nights in

251

a row, though, I remembered the ghost lights Grandma had told me about when I was a kid.

Grandma had said the lights marked the last walk of a murdered hand and his employer, who had killed him after their lamp-lit walk across the bottom east of the house. Moving from Sam Arnold's old place, catty cornered across section lines to the southeast past Thad's, the lights crossed at the foot of the hill under the gaze of Grandma's house. That was the legend, Grandma had said.[cclxxix]

She said that Don Britten had seen ghostly lights bobbing across the fields and the rest of the Britten kids, as well as Dad and Nina, had wanted to see them too. So, they'd all sit on the bridge in the evenings, down in that bottom, giggling, whispering, and waiting for the lights like a bunch of gangly Icabod Cranes. They'd sit there until almost dark, when Grandma or Mrs. Britten would call them in.[cclxxx]

I didn't put much stock in ghost lights and I had a lot of work to do, including a bedroom to get ready. Ben and I were still trying to adjust to the quiet after the storm, and we spent a lot of time in the evenings playing a little kids' version of Pictionary and listening to quiet classical music. The outburst with the rifle hadn't been the first episode.

My family had struggled to blend two sets of kids, his and mine, and we'd added ours. We might have survived that, but we'd moved to the home place where we'd been caught up almost immediately in the farm crisis of the 1980s. The pressure had been too much. My husband, Yogi, said once that he'd walked out the front door every morning and spun on his heel for an hour, trying to decide which crisis to work on that day.

The drinking had begun when Yogi felt threatened, as he did every day. He defended himself by attacking. The kids had worked harder than they'd ever imagined, but mostly he screamed at them for what they couldn't get done.

As I started painting the second coat, I was thinking about the day Yogi had followed Jason into his bedroom, the one I was painting, yelling and screaming at him. I'd stormed up the stairs and ordered him out. He couldn't blame Jason for everything. I'd learned a few months later that Jason and I had both feared the same thing that day; that we'd lose control and seriously hurt him. Jason, at sixteen, stood as tall as Yogi and the farm work had filled him out and toughened him up. He'd have been a tough fighter once he lost control. He never did.

I thought about the letters and numbers, too. I couldn't help it; they were still visible on the wall. Even though I knew the walls had been redone after the Arnolds left, they were on my mind as well. Focus didn't come very easily then and I skipped all over the place.

When I'd walked out of the house months before, I'd had no money, no job, and no credit. I'd been looking for work, but I kept hearing that I was overqualified. So, I'd been thinking about the home place and wondering if a history of one quarter section could make an interesting book. That provided some sense of order in my emotional chaos. I had written a lot of history for NEBRASKAland before my marriage and the step-by-step process of research helped me pull myself together.

I'd dug out the abstract and found out William Arnold had homesteaded the home quarter, the southwest quarter, section two, township three, range ten. I learned, also, that his brother, Thaddius, had taken the southeast quarter. I'd learned that Thad had committed suicide[cclxxxi] and I poked around on a neighboring quarter until I found his gravestone in a tiny, fenced-off plot choked with brush, along with the headstone of his daughter whose death had apparently prompted his suicide. Yes, I had thought, Thad's story could make a chapter, although it involved a

253

neighboring quarter—the one the ghost lights crossed, supposedly.

As I painted under the angle of the eaves on the north side, I thought about those ghost lights and remembered a spring thunderstorm when I'd run upstairs to close windows. Wind had slashed through the screens, carrying the first heavy drops of moisture, as I squatted down to close the low window, wedged under the eaves with its sill resting on the floor, and looked north at Grandpa's ash-and-cedar shelterbelt. I eased the storm windows down and slammed the windows.Through the wind-driven drops on the panes, I'd noticed a glow in the trees. I thought someone must be in the pasture with a pickup, low beams shining back up the lane. But a truck would have to be right in the trees to light up that area and no one could drive into that pasture without me or the dog knowing about it. I'd kept looking at the light, a low, golden earth-glow that remained steady, lighting up the tree trunks. When I went downstairs to shut the kitchen windows, it had disappeared. Perhaps that was a different version of Don Britten's ghost lights.

A few days later, I was putting on the second coat and the numbers had covered. I was almost done when I turned back to the tray to fill the roller. When I faced the wall again, I found a bold streak of ink across the new paint, a streak that hadn't been there when I'd turned away. I looked at the streak for a moment, then, with the ghost stories rattling around somewhere in my head, I said, "Daddy, if you have the power to do this, the least you can do is to not behave like a common vandal," and I wondered where the hell that had come from.

Ben, playing on the floor near the door, looked at me for a moment to see what he'd done wrong, then went back to playing. I finished painting, feeling my father's presence more than usual. I painted over the streak, which didn't cover, zipped around the corner, and hauled everything downstairs to clean up.

As a cloud of paint ran out of the rollers and brushes, I thought about my father. I'd last seen him twenty-five years before, less than two months before my seventeenth birthday. He'd always been somehow inside himself, always out of reach, always waiting for something, maybe the monster swinging through the trees of my dreams. I didn't know why I had always felt a sense of foreboding about my dad. Yet . . . as long as he was alive, I'd felt safe.

On the way to a meeting one night a week or so after I'd finished my bedroom, I described my sequence of ghostly events to my friend, Lyle Linder, Blue Hill's Methodist minister. I laughed, expecting something from him like, "I suppose next you'll want me to do an exorcism," but Lyle surprised me. Instead, he sat silent for a moment, a massive presence in the car. Then with a sharp edge in his voice, he said, "Don't you ever invite any spirit into your house. Even if you think it's your father."

I smiled. "You think it might 'haint' me?"

"You wouldn't believe the things people ask me to deal with out in these old houses," he said. "I can't tell you anything about it, of course. Just believe me when I say I've been asked to conduct exorcisms. You don't want any spirits, even if you think they're friendly."

I certainly didn't feel threatened by my father's ghost, if that's what was in that bedroom. A ghost seemed like the least frightening possibility in my life. In fact, the thought of Daddy hovering around right then seemed pretty comforting, although I felt I was just dealing with my fading memory of him, not a spook.

When we returned from the meeting, we stopped at
Lyle's office and he rummaged through his heaps of books
on the floor surrounding his desk, a desk dwarfed by the
height and breadth of the man behind it. He retrieved one
on hauntings that I took with me. It was about old haunted
houses and spirits that rummaged around in people's lives.
Not in a nice way. I started reading it right away and
promptly scared myself half to death, not so much because
of the book, but more because of Lyle's sincere belief that
there were things in these old houses . . . things he
believed in as strongly as he believed in God, or so it
seemed.

A couple of days after I read the book, I asked my
eleven-year-old nephew, David, to help me move my
bedroom furniture from the room downstairs to the one I'd
just painted. I needed an extra set of hands and a counter-
balance to the awkward weights and shapes of the
furniture. David wasn't large, but he was a blond
whirlwind and he could hold things in place while I
maneuvered them . . . if I could get him to hold still long
enough. We dragged a six-foot oak dresser up those steep
stairs, stood it not quite upright to turn a corner and clear
the doorway, sweating to keep its golden surface
unmarred. We dragged up the night table. We carried up
the drawers, two by two. Then I drained my waterbed,
siphoning the water through a hose. I had to collapse the
frame because it was too wide to get up the steps, even
standing on its side. I hammered it back together, ran a
hose through the floor vent, and took David home. As I
waited for the bed to fill, I thought the water I ran so easily
would have watered seventy of Dad's baby trees. The
shotgun had always been in the bedroom I'd moved out of,
but I had to consciously choose to move it upstairs. I did.

By midnight, I was asleep.

But then I woke up sharply. The lights in the kitchen were on. I went downstairs and turned them off, feeling my way through the rumpus left after the furniture moving. Night after night, I would close my eyes and then pop up in bed realizing a light still burned somewhere in the house. Nearly every night I ran downstairs at least once to turn out a light. The random creaks and groans the old wooden house made when it settled down for the night seemed to develop a cadence, like quiet footsteps up the stairs, like an angry husband.

Around Easter, I heard someone or something rustling around in the kitchen. I took the shotgun and crept down the stairs, avoiding all the spots that creaked . . . I knew them all. I was halfway across the front room when I saw Jason, who lived in Lincoln with his father by then, rummaging around in the 'fridge. I went back to bed and greeted him, with some semblance of sanity, in the morning.

One morning in March, when Ben was at preschool, I just sat down and thought about all the noises and the lights and the marks on the walls. In that bedroom, I focused on Dad, maybe to avoid focusing on my current realities. Instead, I remembered the day my father went out to the hay field alone. Somehow that day was getting all mixed up in my failed marriage anyway.

My mother had told me later that Dad hadn't felt well when he woke up that morning. She'd told him to stay in the house and rest, and she went to work. But, after she left, Daddy went out to haul hay. July 31, 1963. He wanted that field cleared so the hay could grow for another cutting. He was scheduled into the VA Hospital next day for tests. Sitting next to the library table, I left my uncertainty in Dad's old room and moved into the certainty of his last day.

I was cooking and cleaning house then while Mom worked in town, so Dad didn't even ask me to help. That morning, he threw sixty-to-eighty-pound bales over the

257

side of a grain truck, well over his head. When he hauled by himself, as he did that morning, he drove into the field, carried and threw bales until he had an area cleared, drove the truck ahead and repeated the process. All summer Dad had come in from work like that with his back twisted, left hip thrust a little to the side

That summer, he'd begun having chest pains, although my sister, Jo Ann, and I didn't know anything about it. At eleven and sixteen, we were clueless. Mom had told me to watch out for Dad, that he hadn't been feeling well, but not what to do about it if something happened. Dad's doctor hadn't found any cause for the pain, but suspected light heart attacks.

Nobody had told Grandma Hazel. She thought he had kidney trouble the afternoon he was working on the pickup in the yard at her house.

"He was asetting there in the pickup and he was holding his left arm," she said. I walked out and I says, `What's the matter, Cecil?' He said, `Oh, my arm hurts so bad.' I said, `Well, you better go home and lay down,' and I sent him home. I don't know whether he suffered all night that night or whether it quit."[cclxxxii]

He came in from loading bales the next day, limping as usual, looking a little gray, although I just thought it was alfalfa dust at first. After lunch, he lay down on the floor, not uncommon for my father because of his bad back. But this time he held his left arm up in the air. Jo Ann and I watched him lying there for hours or what seemed like hours. I sat rigid, trying to read. I kept peeking over my book, trying not to let him know how alarmed I was getting. I asked if I should call. A doctor. Mom. Grandma.

"No," he said.

Jo Ann and I looked at each other and went back to reading. I looked at all the words in order. Then I looked at them again—and again. I turned a page now and then, not because I knew what was on the previous page, but because I didn't want Daddy to know I was watching him.

Then, finally, "Call," he said. "Call your mother."

I called. I called Grandma, too, she was closer.

"I think I had just come home from getting groceries," she said. "I was putting my groceries away. I just went right out and jumped in the car and went right down there. I went down there without Nina and left her at home. I never told her till afterwards. Nina said, `Why didn't you come and get me. I wanted to be there.' But there wasn't enough time. Wasn't time enough even for your mom to get home. Seems like she come in the door and he got up and walked over to her. He was kind of crying."[cclxxxiii]

When Mom ran through the door ten minutes after I called, dust still rolling over the car where she'd slid to a stop in the yard, he'd struggled to his feet. He met her in the kitchen, by the front door, doubled over, tears spilling, and said, "Momma." Then he went into the living room, lay back down on the floor and quit breathing.

I rolled him over on his belly and tried artificial respiration. All I knew then was back-pressure-arm-lift method. I took my place by his head, turning his face to the side and reached into his mouth to clear his air passage. Then I leaned forward and pressed my full weight on the heels of my hands below his shoulder blades. His body felt like a sack of cornmeal as I pressed down on his back. I leaned back on my heels and pulled his elbows toward me. I heard no breath sounds, but I couldn't stop. I thought the doctor would tell me I'd saved his life, but nothing happened. He didn't begin to breathe on his own like he was supposed to.

I didn't see Jo Ann or Grandma. Mom stood and watched for a moment, maybe longer, then she interrupted, said she'd called Dr. Bennett. She took over for me and sent me to meet him at the tin schoolhouse, so he wouldn't get lost. I ran out of the house with Jo Ann right behind, leaped in his gray '50 Dodge and roared over the hills streaming billows of dust.

When we reached the schoolhouse, we saw the doctor's dust about a half-mile away, around the curves and over the hills. We jumped out and flagged him down, then raced back over the hills, two miles to the east. When we got back, the doctor only confirmed what I already knew but hoped I didn't. My father was dead. He was forty-seven, almost twenty years younger than I am as I write this.

In 1988, I talked to Daddy for the first time in twenty-five years. I curled up in a gold swivel rocker in a corner of my newly-painted bedroom, thinking about him. Maybe Lyle was right. He'd died very young. Maybe he wasn't ready to give it up. I don't suppose that I really believed my dad was hanging out with me that fall and winter. But the lights and noises were beginning to add to my already uneasy sense of danger.

"Dad," I said, following Lyle's advice, "This is getting really weird for me and a little frightening. This is no place for you. I don't know. Are you stuck? You might try to find Christ."

I stopped talking aloud then, but I thought that, if Daddy could hear me, he had to know that I didn't believe in a personal savior, and I knew he'd think I'd lost my mind. I thought, for his benefit, that the marks on the walls and the various noises and lights were making me nervous, and I hoped he'd find someplace where he could be happy. That, at least, was honest.

I moved to the floor in front of the low south window, wedged under the eaves, like the one on the north. I looked out over the fields, at Roy Alber's place and Wilford's and Gerald's, at John Degener's and then out across the swells of hills to where my high school friend, Julene, lived. I wondered, as I had for twenty-five years, about my complicity in Daddy's death.　　　Staring out over the fields, I wondered if it had been an accident. I'd been sure at the time that he'd wanted to die, because he wouldn't let me call for help. But perhaps he'd thought the spell would pass away like all the others.

That day in 1963, though, the spell didn't pass. My father did. And I cleaned house. And cleaned house and cleaned. And I didn't cry and I finished high school as if nothing had happened.

I have only two clear memories of that time. One is when we visited my dad in the funeral home and I couldn't associate the waxen figure with my father. The second is the notes of Taps, played at the cemetery by Tom Johnson, just a high school kid like me. Those simple phrases make me weep now, but then I couldn't cry. I suppose I'd started anaesthetizing myself against loss when my parents split up.

Grandma told me I was mad at Mom then, and that I'd said, "Mom shouldn't have left poor Dad. She shouldn't have left him."[cclxxxiv] She left out the part where I said I hated my mom. I vaguely remember someone telling me then that nice girls don't say things like that. So I went out and raced that old Chevy touring car as fast as I could go.

The touring car was gone the summer Dad died but I still had his old Dodge, until I wrecked it three months later. The wreck was really spooky. I wasn't speeding. There wasn't anything wrong with the car. I just drove off a cliff at the side of the road, taking five other kids with me. It was as if a troll had reached out of that ditch and dragged us in. Fortunately, we all survived, although Donny Buckles suffered a concussion that nagged him the rest of his short life.

That day in my "ghost" room, I probably sat for another hour, looking out over the reddish buffs and tans of the pastures and the stubble fields of corn and milo and wept for my father for the first time since he'd died. I suppose I was crying for a lot of other things, too. When I'd cried myself out, I laid a cold washcloth across my eyes for about half an hour to take down the swelling, took a couple of aspirin for the headache, and tried to calm myself before I went to get Ben.

That night, before I drifted off to sleep in the room that had been my father's, I remembered the times when I still lived with my husband that I'd gotten up in the middle of the night to feed the wood stove and the glow of the coals when I opened the fire door. Almost all the scars from bumping the edges of the stove are gone from my hands now, but the ghost of those nights was fresh then. Those were the nights when my oldest son had gone to live with his father, his sleepless brother puttered around half the night in his room, the one I'd moved into, and Ben, my baby, woke me once or twice every night.

The farm crisis of the 1980s had swallowed up a lot of good farm people. We'd lost almost everything. My husband had lost most of all; he'd lost his sobriety to an undiagnosed anxiety disorder. As the farm failed, he drowned his fear of failure in Schnapps, then defended himself by attacking the kids and me with screamed obscenities and accusations. If we'd just known the demons he fought, perhaps we could have found the specialist who prescribed anti-anxiety medication after our divorce. But we were too busy just trying to survive and rural communities are not hotbeds of good mental health care.

I've begun to realize that summoning my father's ghost might have been my way of comforting myself amid a chaos of emotions that had left me an emotional zombie.

Since then, I've summoned them all, generation on generation of my family, looking for their secrets of emotional safety.

After that day my ghost kind of disappeared. Maybe it was my dad and maybe, once I could remember him, I didn't need a ghost. Anyway, the lights seemed to stay off when I turned them off and the thumpings and creakings seemed more random again.

David eventually confessed to writing his graduation date, 1995, on the bedroom wall. The ink streak did not cover as long as I lived there. I never really tried to paint over it.

Ironically, the only thing I could do for my husband, during those awful months when he was completely out of control, was to leave him and mean it. And I meant it. I'd contained my fury night after night while he stormed and stomped. I had nothing left to give him. I was only beginning to realize that stifling my rage had made it impossible to feel anything. It seemed a final dose of anesthetic.

I guess there's a bit of Scarlett O'Hara in me, waiting until tomorrow to think about the worst losses. Maybe that's the best we can do; stagger forward until we can stand up and run. I don't know if that's depression. There are certainly days, even yet, when I feel deadened and it's often hard to remember the things I used to enjoy. I don't sing when I'm going about my chores like I used to. I even remember singing when I picked up bales during those first days after we moved back to the farm. Now, I have to consciously decide to sing and think of a song before I open my mouth.

Sometimes, I run on the treadmill, but that's not really running, is it? It's exercise. I'll know I'm running when can laugh like my grandfather, rolling on the ground with tears running down my cheeks.

"I don't believe an accident of birth makes people sisters or brothers. It makes them siblings, gives them mutuality of parentage. Sisterhood and brotherhood is a condition people have to work at."-- Maya Angelou

Two Sisters And A Half

Grasshoppers still love green beans and drought and my missing sister is still missing, or more accurately, missing again.

I was wrestling the grasshoppers for my garden when my half-sister, Linda, found us. We spent a day together and we blew the opportunity to be real sisters. Maybe I blew it alone. Maybe it was just the drought.

That summer of 1988, I lived on the place I later inherited from my grandmother. Every day before the sun climbed over the peak of the roof, I rolled the bushes over, gently twisting their flexible stalks, to find the ripe beans. I harvested whatever else the garden had produced— sometimes a baseball-bat zucchini I hadn't seen when it was small. Then I pulled whatever weeds I'd spotted and turned the sprinkler on the still-shaded garden to drive the grasshoppers out before the sun climbed too high. If most of the droplets didn't dry by 10:30 or 11 o'clock, they would burn the leaves to cinders.

Cracks had opened in the yard and even the warm-season grasses crunched underfoot. For two months straight, temperatures topped 100°. The only rain we got fell the first week in July, four inches in a half-hour, a gully-washer that poured down the hills into the ponds, then through the breaks in the dams and on downstream, ripping off topsoil and tearing crevices down to hard, yellow clay, reminding me of a summer, years before, when I'd played in muddy water under a washed-out bridge. Back then, I'd puddled my feet in gelatinous topsoil as it passed on south, cutting through our pasture, washing out the fence and roiling through the neighbor's pasture and over the road a mile away. Meanwhile the corn's brown-edged leaves curled and drooped.

That spring, my marriage had blown up, leaving me with a herd of longhorn cattle my husband had been managing for a local doctor. I'd given them protein cake to supplement the drying grass, but finally in early July, Doc Adam and I agreed that his cows had to return to the Sandhills where at least a little rain had kept the grass from drying up entirely. With the cattle gone, I was doing some marketing and PR work for a company out of North Platte. I'd been on the phone to farmers and ranchers, coast to coast, selling ad space in the National Western Stock Show program trying to win my life back after my second divorcee. Every day, I had commiserated and joked with stock growers about the drought. I'd talked with farmers in Illinois and Ohio who complained that they hadn't had rain in two weeks or more. I smiled to myself, knowing that was a long time without rain in their neck of the woods. One of them told me his sons had been fishing in the creek and the catfish they brought home had ticks on them. In South Dakota, I heard that the trees in town were fighting over dogs for a drink.

Nobody joked about the farm crisis that came before the drought, though. That crisis had emptied still more

266

rural homes and resulted in suicides and stand-offs between law enforcement people and bankers on one side and beleaguered farmers and ranchers trying to hang on to land that had been in their families for generations. Like the rain ripping through topsoil, this agricultural "adjustment" had torn the fabric of rural communities that were already in danger of blowing away.

That crisis had wiped me and my estranged husband off the financial map. We'd gone through bankruptcy proceedings and lost everything we had—except the land, which we'd leased, not bought, from my grandmother. It had undoubtedly contributed to the return of my husband's alcoholism—something he thought he'd put behind him years before. We hung on for a while, Yogi got a job at a feedlot and I was waiting tables in town, but it all blew up one night and I found myself in an emotional desert as sharp as the serrated leaves of yucca, plants my father used to call Spanish bayonet.

Three months later, the grasshoppers were still sneaking into the garden, but they were feasting in the fencerows. One morning, as I rounded the corner of the house, I heard the phone ringing and scurried in with a shirttail load of green beans. My little sister, Jo Ann, didn't even bother with a greeting.

"Faye, I've seen Linda," she said.

Linda, I thought. Jo Ann seemed to think I'd know Linda. Then I did.

"You mean Linda?" I said.

"Yes, Linda."

The half-sister I'd never seen. That summer I was 41, she was 38 and Jo Ann 36. We'd never laid eyes on each other, never spoken on the phone, never exchanged a letter. That drought had been prolonged for decades.

"Faye, I knew her. We pulled up at Grandma's and I saw the license plates and wondered who Grandma knows from Tennessee. Then she got out of the car and I knew her. We just ran up and hugged each other."

My sister doesn't hug much more than I do. It was hard for me to imagine.

"What's she like?"

"She's so . . . refined."

I could tell she meant this as a compliment. Normally, from Jo Ann, "refined" meant stuck up. That day, though, it meant everything she could have expected from our father's other daughter.

Almost thirty years after I learned I had a half-sister, I was about to meet her for the first time. I tried to remember something I knew about her, something from a picture. After the photos, no one had mentioned Linda. I didn't know Mom had told Jo Ann, so I kept my promise not to tell. Apparently, Jo Ann didn't know I knew, either, so we didn't talk about it.

Mom always said she remembered her bus trips back and forth between her parents and how painful the passing back and forth had been for her. She had thought neither one of them wanted her, so each kept sending her to the other.[cclxxxv] Margo had remarried soon after she left dad for good, so Linda had a dad and Mom seemed to think that one dad was all a child could bear. She thought denying Linda her blood father was a kindness. There would be no bus trips from one parent to the other, never knowing if

268

the parent at the end of the trip wanted her or the other parent only wanted to get rid of her.

I think Mom had felt shamed by her parents' divorce. She wouldn't talk about her feelings, but I believe the other kids at school and in her neighborhood must have shunned her and shamed her. Divorce was rare and unacceptable then. She thought my sisters and I would share the grief and humiliation she'd felt if anybody, including us, knew about her divorce, so she tried to keep it secret. My parents even went to somewhere in Kansas to remarry, where the community wouldn't find out, and they waited till the anniversary of their first marriage so their wedding date would be consistent, May 23.[cclxxxvi] I don't know if or how they'd kept their divorce out of the papers.

All of Mom's secrecy to protect the kids always seemed thin to me—more an excuse than a reason—a way to hide her jealousy and fear of Margo and even Linda. Yet, year by year, as Mom has talked to me about my kids, advised me about how to deal with their fathers and their relationships with their fathers, I'm coming to believe that she sincerely thought that secrecy would cause the least pain for us all—including Linda. The secret sabotages my effort to trust my mother. This was her secret. She's been very clear that Linda's exclusion from our family was her ultimatum, not a joint decision. She used the leverage of my father's love to cut him—and her daughters—from our own flesh.

But thirty-eight years after I learned about my sister, when Linda arrived, Daddy was dead. Grandma had moved into town and Mom lived in Republican City with my step-father, "Speck" Copley. I lived in Grandma's and Grandpa's house on top of the hill and Jo Ann lived with her family at the bottom. She'd taken over the cottage Grandma and Grandpa had moved there in 1945 for Daddy

269

and his new bride, my mother. Margo had lived there briefly, too.

In 1988, my father's other daughter was all grown up with a son of her own. She'd come to visit Grandma and Aunt Nina—her grandmother and aunt as well as ours. I don't know if she even intended to see Jo Ann and me.

We'd never tried to find her, maybe she didn't want to find us. By the time I finished high school, it seemed impossible since no one had heard from or about Linda or Margo for years. There was no Internet search function. I hadn't a clue about where I could start looking and no one would tell me. I didn't know then that Nina had a private detective's license. Maybe I could have persuaded her to help me if I'd done what I never did. Throw a fit. Maybe someone would have told me if I'd . . . what? Fasted . . . refused to do chores. Civil disobedience was just a word then. I didn't do anything and nobody helped. I didn't find Linda and more years passed until Jo Ann stumbled into her visit with Grandma.

"Where is she?" I asked, still trying to remember anything I might have ever known about Linda.

"They're staying at the motel."

"They?"

"Margo's with her."

I hadn't seen Margo since I was three, before Linda was born, and I didn't remember her—except a picture I'd seen in Nina's photo album.

I was so thrilled Linda had come, I forgot to be ashamed that she had to come find us. Later I did feel shame that she had to come—uneasy, uncertain of her welcome, worried we would think she wanted something from us. All she wanted was acknowledgement and that word would poison the very beginnings, and apparently the ending, of our relationship.

I called the motel, but Margo and Linda had gone out to eat. I called the Blue Hill Cafe and asked for Linda Murphy. Margo came to the phone and I arranged to meet them at the motel a bit later. Linda and I greeted each other more gravely than she and Jo Ann had, maybe because we had some warning and made some preparation; maybe because I am more reserved than Jo Ann. When I try to remember that meeting now, I can't latch onto many images. I'd counted on Grandma to help me unravel the skein of events surrounding Linda and Margo and my parents' divorce and remarriage, but she could go only so far. Then she'd say, "I don't know. I can't remember." She makes a pushing gesture with her hands. "Maybe I don't want to remember. It was so . . . It hurt to see them."[cclxxxvii]

Now I can't remember either, even what happened in '88. It all happened so fast and unexpectedly that I remember only scattered bits and pieces. Their visit was a lot like the gully washer in July—an emotional abundance that cut deep into a desert of relationships lost.

I know Margo and Linda had been to see Nina at the nursing home. I'm not sure Linda had been prepared for the transformation she saw there. For fifteen years, I'd watched Nina's body twist and slump. Linda had had only her one childhood meeting with a tall, elegant woman who smelled of White Shoulders cologne and who took pictures and insisted on being photographed. At seventy, Nina had become nearly helpless, but I could still remember when she'd danced. I told Linda about the dancing "lessons" with the Arthur Murray book and our dancing alone together on tiptoe. I told her about the dress-up sessions and the pictures—and I told her about Nina's cats. It seemed like,

271

just as a litter of kittens grew up to be cats, some mama cat would bring in a new bunch—every summer, all summer long. Grandma and Grandpa had a "kitty coop," an old chicken house, for the cats. They kept cobs for the cook stove in there, too. Sometimes the mothers hid their litters so well that they got wild before we found them. The wild kittens would scratch and bite and snarl and spit, but we loved them tame, or at least until they resigned themselves to our attentions.

I told about crying, dragging a bloody little wisp of a thing into the house and about Nina taking it away from me and rushing it back to its mother while Grandma explained about birth. I told her about Nina's rowboat. Grandpa had built her a dock at the edge of the stock pond in the heifer pasture. Nina would row the boat around and I would trail my hands in the water. When Jo Ann came along, she always wanted to row.

The day after our first, evening meeting, while Jo Ann was at work, I took Linda and Margo on a tour of the farm. I tried to remember every detail about growing up as Cecil Colburn's daughter—so Linda would know at least something about her father. I told her about how quiet he was and how he seemed always preoccupied, about how hard he'd worked, particularly after our Grandpa died and he had to support the five of us—Mom, Jo Ann and me, as well as Grandma and Nina. I told her about the times it rained him out of the field, so we climbed in the car and went fishing at Harlan Reservoir. I told her about dad drinking beer and standing on the lake shore singing O Sola Mio—just that one phrase, off key. I told her he couldn't carry a tune in a bucket.

Linda told about her childhood and her determination to get an education, even though her family thought college was a waste of time, especially for girls. I found myself

272

thinking that Linda was everything I would have expected my father's other daughter to be.

We spent most of the day together: Margo and Linda and my then four-year-old son, Ben, and me. I showed Linda her father's old bedroom up under the eaves of the house where I lived then and the place on the floor in the cottage at the bottom of the hill where he died. We visited the pastures and the shelterbelts and the trees he'd planted . . . the dams he and Grandpa had built. I told her about my father's wish to turn it all back to trees and grass.

As we drove around the pastures, Linda cringed when fat grasshoppers leaped through the windows, landing in her lap or smacking against her shoulder. She brought up the doors that didn't have locks. She worried that I would be robbed or raped or murdered living alone on that farm with no lock on the door. Maybe she'd read Truman Capote's novel, In Cold Blood. But the Clutter murders were decades past. What made the story so sensational was its absolute rarity.

Originally, the doors all had locks, I said, but to my knowledge, they'd never been locked. I'd asked Grandma once about the keys and she had no idea what had happened to them. The young man who rents the house now doesn't lock the doors either.

As we toured the place, I noticed sagging barbed wire and broken posts. In the barn, I saw empty holes where Dutch doors had been torn off their hinges, from being left open when the winds whipped over the hill. None of my town-grown family had really understood about doors and prairie winds, so they often forgot to hook them. Even the metal storm door on the house had lost a panel. Boards broken from the barn and granary had remained

273

unreplaced for years, and the white paint had weathered and peeled gray.

I found myself feeling inadequate because I hadn't managed to keep all of it from becoming shabby. I felt as though I'd been caretaker of something that belonged to Linda, too, and I hadn't done a very good job. The dams had washed out years before and I had no money to repair them. When my second husband and I had moved onto the home place, we'd expected to repair or replace the old dams, but we'd lost our shirts and he'd lost his sobriety. The ponds had become stagnant and they were drying up.

We'd managed to replace some fencing before we went belly-up, but most of the old fences hadn't seen posts and new wire for at least 25 years. That summer I took out the last of the hedge posts my grandfather had set in 1926. Linda never commented on the disarray, and when I pointed out the losses, Margo assured me I'd get it back up to snuff. I don't think she really understood how completely broke I was or the enormous cost of deferred maintenance. I don't know if Linda did. As I look back at that meeting, I realize I didn't ask about a lot of things. We'd never been together before and hadn't made a habit of talking about things that matter. We had a desert of years between us that we couldn't bridge in one day. Like my mother and father, we had a great canyon of different lives lived that didn't give us any frame of reference for understanding each other.

Later, I tried to write about Linda and the excitement I felt at meeting her, the admiration I felt for the way she'd invented herself under circumstances that were less encouraging than mine. I used the word unacknowledged, not because my family did not acknowledge her but because it was the word she used when she described how she felt. She has not spoken to me since she read that word. I don't think she read beyond it; the hurt is just too

274

deep. If she had, though, I think she'd understand how sorry and disappointed I was and am that we didn't grow up together and how badly I feel that we're not close.

"I always thought I'd see my dad some time,"[cclxxxviii] Linda told me the day we met and I wanted to cry for her.

Margo wrote to Nina for a long time after the divorce, sending the pictures of Linda that finally gave up the secret. Nina took the letters and pictures out to the fields to show her brother. But then the letters stopped coming and my family lost its daughter before we'd ever known her.

Linda said when her son, Sean, was born, she decided it couldn't possibly hurt Jo Ann and me to know about her. We'd all grown up. So she called to present her son to his grandfather. Daddy had been dead for ten years.

"You know, it really hurt when I found out he hadn't even mentioned me in his will," Linda said. "I didn't want anything, just some little trinket to acknowledge my existence."[cclxxxix]

I wish I could help her understand that Dad didn't expect to die. He was only forty-six. He didn't have a will and that, even if Dad died too suddenly and too soon to provide acknowledgment on paper, he certainly acknowledged Linda as his own and lived his life with the empty awareness of a child he could never hold or protect. I think he tried to spare her the pain he actually caused her—by denying himself.

For years I've asked questions and demanded answers from my family. I think I've gotten all the answers I'm going to get. The one person who could answer me—and my sisters—died in 1963.

It was after Linda's and Margo's visit that Margo sent the letters, and I thought I'd read and absorbed them all. As I've written and thought about my family, though, I've searched them more thoroughly and I found one more. Dad's last letter to Margo asking for a divorce. It was undated, but he mentioned an Easter card from Margo that had created an uproar and he mentioned his unborn daughter, so it must have been between Easter and May 4, 1950.

"This is absolutely the hardest letter I have ever written in my life," he began.

He asked Margo to file for divorce "as soon as possible," and explained that he was sure he wanted to be with Mom.

". . . she is afraid of the feeling I have for you," he wrote. "She knows you are a grand girl and for that very reason, lassie, I will have to break completely and cleanly or I will have a nervous wreck on my hands . . ."ccxc

And so he did break "completely and cleanly." Nina was the subversive who kept him in touch.

I think if my father could talk to us now, he would tell us that his agreement to never see his daughter cost him a price he paid for the rest of his life. I think he'd tell us that you can't have one without the other; that when you hold one emotion carefully in check, you can't fully feel any of them. Without seeing Linda's devastation, maybe he could never know that his self-denial didn't hurt him alone. When my father denied himself his own flesh, he condemned himself to the loss of his child, his daughter to the loss of her father, and all of us to growing up without our sisters.

I think it's all connected. I think the silence I described to Linda had to do with pain Dad denied—self denial turned to something that sometimes felt to me like indifference. Like grasshoppers that gobble green beans, our loss of Linda helped to eat up the warmth I craved in my family.

"Health . . . is at once wholeness and a kind of unconsciousness. Disease, on the contrary, makes us conscious not only of the state of our health but of the division of our bodies and our world into parts."--Wendell Berry

Incomprehensible Accidents

On August 11, 1993, my nephew, David Klein, slipped out of the house with two guns—a .22 pistol and a .22 rifle. In the sweltering cool of early evening, he shoved his way through seven-foot canes of sunflowers and ragweed. When he reached the grassy banks of the dugout pond, he laid the rifle on the ground and started looking around for bullfrogs to shoot.

He knew a bullet ricocheting off water could be trouble. He knew he shouldn't load the gun before he was ready to hunt, or release the safety before he was ready to shoot. But the pistol lay, ready to fire, restlessly cradled on his hip, in a holster designed for another gun. As he pulled the pistol from its sheath, it discharged, sending a .22 slug into his left calf.

I can almost see my nephew standing there, golden rays of the slanting sun shining on his yellow hair, maybe poking his finger through the hole in his jeans. I can almost hear him thinking, "Oh, shit! I've done it again." Thinking he'd better get to the house so his mom and dad could get him to a doctor. He didn't think it was bad. He was standing on it, walking on it. He could hardly see any blood.

But in its swift, silent passage through the back of his knee, the bullet threaded its way through a rich network of veins and arteries and nerves. As he limped that half-mile or so from the pond, David began to realize this accident wasn't like all the others. His other daredevil stunts had skinned the hide off his knees and elbows. He'd come perilously close to shredding his kneecap when he'd allowed his friend to tow him behind a car—on his bike.

This time, somehow, he felt weak. Sometimes he felt dizzy and he'd have to sink down among the sunflowers and rest for a while. Then he'd walk some more. He knew he needed to make it to the house before his parents left for work. They'd never look for him because he seldom, if ever, left a note when he went out with his friends while they were asleep.

When he finally made it to the house, he woke his parents, Jo Ann and Ken Klein, who were sleeping off the heat before a night shift making plastic PVC pipe. He limped to the pickup. It was the last time he walked on both legs.

My sister doesn't cry often, but I'll never forget her strangled voice when I answered the phone at about ten that Wednesday night.

"David shot himself," she announced.

I gasped as I heard Ken yank the phone away from her.

"He's all right," Ken began. "He had an accident. Shot himself in the leg with the .22."

I heard .22 and began breathing again.

280

"How bad?"

"I don't know. He's in surgery. He walked to the house from the pond and he walked to the pickup."

I woke my son, Jason, and explained why I'd have to take him to work that night. I thought briefly of my sister and brother-in-law, sitting in the hospital waiting room. I pictured and dismissed as completely unlike, the hot afternoon when Dan Erven caught his arm in a corn picker. His family may have stood around shuffling their feet while the doctor examined him—maybe on the kitchen table where they'd carried him after the accident. I wondered if it's harder when you can't see what's happening.

Getting organized in this emergency felt like going through the same motions only nine months before. Jason had heard the phone that time and was standing in my bedroom doorway when I answered.

"Faye," Ken had. "Jo Ann caught her hair in a spindle."

My son watched my face contort with the death sentence I knew I'd heard as I gasped.

"No," Ken said. "She's all right. She scalped herself."

On November 17, 1992, just after midnight, my sister and her husband, Ken, had been at work only a few minutes when Jo Ann caught her hair in the spindle of a pipe puller.

I heard this sound, Ken said later. "It didn't sound like anything I'd ever heard before. Then I heard it again and I

281

knew it was human and someone was in trouble. I didn't know then that it was my wife."ccxci

Jo Ann's headband had slipped and long, silky, black hair tumbled into the machine's spindle. When the machine yanked, she yelled and yanked back, tearing off half her scalp and the left side of her forehead. The instant she could reach the button, she slapped the machine off and ran to her locker for a flannel shirt to pressure-pack her head.ccxcii

She shouted at her husband, by then running to help her, "Back my hair out of the machine." He didn't understand; the shirt around her head hid her torn and bleeding skull. He had no idea what had happened to her. He said it looked like she'd cut herself on the forehead. Once he understood, though, he backed up the "puller." With bloody scalp in hand, Jo Ann gave Ken directions to the hospital and walked herself into the emergency room.ccxciii

"I hadn't even got my door open and the hospital door was slamming shut behind her," Ken said. "She just grabbed her scalp and ran."ccxciv

The doctor packed her scalp in dry ice and sent Jo Ann off by Medivac to the University of Nebraska Medical Center in Omaha. Ken took her to the airport and saw her off. Then he drove himself to Blue Hill. At five a.m. on her 96th birthday, Grandma Hazel awoke to Ken stumbling around trying to get to the phone. He filled her in, called me and left for home.ccxcv

By six o'clock, he had David aroused, I had delegated Jason to getting Ben off to school, and we were driving toward Omaha. We stopped in Lincoln at about 8:15 and waited for David's sister, Jenifer, to get back from an early class. Then we went on to Omaha and waited. In Omaha, three surgeons spent eight hours trying to find a viable artery so they could get blood to Jo's scalp. By the time she came out of surgery, we all, Ken, her daughter, Jenifer, her son, David and I, stood in the hall by a tiny waiting area. A nurse wheeled up with a gurney. I barely recognized the mound of pasty flesh on the cart. Swollen and puffy from bruising and IV fluids, my sister appeared shapeless and gray. Her head looked much like a basketball with seams everywhere.

While David examined her stapled scalp, Jenifer disappeared. I followed her into the restroom.

"You all right?"

"I just didn't want her to know she looked so bad I had to cry about it."

Days later, Thanksgiving Day, with more than 150 miles of sheet ice between Blue Hill and Omaha, Jo Ann, alone with morphine demons, replayed the accident over and over and over. She says part of her seemed to feel that by rerunning the movie she could rewrite the outcome through sheer force of will.ccxcvi Perhaps David, too, on that last night before his amputation, replayed his frog hunt in his dreams—or maybe in a waking nightmare.

That last night, I remained at home with Ben and again my mind filled with details, the getting organized, the figuring out what needed to get done and doing it.

I called who needed calling, and I held off the possible consequences to the people I love in some corner of my mind, some place just off center across a thin membrane where it couldn't seep into the thinking and the doing. Sometimes I felt the membrane bulge as though it might burst, pouring fear and hysteria into the order I fought to maintain.

Looking back, I wonder now if that was Grandma Sicily's weapon against the "Beast," the child to big to bear, the fevers that might take a woman in the prime of her life. Was it an orderly progression of tasks tended, lists ticked off in her head that allowed her to bear the pressure of tending women in childbirth and her neighbors in sickness and death?

I remember times when the membrane bulged, like the Friday night I visited David in the hospital. As he described the accident, I pictured the terrain he'd had to cross to get home. I'd been out there earlier in the month, looking for a missing calf. I'd sputtered and choked on pollen and had become weak from the intense heat. In August, sunflowers and ragweed dry out and rattle together like half-inch dowels stood on end. Unless he'd cut a path before, his trail must have been almost impenetrable. Even in the cool of evening, he must have nearly stifled.

I remember the ragged smell in David's room that I would just sense and then lose track of. I remember his mottled purple flesh and how Grandma Hazel said, over and over, how she didn't like the look of that leg. Yet I thought it must be all right because the doctor wasn't alarmed.

What I didn't know then was that Jenifer had been in the room when David's surgeon did rounds the next morning. As he started to leave, the nurse accompanying him asked, "Shouldn't we be concerned that we can't get a pulse in this boy's foot?"

"You can be concerned if you want to," the doctor responded as he kept walking. ccxcvii

Next morning, the doctor cut away a large part of David's rotting calf muscle. After that surgery, my alarmed sister and brother-in-law moved David to Lincoln where a new physician whisked him into another surgery. ccxcviii

My sister called me that Saturday night. A major artery had continued to bleed after the two earlier surgeries, the surgeon at Bryan East had said. The leg could have been saved if David had been brought to Lincoln the morning after his accident, he said, but by then, it was too late. He would amputate in the morning.^{ccxcix}

The membrane burst as I sat and absorbed this, with my sister on the other end of the 'phone line, crying. We talked for a little bit— but we had nothing to say. She asked me to make the calls again. Once off the phone, I tried to imagine some miracle that would save David's leg. I couldn't. I sat looking out my window over the black prairie and its expanse of stars. I knew Venus hung, spinning and flying, on my right hidden by the other wing of the house. The big and little dippers were behind me.

For a few moments my mind melted into those pinpricks of light. I remembered other lights from months before, the glints of blue in my sister's fine, silky hair, shining against the black when I combed blood and bits of flesh from it. I cried as I rinsed the long, soft strands in my sink and watched the water turn bright. Time after time I washed the hair Jo Ann's doctor had trimmed from her scalp before he tried an unsuccessful graft. I'd hoped to have a wig made for her, but I never found a wig maker. The nearest one was in Hong Kong and "Locks of Love" hadn't been organized yet. For years, her hair remained coiled in plastic bags in a drawer.

From the blue lights in Jo Ann's hair, I focused on hot, golden lights. I remembered David playing varsity basketball as a sophomore. I remembered watching him move over the honeyed oak of the Blue Hill gym floor, doing lay-ups, jumping for tip-offs. The broken membrane flooded my head with images, little bees that buzzed wildly, careening off the structures in my head, stinging whenever they made contact. All the radiant images became weapons. I saw David's fluid movement, so like my father's that Grandma sometimes called him "Cecil." I tried to picture Cecil, my father, the skinny, black-haired kid who played on a state championship basketball team. I'd known for a long time they were the same—one blond, one dark. The smile lines looked the same. The bashful duck of the head was the same. They'd moved the same, but not after Sunday, and maybe not for a long time—maybe not ever.

I pulled myself together and made the necessary calls, remembering when I had called Mom about Jo Ann's accident.

"So that's what's the matter with me," Mom had said, as though I would understand how she could be disturbed by something she didn't even know of yet. "I've been wandering around all day, jumping from one thing to another, nervous as a jumping bean,"ccc she said. I remembered that Grandma May called after Dad died and she hadn't wasted any words. "Ella Mae, what's wrong?" she'd asked. We all thought of that call when we talked about my call to Mom.

As I sat in my living room thinking about those connections, I thought of generations who have sat up through black nights, sharing a grievous loss or a crisis. In Sicily's time, we mostly sat together—by candlelight, or by kerosene lantern. We laid hands on each other. We supported each other with our backs; lifted and turned each other; did for each other the things that nurses, mostly strangers, now do. I thought about the cold green of fluorescent lights in an operating theater where my nephew had lain, unconscious and helpless, surrounded by gleaming machines and strangers, including a surgeon who performed cardio-vascular surgery he wasn't qualified to perform, then failed to get David to qualified help when he discovered his surgery hadn't worked.

Did it matter that he was a stranger?

I wondered if the power of our joined consciousness becomes diffused by separation. Only Jo Ann and Ken were with David when he had his first surgery and they were excluded from the room, helpless. I wondered if we can focus our spiritual power when we're worlds apart and we can't touch each other. I wondered how much of that power we lose when we cannot or do not "do" for each other in crisis. I wondered if we know how, if we've lost the art of healing and of grieving together.

I thought, again, about Dan Erven, whose arm lay buried under a little chunk of rock near the south fence of Eckley Cemetery. Did he ever become whole again? How did his family help him find the lost part of himself? Did the simple act of wrapping the torn and shattered flesh and bone—in muslin, perhaps—help him rebuild himself? I thought, again, about Erven's family and wonder who dug the hole and who gently laid the arm into it and covered it over and who laid the stone in place. I thought Erven must have got about his business of farming very clumsily at first.

I wondered how David would get on with his life. I don't know if it made any difference that the doctors whisked his leg away to be disposed of so that he had nothing to bury, no physical things to grieve over. I do know his mother had provided him with a wonderful example of courage and grace in the face of terrible loss. After her accident, back at home with instructions to let her husband change her dressings, she insisted on seeing the damage—and it was considerable. Then she went back to work—two weeks after her accident. One of her friends asked her how she could come back. Wasn't she afraid of that machine?

"No," she said, "it's just a machine."

I asked if it wasn't a little soon.

"What should I do," she asked, "sit around and make myself miserable?"[ccci]

In David's time, it took just a few days to learn how his natural grace and balance would stand him well. He often set his crutches aside and hopped from place to place. I marveled at his casual ability to stop and stand, balanced, for what seemed impossible periods of time. I laughed with him as his mother recounted the time he hopped furiously across the living room and only stopped in time to keep from driving his nose through the glass of the gun cabinet. He'd started to tip slightly forward and "stepped ahead" to catch himself on the left leg that wasn't there. That he found his mistake funny gives a new dimension to the concept of black humor.

I still wonder what kind of humor David and Ben shared the day after David's surgery. Ben was not quite nine when David lost his leg. He'd idolized his cousin and taken his share of teasing from him. When we arrived at the hospital in Lincoln, he did not want to go into that room.

"Ben," I said. "If you had lost your leg, how would you feel if nobody wanted to see you without a leg?"

"Not very good," he said, hanging his head.

"David's the same David, he just doesn't have part of his leg."

I may never be more proud of Ben than when he walked into that room. And, if not, that will be just fine. He doesn't know too much about the art of grieving, but he does know about how to support a cousin.

I stepped in behind him, so I didn't see what he did, but when David saw him, he chuckled and grinned at him. Neither remembers what elicited the chuckle—or maybe they're just not telling.

I can't help wondering if Ben's visit made any difference to David. That chuckle might have been his first, post-amputation.

Time after time after time, I'm drawn back to the role of will on our lives, the role of our own and that of people who will us well—or ill. And I'm forced to consider the meaning to us as families of the fractures in our families—the distances in place and time.

Close by, David did have his mom and dad and sister, a grandma and a great, his cousins, Ben and Jason and me. Maybe more importantly David had his friends, friends who came to see him, who treated him as they'd always treated him, who took him with them when they went places.

We all treated his loss very matter-of-factly, and so did David. He never hid his stump. If anything, he went out of his way to expose it. I never asked, but I suspect he figured people could get the gawking out of the way and get back to seeing him instead of his wounded leg if he made it easy. And he made it easy for all of us.

We all asked him honest questions and he always answered openly. I don't know if he did it purposefully, or accidentally, but when you answer questions openly and fully, there isn't too much to say about an amputation. You can dispose of the subject rather quickly and get on to more important matters—like what there is to do on a Saturday night that's more fun than sitting around looking at your friend's stump.

And they did. They continued to scare the hell out of us with their foolishness. As David healed, waiting for his prosthesis, they discovered potato bombs. I think, perhaps, Jason worried more about David than any of us—maybe because he saw more of what his cousin did than the rest of us. He worked then with Jo Ann and Ken and he grumbled almost continuously about whether David would be better off with only one arm as well as one leg.

No one, not even Jason, seemed able to keep up with David. It seemed that he had to prove to everyone, mostly himself, that he was the same daredevil kid the town cop had dragged off the roof of the hardware store, with his friends, on the Fourth of July several years before.

I wonder if all Jason's grumbling kept David safe during that vulnerable time when he had to "prove up," or if Grandma and Jason, worrying together, had any effect. Did David's friends go along with him and protect him in ways we never knew about? Or did David just get lucky?

In the aftermath, Grandma said of David, "He's like your dad. Cecil never was a whiner."[cccii]

Grandma's right. David did not whine. Instead, he joked—flippant about his loss. For example, he had chores he liked to ignore. My sis told him one afternoon that, if he didn't get them done on schedule, she'd chain him by the leg so he couldn't leave until they were done.

He grinned. "That depends on which leg you chain!"

Like I said, "black humor."

From as early as I can remember, David had planned to become a marine biologist. But he hasn't made any attempt to follow that career since his accident. Instead, he chooses family—staying close to home. He has two little daughters now and what I see is a good father. I think he has accepted his accident better than I have. Not long ago he told me it might have been a good thing. He said he'd been heading in a bad direction and the accident made him stop to recalibrate.

But when we accept these losses, what then? Our lives don't necessarily go on as before. David's obviously hasn't. His stump is too short to make a good connection with his prosthesis, so he has to slow down so it can catch up. He's gone from a sophomore in high school playing basketball and being scouted by a Big Twelve college team to a guy who doesn't run any more. But he's made that transition with all the grace and courage his mother exemplified for him. I'm proud to be related, not only to young Joseph Swope and Hokolesqua, but to my sister and her son.

Their grace and courage has appeared over and over again during the centuries of my family's history. During our last interviews, Grandma and I may have found one source for some of that strength.

I feel that clash between the expansiveness, the limitless possibility of the American present and future and that deep sense of honoring the past and how important it is not to feel oneself adrift in history. -- Yossi Klein Halevi[ccciii]

Threshold

I can never hear a mourning dove's call without thinking of angels and Grandma Hazel. That's because she thought the doves were, literally, angels. When she and her brother, Earl, were toddlers, Great-grandma Frank and Great-grandpa Will would set the two children on a quilt on the back stoop and tell them to stay. I imagine it was Will who told them not to be afraid.

"Do you hear that sound?" he'd ask. "Those are your guardian angels and they'll be watching over you while we do the chores. Even when you can't see us, they'll be there looking out for you."

Grandma told me she was almost grown before she realized her angels were drab little gray birds who sing beautiful, peaceful songs.[ccciv]

Angels. The angels of my better nature exist only in community, a particular community of people with whom I've served in a food pantry and a soup kitchen, with whom

293

I've welcomed young people and made covenant with them that I would watch them grow and watch out for them. We sang songs together and worked together in order to assure that the most vulnerable among us got the care they needed. We sat with members of other communities, like survivors of the atom bombing of Hiroshima and Nagasaki and refugees from all over the world, to learn about their lives.

The most memorable of those times is the weekend we demanded a citizens' inspection of the brains of America's nuclear arsenal at Offutt Air Base near Omaha. The evening before, we rallied downtown with survivors of the atomic bombings of Hiroshima and Nagasaki. As one of the survivors spoke through his interpreter, I held a poster that depicted a child, lying tangled in his bicycle, his skin a mass of peeling burn blisters. At the end of his speech, the man came to me and pointed to the poster, then to himself several times. He signed that he wanted to take the poster and I released it. Then he took it around the crowd, pointing at himself and at the poster.

Stunned, I thought he was telling us that I'd been holding a picture of him. When I asked his interpreter for confirmation, though, she said the poster was not him, but that's what he'd looked like. I've experienced second degree burns and I can think of nothing more excruciating. I had only two small burns, I can barely imagine his pain and how he survived it. Meeting him under those circumstances took my breath away and still does.

Those days in my dad's old bedroom set me up for the months after 9/11 when I stood at the Kinney Gates with those strong, courageous men from Hiroshima and Nagasaki. I thought of him when I petitioned against the Patriot Act. Every time I carried a clipboard into the streets, I did so with a strong conviction that Dad would be right there with me if he'd lived long enough.

There is an antidote to invasions like the Patriot Act and our country's ceaseless wars in my family's stories, something kinder than the random acts of violence and senseless cruelty we're battered with daily. Those alternatives occur in others' stories as well.

Majda Obradovic taught me something about grace under pressure. She and her daughters, Lana and Leah, escaped Bosnia in the midst of genocide with what they could carry in a backpack. Majda refused to accept the protection of any of the Bosnian factions. She insisted she wasn't a Serb, or a Muslim, or a Croat. She was, and probably always will be, Yugoslavian.

Once she'd learned English, her fifth language, she translated in the hospitals and the courts for people who had not yet learned English, including some people who terrified her. Lana goes back to Bosnia every summer to gather children from all the ethnic groups and teaches them how to get along.

Majda's collection of brass shell casings reminds me of how people can draw beauty from the most horrible cruelty. Those bits of brass are engraved, the largest with a model of Sarajevo before the war, with its Mosque, its Synagogue and its Cathedral, and the people all walking together on the promenade.

Majda made me think of something else that we bring into our communities. When we think of the survivors of the Bosnian genocide, or the Nazi Holocaust, or Hiroshima and Nagasaki, we remember the people the way they were during and after those horrific catastrophes. It's almost like we kill them again when we can't imagine their grandfathers who picked them up and set them on their laps and sang to them. Perhaps if we can remember their lives as well as what happened to them at the end, we can give them back those lives in some way. And we can remember that horror and death aren't all there is in the world. Maybe we can even interrupt the horror and death.

295

I learned from my grandmother that, by expecting people to be good, you can help them to be better human beings than even they thought possible. I learned by experience that you can sometimes be deeply disappointed but that it's none-the-less worth the risk. I think open-handedness and open-heartedness like I witnessed in my grandparents and that I learned about in my search for the meaning of family and community is the glue that holds us together.

I don't suppose he thought about it, but if he had, Grandpa George would have agreed that committing random acts of kindness and senseless beauty is the only rational response to a world that allows the kind of brutality we see in the news. Grandma told me that, after he was gone, people would come to her and give her money that he'd loaned to them, or just given to them. She said she hadn't known anything about the money, but there it was, a gift from her husband when she needed it.

Grandma's and Grandpa's house was always filled with magazines. "Well," Grandma told me, "every time the kids came around with a magazine drive to buy band uniforms or a bake sale to send some kid to County Government Day, Grandpa would buy stuff so they could have what they needed."[cccv]

Because of them, I have an alternative reality to offer my sons. So I celebrate my grandfather, tears coursing down his cheeks, laughing helpless on the ground, and Grandma's vacation, hatless and sun-kissed, picking olives in the Sacramento Valley with her sisters.

When I was in grade school, my dad paid the neighbor kid to drive me to school and back. It was the bargain Dad made with Alvin Witte so that his son could finish high school. I wasn't too impressed at the time with hanging around an empty playground after school waiting for Lou to finish football practice, but I guess now that it wasn't a bad bargain. In that case, Dad actually set out to help a kid

296

who needed to finish school, but there are also ways we influence other lives, completely unawares, when we're just going about getting on.

My friend, Roger Shaffer, who'd had polio when he was six years old, spent a year in an iron lung and came out with a wasted right arm. He had a wicked wit and the most optimistic attitude I've ever encountered. The day he met my kids, he taught them that, when you meet someone who can't reach out and shake your hand, you reach out and shake his. Sean remembered when he applied for a job and interviewed with the company CEO, a quadriplegic. Gordon hired him when Sean reached down for his hand and shook it. He became one of my son's best friends. I doubt Roger would have ever predicted that outcome from his simple gesture.

I think of how all of us have scattered hither and yon now and the connections we miss. They're all dead now, but the years when my family members were sick and dying were a long cycle of stress and depression. I lived hours away from home because I couldn't make a living on the home place. Grandma was alone in her house in Blue Hill and Mom was alone in her house an hour away. I'd think of my step-dad, lying alone day after day in the Old Soldiers' and Sailors' Home and how, just a generation ago, the family would have closed around him and worked it out so that somebody would be there every day. If all of us were together, we might even manage to care for him at home. I punished myself sometimes for not being there for people who had carried me over the mud puddles. In fact, I allowed myself to fall into what I call a "purple funk." I couldn't shake this one by reading the bloodiest murder mystery I could find.

What it was, I realize now, was depression. My youngest son was just entering adolescence then and he got to witness all the crying. I didn't really weep, just doled out a few tears here and a few there when something touched me, usually some sappy TV program involving a sweet family relationship.

"But that's life," Grandma told me. "You can't help it. The families can't stay together. You see, that happens in families. I can say one thing. I've had a family. They've been around me pretty good."[cccvi]

I asked her if families have changed in her lifetime.

"It seems like it. It seems like families don't stick together anymore. Our bunch isn't no family together . . . It's not necessarily blood. Just like Clara Skrdlant. She says she's taken me over as her mother—as her second mother. She's been such a good friend."[cccvii]

"What does it mean to be a family?" I asked. "What was it that held your family together back when you had all that family?"

"I suppose it was love. We all loved each other, all of us. If somebody was sick, there was always somebody to go there and help take care of them. It was a duty, but we wanted to do it. We wanted to help each other."

Years ago, I heard a broadcast on National Public Radio about a group home for homeless men suffering from AIDS. I was so impressed by the way that home brings sickness and dying right back into a brown brick building they call Joseph's House, that's like one of Sicily's birthing rooms, I got a transcript of the program. Patricia O'Dell often sits with the men who are dying, like Sicily sat with her patients. "I always align my breathing with the breathing of the person who is dying," she said. "And it—as verbal communication becomes impossible, I try to establish a sense of communion and a sense of actually being together, so that fear of abandonment is reduced. And what I do is, I put my breathing as much in step with theirs as I can, and I sort of exhale audibly, so that it just sounds like `Ah' as they breathe. And then—then this person doesn't breathe anymore and I find myself still breathing, still saying, `Ah.' And they're gone . . . I've often thought, this must be what it's like to be a midwife."[cccviii]

At Joseph's house, Howard Janifer, a homeless AIDS victim himself, washes and dresses the men for burial. Before they die, they come to ask him if he will "fix" them. Asked why he does it, he said, "`Cause they are my brothers, my brothers in heart and my brothers in pain."[cccix]

When I heard that broadcast, I thought that the men at Joseph's House are dying much, much better than my dad, who had a house he'd have liked to call home, a wife, two step-daughters and five grandchildren and a monthly income. I've thought often about how my family could have made dying less lonely for Dad and never found an answer, scattered as we were.

Dying has become industrialized because we're so fragmented. Most of us send our dead to the funeral home to be prepared for burial, often right out of the hospital. But a friend of mine, with help from his neighbor, washed his wife's body and dressed her himself. A carpenter, he made her coffin, and took her to the crematorium in the back of his pickup.

"That's what Alice would have wanted," he said.

That joint experience between neighbors has altered forever the relationship between those two people, creating something more than the sum of the parts, more than Tom and Kathy and Alice. That something is a kind of presence, separate from any of the actors.

For generations we've defined a family as mom and pop and the kids, all looking out for each other. What we've been calling a family is a stripped down version of a much richer creation. It's like calling a field of bluestem a prairie. It couldn't function. It's the rich diversity of grasses and forbs that makes a prairie work, just as it's the rich diversity of parents and children, grandparents and cousins, aunts and uncles providing nourishment and support that makes a family work.

In my grandma's day, a family was rich like a prairie. Not only did the extended family live in close proximity, there were also "relatives" that were sort of adopted. Grandma always included Philip Hunt in her family, even though he wasn't blood kin. When I think of a family in that way, I can't ignore the realities of Joseph Swope's adopted family with its escaped slave woman and its captured white children. Hokolesqua's family welcomed all comers, fully accepting each for him or herself.

Not all families functioned as well as Grandma's, or even Hokolesqua's in the midst of war. My recent discovery of Great-grandma Ella May Shank-Ford revealed one more secret I hadn't suspected, but probably should have. My mother had always said that she never saw her grandparents, that she never knew her mother's mother. Only recently did I gather enough information to send for Grandma May's birth certificate and once I found that, I tracked down her parents. That's when I found a census record and Ella May Ford's death certificate. Mom's grandmother lived for more than thirty years in a mental institution, Mayview State Hospital, where she'd been diagnosed with paranoid schizophrenia.[cccx] I did the math and realized that she'd lived at home with her husband and children, though, until Mom's mother, my Grandma May, was sixteen. I cannot begin to imagine how terrifyingly chaotic that household must have been, especially for the children.

That's also when I found the girl in the madhouse. Grandma May's little sister, Mildred. She was committed to the Polk Home for the Feeble-Minded when she was eight years old.[cccxi] Mildred was two when her mother was committed and I wonder how much of her arrested development hinged upon her mother's illness. Those homes, in those days, offered little besides warehousing and her diagnosis in 1990 of severe mental retardation and bi-polar disorder might have been accurate at the time, but I can't help thinking I'd be crazy too and unable to communicate even the most rudimentary intelligence if I'd been locked away for seventy years.

When I told Jo Ann about Great-grandma Ella May's illness, she said that Mom had mentioned a visit to her grandmother at the hospital. Apparently, during the last years of her life, as Alzheimer's released some of her inhibitions and cleared her very long term memory, Mom was finally able to talk about something she would never have mentioned when she was lucid. I've known all my life that Mom was terrified of mental illness. I guess that's why I invented the secret girl when I had no reason to believe there was one.

Only now can I begin to understand Grandma May's inability to form a stable home. And when I think about how the devastation of my great-grandmother's mental illness has spilled down through generations, I marvel at how the loneliness and fear that took over her family have affected mine. The balance has come from the broader family and community that supported my mom and dad as they tried to work things out between them.

When Grandma and I tried to define that family and community, Grandma talked about loyalty.

"If one of us was in trouble," she said, "the other ones tried to help. Like George, your Grandpa. He helped his folks financially so much. He took care of John's family for years."[cccxii]

"And he still prospered, though."

"Yes. I think you get paid back for doing things like that, in a way.

"I sometimes study about things like that and . . . I'm sure I don't know either . . . I think one thing that holds the family together, you think of the future. You think maybe there'll be another generation. Another generation. See now, like with Heather, I've got a great-great-grandchild. And with Chuck. It's still a family. Here's a grandma and a mom and dad and kids and grandkids and great grandkids. [Even though Heather and Chuck are my step-children, Grandma claimed them, just like she claimed Philip Hunt].

" It was just like your Grandpa George with the land. He always said, `We never own the land. We're just give it to take care of for the next generation.'

"You know what Jason said to me a couple years ago?" she asked. "He said, `Grandma, I wish it was like it used to be so you could go out to the pasture and look around.' We used to go out and pick wildflowers and everything. He hadn't forgot it.

"That's part of a family. Teaching kids, not just the hard work but some of the pleasures of it. I think that's where everybody has lost out. They've lost their sense of pleasure with little things. With just little things. Heck. You never see kids get out here and snowball anymore."[cccxiii]

Grandma used to remind me of the time Sean, my oldest son, wheeled his bicycle to the top of the tall hill in front of the home place. He hesitated a moment then climbed on and rode down "lickety split." As she helped him untangle from the bicycle at the bottom of the hill, she asked, "Why did you do that?"

"Well, I said to myself, `Are you a man or are you a mouse,' he answered. `I guess I'm a mouse.'"^{cccxiv}

I remember standing in the yard of that same old place and teaching Ben to find the Big Dipper and the North Star. We'd stare at the horizon where the prairie shoulders into the star-splattered dark and listen to coyotes gathering up for their evening hunt.

It seems like the things that happen have a life of their own and the stories are almost conscious entities. You set out to pin them down and they rebel. Sometimes I worry that writing them down restricts them, makes them static instead of fluid, but I don't want to lose them.

As I've explored and written, I've found squishy facts. Even written down, these stories are organic. For example, as I interviewed Grandma, I sometimes found two absolutely valid stories to depict the same event.

When Sicily and Hiram came to Nebraska, they acquired 160 acres of land. According to the 1860 census, they owned that land before the Homestead Act passed. Hiram probably pre-empted when he arrived. But Grandma said that Sicily homesteaded land, herself, after Hiram's death; that she was the first woman to homestead in Nebraska and perhaps Sicily did homestead. I haven't bothered to dig out the records because it doesn't matter. What does matter is that Grandma has lived her entire life believing that a woman, her great grandmother, had the strength and independence to found a dynasty of sorts by herself. What does matter is that Grandma told me that story, and I've believed it. I still believe the essence of that story and, because I do, I accept no limits. I firmly believe I can do anything, if I decide it's important enough to pursue over whatever obstacles come into my way. If I didn't believe Grandma's story, I could count on my mom who insisted I could do anything I wanted if I was willing to work hard enough.

Grandma and I talked for weeks, trying to define family, our family. She told me that she still feels connected to all of us, despite the distances, and that she still feels connected to the family that is gone. She said she thinks all the time about all of us and that it doesn't matter much whether she's thinking about family that is still alive or family that is dead. She feels about the same quality of connection.

She said that she thinks about things we've done. She mentioned specifically shucking corn with Grandpa. She remarked that often when you're doing something you talk more and get more said than you do when you set out to talk things over. I also know you don't have to say a word. It seems really silly, yet one of my warmest memories of Grandma is of buying her favorite fruits with her. She loved bananas, but I remember even more vividly eating green grapes with her on the way home from the store. I still associate the skin's pop and the flood of flavor with Grandma and the Chrysler New Yorker she drove after Grandpa died.

She remained philosophical about the family being scattered. She just said, "That's life. If we hadn't been willing to scatter, we'd all be living piled on top of each other in Virginia or someplace."[cccxv]

Asked what these connections to distant people, distant in space and time, meant in her life as it is now she responded, "It would be pretty bare without them."[cccxvi]

That remark of hers has stuck in my mind and I think of how bare my life would be without these stories. I have stories about my children and my parents and my nephew and niece, about people I've never seen, people who lived centuries ago. And I realize that, without them, my life, too, would lack depth, an assurance that comes from knowing just who you are and where you came from, even if that place is a little scary.

About the Author

As the first-born daughter of a big band canary and a Nebraska farmer, Faith A. Colburn spent a lot of a time with her grandmother while her parents adjusted their lifestyles. With Grandma, she walked the prairies, learning about plants like Spanish bayonet and buffalo beans, as well as animals like mud puppies and jackrabbits. As a public information officer for the state Game and Parks Commission, she canoed the Dismal, rode the Sandhills a-horseback, cross country skied the Missouri bluffs, seined carp, fixed nets, picked trout eggs, and camped out along Bone Creek. She has photographed wildlife, from Sandhill cranes to elk and, tramping the prairies, she gained intimate knowledge of the landscape that often appears as a character or catalyst in her work.

She says that her grandparents' neighborhood and their families have served her well as a pattern for the way families and communities work when they work well. When she writes about them, she attempts to imagine a future, however distant, that's free of hate.

"We can't create what we can't imagine," she says, "so I try to imagine an evolved world where we've learned to get along."

Author of two Nebraska memoirs, Colburn has lived her entire life on the Great Plains. She earned a Master of Arts from the University of Nebraska-Kearney, winning the Outstanding Work of Fiction Award in 2009. She earned a Master of Arts in Journalism and a Bachelor of Arts in Journalism and Political Science from the University of Nebraska-Lincoln. Ms. Colburn wrote a centennial history of the Nebraska Game and Parks Commission and numerous articles for NEBRASKAland, Nebraska newspapers. She earned a number of awards from the Nebraska Press Women for content she produced for a social ministry organization's quarterly news magazine about people with developmental disabilities.

Also by Faith A Colburn:

Prairie Landscapes

A mash-up of Ted Kooser's *Local Wonders*, Roger Welch's *Shingling the Fog* and my own lifetime of environmental journalism, *Prairie Landscapes* represents the ramblings of one mind prowling around on the Great Plains. With its focus on families and landed communities, it brings you face to face with the prairie and its creatures. A little prose poetry, a little weird science, a bit of animal antics, some environmentalism and a touch of folklore, *Prairie Landscapes* is comprised of 133 short pieces of about 500 words.

From Picas to Bytes: Four Generations of Seacrest Newspaper Service to Nebraska

If you want to know how a newspaper can help a community thrive, here's how it is done— A newspaper is a big business in a mid-sized community and Seacrest donation of time and money to community projects provided enormous support to Lincoln. The Seacrest family owned the *Lincoln Journal* for 100 years. They formed coalitions to promote Nebraska's almost unique open meetings and open records law. Their advocacy for open courts also gave the public more access than in most states. They worked tirelessly to support press freedoms. Early adoption of new technologies helped keep a mid-sized daily newspaper in business long after most of their peers turned off the presses and closed their doors.

To learn about Ms. Colburn's upcoming books, to visit her blog, for excerpts and short stories, as well as articles about her and her work, visit her Website at http://faithanncolburn.com/wordpress/.

Reader's Guide

Set mostly on the Great Plains, specifically Nebraska, *Threshold* makes a lot of observations through the lens of one family. Does the author examine economics and politics, family traditions, the arts, or religious beliefs?

Did you feel this book truly belonged in the nonfiction genre? What was the motivation for the writing of this book? What threshold do you think the author hopes to help you across?

Does the author criticize or admire the family she describes? Does she wish to preserve or change their way of life? Either way, what would be risked or gained?

What is **different** from your own family? What do you find most surprising, intriguing or difficult to understand?

What are the **central themes** discussed in the book? What issues or ideas does the author explore? Are they personal, sociological, global, political, economic, spiritual, medical, or scientific?

What kind of **language** does the author use? Is it objective and dispassionate? Or passionate and earnest? Does the language help or undercut the author's premise? Did the essays read like stories, newspaper articles, reports, something else? Give examples.

What are the **implications** for the future? Are there long- or short-term consequences to the issues raised in the book? Are they positive or negative...affirming or frightening? What life lessons can be learned from these stories?

Talk about **specific passages** that struck you as significant—or interesting, profound, amusing, illuminating, disturbing, sad...? What was memorable?

What have you **learned** after reading this book? Has it broadened your perspective about a difficult issue—personal or societal? Has it introduced you to a regional culture in your own country?

If you would like to have the author speak to your club, you can contact Ms. Colburn at faithanncolburn@gmail.com or visit her Website at http://faithanncolburn.com/wordpress.

ENDNOTES

Introduction

[i] Murphy, Pat. "One Odd Shoe." *The Coyote Road: Trickster Tales.* Ed. Ellen Datlow and Terri Windling. New York, New York: Viking. 2007. Pp. 33.

[ii] Gutkind, Lee. *The Art of Creative Nonfiction.* New York, New York: John Wiley and Sons, Inc., 1997. Pp. 10.

[iii] Ibid. Pp. 65-66.

[iv] Eiseley, Loren. "The Slit." *The Immense Journey.* New York:Vintage Books, 1958. Pp. 3-14.

[v] Griswold, Sandy. Weekly sports columns. *Omaha World Herald.* 1890.

[vi] Wexler, Laura. "Saying Good-Bye to 'Once Upon a Time,' or Implementing Postmodernism in Creative Nonfiction. " *Writing Creative Nonfiction.* Ed. Carolyn Forché and Philip Gerard. Cincinnati, Ohio: Story Press. 2001.

[vii] Ibid.

[viii] Kittredge, William. "Owning it All." *Owning it All.* St. Paul, Minnesota: Graywolf Press. 2002. Pp. 57-72.

[ix] Shaller, Susan. *A Man Without Words.* New York, New York: Summit Books. 1991.

[x] Hedge Coke, Allison Adele. *Rock, Ghost, Willow, Deer.* Lincoln, Nebraska: University of Nebraska Press. 2004.

[xi] Toffler, Alvin. "The Rise of the Prosumer." *The Third Wave.* New York, New York: William Morrow and Company, Inc. 1980. Pp. 251-273.

[xii] Toffler, Alvin. "The Electronic Cottage." *The Third Wave.* New York, New York: William Morrow and Company, Inc. 1980. Pp. 181-193.

Chapter One

[xiii] All references to the elephants of the Platte or seeing the elephant, and westward migration through the Platte Valley, including the epigram, were gleaned from Matties, Merrill J. "Elephants of the Platte." *The Great Platte River Road: The Covered Wagon Mainline Via Fort Kearny to Fort Laramie.* Lincoln, Nebraska: Nebraska State Historical Society, 1969. Pp. 61-102.

[xiv] Information about Webster County Archeology came from a 1988 conversation with Jim Potter, then archivist of the Nebraska State Historical Society.

[xv] Colburn, Hazel Izetta. Interviews taped between October, 1994 and May, 1995. This memoir began with a series of twenty-one, ninety-minute interviews with my grandmother, who was ninety-six when the interviews began. The tapes and a transcript are now housed in the Nebraska State Historical Society Archives.

[xvi] Richardson, Robert H. Tilton Territory: A Historical Narrative, Warren Township, Jefferson County, Ohio, 1775-1838. Philadelphia : Dorrance, ©1977. Pp. 19.

[xvii] Morton, Oren Frederic. "Three Wars with the Indians." *A History of Monroe County, West Virginia*. Dayton, Virginia: Ruebush-Elkins Co., 1916. Pp. 33-41. Haynes, Edith Jones. "Wolf Creek Community." *Gleanings of Monroe County West Virginia History*. Ed. Charles B. Motley. Radford, Virginia: Commonwealth Press, 1973. Pp. 171-172.

[xviii] Gribben, John. "Prologue: The Problem." *Schrödinger's Kittens and the Search for Reality: Solving the Quantum Mysteries*. Boston, Massachusetts: Little Brown and Co. Pp. 1-30.

[xix] Eiseley, Loren. "The Bird and the Machine." *The Immense Journey*. New York:Vintage Books, 1958. Pp. 179-193.

[xx] Whitman, Walter. "Song of Myself." *Leaves of Grass*. Bantam Books: New York, 1983. Pp. 73.

Chapter Two

[xxi] Hiscox, Elizabyth, Cynthia Hogue and Lois Roma-Decley. "A Conversation with Martha Collins." *Writer's Chronicle*. May/Summer, 2011-11-09. Accessed 01/14/2012 at http://elink.awpwriter.org/m/awpChron/articles/hiscoxhogueromadeeley01.lasso.

[xxii] Cavendish, Richard. "General Braddock defeated: July 9th, 1755." *History Today* 55.7 (2005): 60. *Academic OneFile*. Web. 13 Jan. 2012. Accessed: 09/11/11. http://go.galegroup.com/ps/i.do?id=GALE%7CAI33978214&v2.1&u=unl_kearney&it=r&p=AONE&sw=w

[xxiii] Rowlandson, Mary. "A Narrative of the Captivity and Restoration of Mrs. Mary Rowlandson." *The Norton Anthology of American Literature: Sixth Edition, Volume A*. Ed. Nina Baym. New York, New York: W.W. Norton and Co. 2003. Pp. 308-340. Rowlandson's description of her capture is only one of many examples in the late seventeenth and early

eighteenth century literature. Although the people on the frontiers probably didn't read those narratives, they'd have known the stories, which were common "knowledge" among the settlers.

xxiv Addington, Luther F. *The Shawnee Captivity of Tommy Ingles*. Radford, Virginia: Commonwealth Press, Inc., 1975.

xxv Morton, Oren Frederic. "Three Wars with the Indians." *A History of Monroe County, West Virginia*. Dayton, Virginia: Ruebush-Elkins Co., 1916. Pp. 32.

xxvi Ibid. Pp. 34.

xxvii Morton, Oren Frederic. "Ten Years of Indian War." *Annals of Bath County*. Staunton, Virginia: The McClure Company, Inc. 1918. Pp. 80.

xxviii Morton. "Three Wars." Pp. 34.

xxix Morton. "Ten Years." Pp. 82.

xxx Op.Cit. Addington, Pp.12.

xxxi Ibid. Pp. 18.

xxxii Morton. "Three Wars." Pp. 33-34.

xxxiii Op. Cit. Addington. Pp. 13.

xxxiv Ibid. Pp. 18-19.

xxxv Axtell, James. "The White Indians of Colonial America." *The William and Mary Quarterly*. Vol. 32, No. 1. Accessed online 9/22/11. http://www.jstor.org/stable/1922594 Pp. 72.

xxxvi *Native American Indian and Melungeon History-Genealogy*. Accessed 05/20/2009 at http://mornstarz.blogspot.com/2008/04/4-thomas-pasmere-carpenter-corn-planter.html. Genealogy going back to the colonial era is difficult at best and discovering Indian and mixed-blood relationships even more so. The source of the Carpenter/Hokolesqua connection is questionable, but I use it to acknowledge the interracial mixture that took place at the very beginning of the nation.

xxxvii *Native*. This reference, again, recognizes the ways in which races mixed. For more, see Hallowell, A. Irving. "Papers of Melville J. Herskovits: American Indians. White and Black: the Phenomenon of Transculturation." *Current Anthropology*. Vol. 4, No. 5 (Dec., 1963). Pp. 519-531.

xxxviii Op. Cit. Morton. "Three Wars." Pp. 34.

xxxix Op. Cit. Axtell. Pp. 60.

xl Ibid. Pp. 62.

xli Ibid. Pp. 57.

xlii Ibid.

xliii Morton, Oren Frederic. "The Swope Family."*A History of Monroe County, West Virginia.* Dayton, Virginia: Ruebush-Elkins Co., 1916. Pp. 494.

xliv Ibid. Pp. 499.

xlv Ibid. Pp. 497.

xlvi Ibid.

xlvii *Rodale's Illustrated Encylopedia of Herbs.* Ed. Claire Kowalchik and William H. Hylton. Emmaus, Pennsylvania: Rodale Press, 1987. "Beebalm." Pp. 39. "Birch." Pp. 44. "Blue Cohosh." Pp. 50.

xlviii Eckert, Allan W. *A Sorrow in Our Heart.* New York, New York: Bantam Books. 1993. Pp. 86-89. Eckert has not provided separate citations for specific passages in this book, so it is hard to judge the reliability of his information.

Unlike other sources such as Elizabeth Eggleston Seelve's book *Tecumseh and the Shawnee Prophet* published in 1878 by Dodd, Mead and Company in New York, he provides the Shawnee point of view.

xlix Haynes, Edith Jones. "Wolf Creek Community." *Gleanings of Monroe County West Virginia History.* Ed. Charles B. Motley. Radford, Virginia: Commonwealth Press, 1973. Pp. 172.

l Morton. "Three Wars." 38-41 and Eckert 95-106.

li Morton, Oren Frederic. "Monroe in the Revolution." *A History of Monroe County, West Virginia.* Dayton, Virginia: Ruebush-Elkins Co., 1916. Pp. 46-47.

lii Ibid.

liii Eckert. Pp. 466-469.

liv Kemper, General William Harrison. *History of Delaware County [Indiana].* Chicago: Lewis Publishing Company, 1908. Pp. 337-338.

Chapter Three

lv Leopold, Aldo. "Forward to Sand County Almanac." *A Sand County Almanac: with Other Essays on Conservation from Round River.* New York: Oxford University Press, 1966. Pp. x.

lvi "An Act to Appropriate the Proceeds of the Sales of the Public Lands, and to Grant Pre-emption Rights." *The Preemption Act of1841.* 27th Congress, Ch. 16, 5Stat. 453 ,1841. Accessed online on 11/30/2011 at

http://www.minnesotalegalhistoryproject.org/assets/Microsoft%20Word%20-%20Preemption%20Act%20of%201841.pdf

lvii Colburn, Hazel Izetta. Twenty-one ninety-minute interviews recorded between fall 1994 and spring 1995.

lviii Ibid.

lix Luttig, John C. *Journal of a Fur Trading Expedition on the Upper Missouri*. 1812-1813. Accessed online on 11/30/2011 at http://user.xmission.com/~drudy/mtman/html/Luttig/luttig.html.

lx Op. Cit. Colburn.

lxi Ibid.

lxii Andreas, A.T. "Otoe County." *Andreas' History of the State of Nebraska*. Online publication by Kansas Collection Books. http://www.kancoll.org/books/andreas_ne/otoe/otoe-p1.html#event. Captured: November 21, 2011.

lxiii Dale, Raymond Elmer. *Otoe County Pioneers: A Biographical Dictionary*. Lincoln, Neb.: [s.n.]

1961-1965. Pp. 1194-95.

lxiv Ibid.

lxv "Douglas, Otoe County." *Nebraska our towns . . . East Southeast.* Project coordinator: Jane Graff. Seward, Nebraska: Second Century Publication Committee, 1992. Pp. 150-151.

lxvi Ibid.

lxvii Leopold. Op. cit. Pp. x

lxviii Colburn, Cecil. Correspondence. March, 1941–August, 1949.

lxix Steele, Volney, M.D. "Homestead Doctors: House Calls on the Great Plains." *Bleed, Blister and Purge: A History of Medicine on the American Frontier*. Missoula, Montana: Mountain Press Publishing Company, 2005. Pp. 190.

Chapter Four

lxx Celano, Paula J.and Janet R. Sawyer. "Vaginal Fistulas." *The American Journal of Nursing*. Lippincott Williams & Wilkins. Stable URL: http://0-www.jstor.org.rosi.unk.edu/stable/3421433. Accessed 11/30/2011.

lxxi Ulrich, Laurel Thatcher. *A Midwife's Tale: the Life of Martha Ballard, based on her Diary, 1785-1812*. New York: Alfred A. Knopf, 1990. Pp. 80.

313

lxxii Hoffert, Sylvia D. "Childbearing on the Trans-Mississippi Frontier, 1830-1900." *The Western Historical Quarterly.* Vol. 22, No.3 (Aug., 1991). Pp. 273-288. Publisher: Western Historical Association. Pp. 276.

lxxiii Steele, Volney, M.D. "Indian Medicine: Native American Health Before and After the White Man." *Bleed, Blister and Purge: A History of Medicine on the American Frontier.* Missoula, Montana: Mountain Press Publishing Company, 2005. Pp. 21.

lxxiv Colburn, Hazel Izetta. Twenty-one ninety-minute interviews recorded between fall 1994 and spring 1995.

lxxv Ibid.

lxxvi Steele, Volney, M.D. "Granny Remedies: Pioneer Women and Folk Medicine." *Bleed, Blister and Purge: A History of Medicine on the American Frontier.* Missoula, Montana: Mountain Press Publishing Company, 2005. Pp. 139.

lxxvii Op. Cit. Colburn.

lxxviii "Death of Mrs. Hendricks Otoe County Pioneer." *The [Nebraska City] Daily Tribune.* Monday, January 8, 1906. Pp. 1.

lxxix Ibid.

Chapter Five

lxxx Dale, Raymond Elmer. *Otoe County Pioneers: A Biographical Dictionary.* Lincoln, Neb.: [s.n.] 1961-1965. Pp. 1305.

lxxxi "Historical Sketch Twelfth Regiment Iowa Volunteer Infantry." *Roster and Record of Iowa Soldiers in the War of the Rebellion Together with Historical Sketches of Volunteer Organizations 1861-1866. Vol. III, 9th–16th Regiments–Infantry.* Des Moines: Emory H. English, State Printer. 1910. Pp. 529, and "Historical Sketch Twenty-Seventh Regiment Iowa Volunteer Infantry." *Roster and Record of Iowa Soldiers in the War of the Rebellion Together with Historical Sketches of Volunteer Organizations 1861-1866. Vol. III, 17th–31st Regiments–Infantry.* Des Moines: Emory H. English, State Printer. 1910. Pp. 1211.

lxxxii Op. Cit. Dale. Pp. 2384.

lxxxiii Colburn, Nina. Genealogy notebooks accumulated from family bibles, interviews with family members and visits to the National Archives.

lxxxiv Op. Cit. Colburn, Hazel Izetta.

Chapter Six

[lxxxv] "Three are Killed in Prison Uprising." *The Lincoln Daily Star.* Wednesday Evening, March 14, 1912.

[lxxxvi] Colburn, Hazel Izetta. Twenty-one ninety-minute interviews recorded between fall 1994 and spring 1995. Except for prison escape and Bessey Forest, Grandma Hazel narrates this story.

[lxxxvii] "Fruitless Search for Murderers Still On." *The Lincoln Daily Star.* Saturday Evening, March 16, 1912.

[lxxxviii] "Death at the End of Convicts' Road." *The Nebraska State Journal.* Tuesday Morning, March 19, 1912.

[lxxxix] "Sassafras." *Rodale's Illustrated Encylopedia of Herbs.* Ed. Claire Kowalchik and William H. Hylton. Emmaus, Pennsylvania: Rodale Press, 1987. Pp.451.

Chapter Seven

[xc] Dobesh, Wilma. "Colburn Family Memories." Booklet of information gathered for a June 20-21, 1998, family reunion.

[xci] Pudup, Mary Beth. "The Limits of Subsistence: Agriculture and Industry in Central Appalachia." *Agricultural History.* Vol. 64, No. 1 (Winter, 1990), pp. 61-89. This paragraph comes from several sources, including "Colburn Family Memories" cited above, and a Wikipedia article "Agriculture and Farming in Ohio." Accessed online at http://en.wikipedia.org/wiki/Appalachian_Ohio#Culture_and_History_of_Appalachian_Ohio on June 15, 2010.

[xcii] Ibid.

[xciii] Colburn, Hazel Izetta. Twenty-one ninety-minute interviews recorded between fall and spring 1995. Nearly everything in this chapter comes out of interviews with Hazel and ruminations upon what she said.

[xciv] Campbell, Estella. "Eclampsia." *The American Journal of Nursing.* Vol. 7, No. 1 (Oct., 1906) Pp. 24-25.

[xcv] Carew, Dave. "Adoptee grateful for Nebraska Industrial Home." *The Lincoln Journal-Star.* Saturday, March 29, 2008 Accessed online on March 29, 2009 at http://journalstar.com/news/local/article_e0996b5b-a7cb-5821-918d-a3c3358265d3.html.

[xcvi] Ibid.

[xcvii] Ward, Superintendent Lena E. *Twelfth Biennial Report of the Nebraska Industrial Home at Milford, Nebraska.* Biennium Ending November 30, 1912.

[xcviii] Ibid.

[xcix] Ibid.

[c] Ibid.

[ci] Campbell, Estella. "Eclampsia." *The American Journal of Nursing.* Vol. 7, No. 1 (Oct., 1906) Pp. 24-25.

[cii] Ibid.

Chapter Nine

[ciii] "General Summary." *Climatological Data, Nebraska Section.* January-April, 1928 Editions. Lincoln, Nebraska: U.S. Department of Agriculture, Weather Bureau. 1928.

[civ] Colburn, Hazel Izetta. Twenty-one ninety-minute interviews recorded between fall 1994 and spring 1995.

[cv] Op. Cit. "General Summary."

[cvi] Op. Cit. Colburn.

[cvii] Op. Cit. "General Summary." March.

[cviii] Larne, Phoebe. When I told Phoebe about Grandma's breakdown, she asked her grandmother, Emily, my grandma's sister-in-law, if she remembered anything about it. Phoebe quoted her response to me over the phone.

[cix] "The Influenza Pandemic of 1918." Online article published by Stanford University at http://virus.stanford.edu/uda/. Accessed 12/01/2011.

[cx] Witte, Walt. This detail came from a conversation on my front step at the home place sometime in 1992.

Chapter Ten

[cxi] Colburn, Cecil William. Correspondence. March, 1941–August, 1949.

[cxii] Ibid. .

[cxiii] Colburn, Hazel Izetta. Twenty-one ninety-minute interviews recorded between fall 1994 and spring 1995.

[cxiv] "Civilian Conservation Corps." Online encyclopedia, *Wikipedia.* Accessed at http://en.wikipedia.org/wiki/Civilian_Conservation_Corps on 09/20/2001. This is a well-sourced, general article.

cxv Op.Cit. Colburn, Cecil William.

cxvi Ibid.

cxvii Colburn, Cecil William. Undated letter published in *The Blue Hill Leader*. Undated clipping in family scrapbook.

cxviii Op. Cit. Colburn, Cecil William.

cxix Ibid.

cxx Ibid.

cxxi Ibid.

cxxii Ibid.

cxxiii "Bushmaster." *Encyclopædia Britannica. Encyclopædia Britannica Online*. Encyclopædia Britannica Inc., 2011. Accessesd on October 12, 2011, at http://www.britannica.com/EBchecked/topic/86178/bushmaster. "Lachesis." *Webster's New Universal Unabridged Dictionary*. New York: Barnes and Noble. 1996. Pp. 1073.

cxxivOp. Cit. Colburn, Cecil William.

cxxv Ibid.

cxxvi Arthur, Anthony. *Bushmasters: America's Jungle Warriors of World War II*. New York: St. Martin's Press, 1987. Pp. 1.

cxxvii Ibid. Pp. 2.

cxxviii Arthur, Anthony. "Lineage and Chronology." *Bushmasters: America's Jungle Warriors of World War II*. New York: St. Martin's Press, 1987. Pp. xi, and Patrick, Joe. *The Bushmasters: Arizona's Fighting Guardsmen Online*. 158th Regimental Combat Team (RCT) "Bushmasters" Forum within World War II Forums. Acessed 08/10/2010 at http://www.ww2f.com/land-warfare-pacific/23282-158th-regimental-combat-team-rct-bushmasters.html.

cxxix Ibid. Patrick.

cxxx Ibid.

cxxxi Braun, Captain Harold. *Braun's Battlin' Bastards: The Bushmasters of Company B, 1st Batallion, 158th R.C.T.* Ed. Jim Culberson. Melbourne, Florida: Sea Bird Publishing, Inc., 2005. Pp. 76.

cxxxii *Blue Hill Leader*. Weekly newspaper. Blue Hill, Nebraska: Ostdiek Publishing Company. March, 1941–December, 1945. Available on microfilm at the Blue Hill Public Library. Undated item in family scrapbook. Must have been January, 1945.

317

cxxxiii Op. Cit. Arthur. Pp. 44.

cxxxiv Ibid. Pp. 44-45.

cxxxv Mendez, Joe. Telephone interview, 11/05/2011.

cxxxvi Arthur. Op. Cit. Pp. 45-46.

cxxxvii Bunkin, Irving A. and Donald L. Miller. "Under the Knife." *World War II*. March/April 2011. Vol. 25, No. 6, Pp. 39-49. Accessed online on October 15 at http://rpkearn.unk.edu/ebsco-web/ehost/detail?sid=7167901c-1730-44dc-aea9de1ce6216bfc%40sessionmgr15&vid=2&hid=11&bdata=JnNpdGU9ZWhvc3QtbGl2ZSZzY29wZT1zaXRl#db=aph&AN=58110937

cxxxviii Sledge, Eugene. "Life in the Infantry." *The War*. PBS documentary online support site. Accessed October 13 at http://www.pbs.org/thewar/at_war_infantry.htm.

cxxxix Phillips, Sidney. "Life in the Infantry." *The War*. PBS documentary online support site. Accessed October 13 at http://www.pbs.org/thewar/at_war_infantry.htm.

cxl Op. Cit. Bunkin.

cxli Op. Cit. Arthur. Pp. 57.

cxlii Op. Cit. Bunkin.

cxliii Op. Cit. Mendez.

cxliv Arthur. Op. Cit. Pp. 50.

cxlv Ibid.

cxlvi Lansford. Bill. "Life in the Infantry." *The War*. PBS documentary online support site. Accessed October 13 at http://www.pbs.org/thewar/at_war_infantry.htm.

cxlvii Mendez. Op. Cit.

cxlviii *Leader*. Op. Cit. August 31, 1945.

cxlix Op. Cit. Arthur. Pp. 85-86.

cl Ibid. Pp. 87, 96

cli Ibid. Pp.. 97.

clii Ibid. Pp. 113.

cliii Ibid. Pp. 115-125.

cliv Ibid. Pp. 125-126.

clv Sullivan, Gordon R., General, United States Army. *New Guinea: The U.S. Army Campaigns of World War II.* On-line brochure published by the U.S. Army Center of Military History. http://www.history.army.mil/brochures/new-guinea/ng.htm. Captured 12/21/2011. Pp. 25.

clvi Ibid. Pp. 26.

clvii Shankle, Glenn. "Landing at Lingayen Gulf" *Pacific Wrecks 1995-2011: 17 years preserving the living legacy of World War II.* http://www.pacificwrecks.com/people/veterans/shankle.html. Accessed 08/10/2011.

clviii Op. Cit. Arthur. Pp. 136.

clix Ibid. Pp. 139.

clx Ibid. Pp. 148.

clxi Ibid. Pp. 150.

Chapter Eleven

clxii Colburn, Hazel Izetta. Twenty-one ninety-minute interviews recorded between fall 1994 and spring 1995. Preceding paragraphs are all from these interviews.

clxiii *The Blue Hill Leader.* Weekly newspaper. Blue Hill, Nebraska: Ostdiek Publishing Company. March, 1941–December, 1945. Available on microfilm at the Blue Hill Public Library.

clxiv Ibid. Date.

clxv *Leader.* Compiled from August, 1941 – May, 1942.

clxvi Ibid.

clxvii "Early Settlers." *The Heritage of Blue Hill.* Blue Hill, Nebraska: The Blue Hill Bicentennial History Committee. 1977. Pp 18-19.

clxviii "Business Directory." *The Heritage of Blue Hill.* Blue Hill, Nebraska: The Blue Hill Bicentennial History Committee. 1977.

clxix "The Attack on Pearl Harbor." *Wikipedia:The Free Enclycopedia.* Accessed at http://en.wikipedia.org/wiki/Attack_on_Pearl_Harbor on March 8, 2012.

clxx Ibid.

clxxi Op. Cit. *Leader.*

clxxii Ibid. December 12, 1941.

clxxiii "Elm Creek Precinct." *Standard Atlas of Webster County Nebraska.* Chicago, Illinois: Geo. A. Ogle and Co.

clxxiv "Reminiscences." *The Heritage of Blue Hill.* Blue Hill, Nebraska: The Blue Hill Bicentennial History Committee. 1977. Pp. 91.

clxxv Cressman, Robert J. "A Magnificent Fight: Marines in the Battle for Wake Island." *World War II Commemorative Series.* Washington, D.C.: Marine Corps Historical Center. 1992. Accessed online at http://www.ibiblio.org/hyperwar/USMC/USMC-C-Wake.html on March 8, 2012.

clxxviOp. Cit. *Leader.* January 2, 1942.

clxxvii Ibid. January 9, 1942.

clxxviii "The Philippeans." *U.S. Army Campaigns of World War II.* Washington, D.C.: U.S. Army Center for Military History. Last updated October, 2003. Accessed online at http://www.history.army.mil/brochures/pi/PI.htm on March 8, 2012. Pp. 9-15.

clxxix Op. Cit. *Leader.* Compiled from January – March, 1942.

clxxx Ibid. January 9, 1942.

clxxxi Grandstaff, Judy. Personal conversation October 19, 2011.

clxxxii Op. Cit. *Leader.* Compiled from March – May, 1942.

clxxxiii Ibid. June 12, 1942.

clxxxiv Chen, C. Peter. "Caribbean Sea and Gulf of Mexico Campaigns: 16 Feb 1942 - 1 Jan 1944." World War II Database. Accessed at http://ww2db.com/battle_spec.php?battle_id=276 on March 8, 2012

clxxxv Op. Cit. *Leader.* July 3, 1942.

clxxxvi "Battle of the Coral Sea, 7-8 May, 1942: Overview and Special Image Selection." *Naval History and Heritage.* Naval Historical Center. Accessed online at www.history.navy.mil/photos/events/wwii-pac/coralsea/coralsea.htm on March 8, 2012 and "Battle of Midway, 4-7 June 1942: Overview and Special Image Selection." *Naval History and Heritage.* Published by the U.S. Navy. Accessed online at http://www.history.navy.mil/photos/events/wwii-pac/midway/midway.htm on March 8, 2012.

clxxxvii Op. Cit. *Leader.* July 17, 1942.

clxxxviii "The History Place: World War II in Europe. Timeline with photos and text." *The History Place.* 1996. Accessed online at http://www.historyplace.com/worldwar2/timeline/ww2time.htm on March 8, 2012.

clxxxix Op. Cit. *Leader*. August 21, 1942.

cxc Ibid. September 11, 1942.

cxci Ibid. October 30, 1942.

cxcii Ibid. November 27, 1942.

cxciii Ibid. December 11, 1942.

cxciv Ibid. December 18, 1942.

cxcv Ibid. January 1, 1943.

cxcvi "Honor Roll." *The Blue Hill Leader*. January 1, 1943.

cxcvii "Business." *The Heritage of Blue Hill*. Blue Hill, Nebraska: The Blue Hill Bicentennial History Committee. 1977. Pp. 224.

cxcviii Op. Cit. *Leader*. January 15, 1943.

cxcix Sullivan, Gordon R., General, United States Army. *New Guinea: The U.S. Army Campaigns of World War II*. On-line brochure published by the U.S. Army Center of Military History. http://www.history.army.mil/brochures/new-guinea/ng.htm. Captured 12/21/2011.

cc Op. Cit. *Leader*. February 12, 1943.

cci Ibid. March 12, 1943.

ccii Ibid. April 16, 1943.

cciii Op. Cit. *Leader*. Compiled from September – October, 1943.

cciv Colburn, Cecil. *The Blue Hill Leader*. April 23, 1943.

ccv Ibid.

ccvi Colburn, Hazel.

ccvii Op. Cit. *Leader*.

ccviii Op. Cit. Colburn, Hazel.

ccix Op. Cit. *Leader*. May 14, 1943.

ccx Ibid.

ccxi "Honor Roll." June 4, 1943.

ccxii Op. Cit. *Leader*.

ccxiii Ibid. August 20, 1943.Op.

ccxiv Op. Cit. "Reminiscences." Pp. 84-85.

ccxv Ibid.

ccxvi Ibid. April 9, 1943.

ccxvii Ibid. September 24, 1943.

ccxviii Ibid.

ccxix Op. Cit. Colburn, Hazel.

ccxx Ibid.

ccxxi Ibid.

ccxxii Ibid.

ccxxiii Meents, Bud. Personal conversation, summer of 1988.

ccxxiv Op. Cit. Colburn, Hazel.

ccxxv Op. Cit. *Leader*. August 24, 1945.

ccxxvi Ibid.

ccxxvii Op. Cit. *Leader*. May 4, 1945.

ccxxviii Op. Cit. *Leader*. Compiled from weekly newspapers from December, 1941 through December, 1945.

ccxxix Op. Cit. *Leader*. May 4 and June 15, 1945.

ccxxx Op. Cit. *Leader*.

ccxxxi Op. Cit. *Leader*.

Chapter Twelve

ccxxxii Colburn, Cecil William. Correspondence. March, 1941–August, 1949.

ccxxxiii Colburn, Ella Mae Bowen. Most of this story is from my memory of what my mother has told me over a lifetime. Any quotes are remembered from incidental conversations that were never recorded.

ccxxxiv Op. Cit. Colburn, Cecil William.

ccxxxv Colburn, Hazel Izetta. Twenty-one ninety-minute interviews recorded between fall 1994 and spring 1995.

ccxxxvi Ibid.

ccxxxvii Ibid.

ccxxxviii Ibid.

ccxxxix Ibid.

ccxl Ibid.

ccxli Ibid.

ccxlii Ibid.

ccxliii Ibid.

Chapter Thirteen

ccxliv Colburn, Hazel Izetta. Twenty-one ninety-minute interviews recorded between fall 1994 and spring 1995.

ccxlv "Liver Cancer Treatment Information." Published by Cancer Answers.com. www.canceranswers.com/Liver.Cancer.html. Captured 11/9/2011.

Chapter Fourteen

ccxlvi Churchill, Winston. From October 1, 1939 radio broadcast. *Bartlett's Familiar Quotations, Fifteenth Edition.* Ed. John Bartlett. Boston:Little, Brown and Company, 1980. Pp. 743.

ccxlvii Colburn, Hazel. 1994-95 taped interviews. All quotes in this chapter come from those interviews, unless otherwise noted.

ccxlviii Roosevelt, Eleanor. Letter to "Miss G." About 1954. Letter stolen in 1994.

ccxlix Murray, Arhur. *How to Become a Good Dancer.* New York: Simon and Schuster, 1959.

Chapter Fifteen

ccl Colburn, Ella Mae. Most of this story comes from my mother and my grandmother. My step-mom managed to fill in a few details, as well. I've indicated which is speaking throughout.

ccli Colburn, Nina Marie. Nina only mentioned my half-sister once, but the occasion was very memorable.

cclii Colburn, Ella Mae. Mom told this story several times, quoting Jumbo each time.

ccliii Colburn Hazel Izetta. Twenty-one ninety-minute interviews recorded between fall 1994 and spring 1995.

ccliv Goodman, Margo. Conversations on her visit to Nebraska in August, 1988.

Chapter Sixteen

cclv Colburn, Cecil William. Undated correspondence. March, 1941– August, 1949.

cclvi Copley, Ella Mae Bowen Colburn. Numerous conversations, none recorded, over a period of decades.

cclvii Colburn, Hazel Izetta. Twenty-one ninety-minute interviews recorded between fall 1994 and spring 1995.

cclviii Ibid.

cclix Op. Cit. Colburn, Cecil William.

cclx Ibid.

cclxi Ibid.

cclxii Ibid.

cclxiii Ibid.

cclxiv Ibid.

cclxv Ibid.

cclxvi Ibid.

cclxvii Goodman, Margo. Conversations both in person and by telephone in August/September, 1988.

cclxviii Op. Cit. Colburn, Cecil William.

cclxix Ibid.

cclxx Ibid.

cclxxi Ibid.

cclxxii Ibid.

cclxxiii Op. Cit. Goodman.

cclxxiv Op. Cit. Copley.

cclxxv Op. Cit. Colburn, Hazel.

cclxxvi Op. Cit. Colburn, Cecil.

Chapter Seventeen

cclxxvii Colburn, Hazel Izetta. Twenty-one ninety-minute interviews recorded between fall 1994 and spring 1995.

cclxxviii Land abstract, southwest quarter, section two, township three, range ten.

cclxxix Op. Cit. Colburn.

cclxxx Ibid.

cclxxxi Arnold, Leon. Ten taped interviews in 1992.

cclxxxii Op. Cit. Colburn, Hazel.

cclxxxiii Ibid.

cclxxxiv Ibid.

Chapter Eighteen

cclxxxv Copley, Ella Mae Bowen Colburn. Remembered conversations over a period of decades.

cclxxxvi Ibid.

cclxxxvii Colburn, Hazel Izetta. Twenty-one ninety-minute interviews recorded between fall 1994 and spring 1995.

cclxxxviii Murphy, Linda. Conversations, August 1988.

cclxxxix Ibid.

ccxc Colburn, Cecil William. Correspondence. March, 1941–April, 1950.

Chapter Nineteen

ccxci Klein, Ken. Several conversations in November, 1992.

ccxcii Klein, Jo Ann. Several conversations in November, 1992.

ccxciii Op. Cit. Klein, Ken.

ccxciv Ibid.

ccxcv Ibid.

ccxcvi Op. Cit. Klein, Jo Ann.

ccxcvii Klein, Jenifer. Conversation August 12, 1993.

ccxcviii Klein, Jo Ann. Phone conversation, August 14, 1993.

ccxcix Ibid.

ccc Copley, Ella Mae Bowen Colburn. Phone conversation August 14, 1993.

ccci Op. Cit. Klein, Jo Ann.

cccii Colburn, Hazel Izetta. Twenty-one ninety-minute interviews recorded between fall 1994 and spring 1995.

Chapter Twenty

ccciii Halevi, Yossi Klein. "Thin Places/Thick Realities." *On Being.* Interview with Krista Tippit. May 12, 2011. American Public Radio.

ccciv Colburn, Hazel Izetta. Twenty-one ninety-minute interviews recorded between fall 1994 and spring 1995.

cccv Ibid.

cccvi Ibid.

cccvii Ibid.

cccviii O'Dell, Patricia. "Joseph's House Provides Home for Men with AIDS." *All Things Considered*. Interview with Daniel Zwerdling. January 8, 1995.

cccix Janifer, Howard. "Joseph's House Provides Home for Men with AIDS." *All Things Considered*. Interview with Daniel Zwerdling. January 8, 1995.

cccx Commonwealth of Pennsylvania. Certificate of Death. August 18,1949.

cccxi U.S. Census. 1930. Polk, Venango, Pennsylvania

cccxii Op. Cit. Colburn, Hazel.

cccxiii Ibid.

cccxiv Ibid.

cccxv Ibid.

cccxvi Ibid.

BIBLIOGRAPHY

Addington, Luther F. *The Shawnee Captivity of Tommy Ingles.* Radford, Virginia: Commonwealth Press, Inc., 1975.

Alder, Henry Clay. *A History of Jonathan Alder: His Captivity and Life with the Indians.* Ed. Larry L. Nelson. Akron, Ohio: The University of Ohio Press, 2002.

Andreas, A.T. "Otoe County." *Andreas' History of the State of Nebraska.* Online publication by Kansas Collection Books. http://www.kancoll.org/books/andreas_ne/otoe/otoe-p1.html#event. Captured: November 21, 2011.

"Are Scouring Country for Fleeing Convicts." *The Lincoln Daily Star.* Friday Evening, March 15, 1912.

Arthur, Anthony. *Bushmasters: America's Jungle Warriors of World War II.* New York: St. Martin's Press, 1987.

Axtell, James. "The White Indians of Colonial America." *The William and Mary Quarterly.* Vol. 32, No. 1. Pp. 55-88. Accessed online 9/22/11. http://www.jstor.org/stable/1922594

"Battle of the Coral Sea, 7-8 May, 1942: Overview and Special Image Selection." *Naval History and Heritage.* Naval Historical Center. Accessed online at www.history.navy.mil/photos/events/wwii-pac/coralsea/coralsea.htm on March 8, 2012 and "Battle of Midway, 4-7 June 1942: Overview and Special Image Selection." *Naval History and Heritage.* Published by the U.S. Navy. Accessed online at http://www.history.navy.mil/photos/events/wwii-pac/midway/midway.htm on March 8, 2012.

Benyus, Janine M. "How Will We Heal Outselves? Experts in our Midst: Finding Cures Like a Chimp." *Biomimicry.* New York: William Morrow and Company, 1997. Pp. 146-184.

Blue Hill Leader. Weekly newspaper. Blue Hill, Nebraska: Ostdiek Publishing Company. March, 1941–December, 1945. Available on microfilm at the Blue Hill Public Library.

327

Braun, Captain Harold. *Braun's Battlin' Bastards: The Bushmasters of Company B, 1ˢᵗ Batallion, 158ᵗʰ R.C.T.* Ed. Jim Culberson. Melbourne, Florida: Sea Bird Publishing, Inc., 2005.

Bunkin, Irving A. and Donald L. Miller. "Under the Knife." *World War II.* March/April 2011. Vol. 25, No. 6, Pp. 39-49. Accessed online on October 15 at http://rpkearn.unk.edu/ebsco-web/ehost/detail?sid=7167901c-1730-44dc-aea9-de1ce6216bfc%40sessionmgr15&vid=2&hid=11&bdata=JnNpdGU9ZWhvc3QtbGl2ZSZzY29wZT1zaXRl#db=aph&AN=58110937

"Bushmaster." *Encyclopædia Britannica. Encyclopædia Britannica Online.* Encyclopædia Britannica Inc., 2011. Accessesd on October 12, 2011, at http://www.britannica.com/EBchecked/topic/86178/bushmaster.

"Business Directory." *The Heritage of Blue Hill.* Blue Hill, Nebraska: The Blue Hill Bicentennial History Committee. 1977.

Campbell, Estella. "Eclampsia." *The American Journal of Nursing.* Vol. 7, No. 1 (Oct., 1906) Pp. 24-25.

Carew, Dave. "Adoptee grateful for Nebraska Industrial Home." *The Lincoln Journal-Star.* Saturday, March 29, 2008 Accessed online on March 29, 2009 at http://journalstar.com/news/local/article_e0996b5b-a7cb-5821-918d-a3c3358265d3.html.

Cavendish, Richard. "General Braddock defeated: July 9th, 1755." *History Today* 55.7 (2005): 60. *Academic OneFile.* Web. 13 Jan. 2012. Accessed: 09/11/11. http://go.galegroup.com/ps/i.do?id=GALE%7CAI33978214&v2.1&u=unl_kearney&it=r&p=AONE&sw=w

Celano, Paula J.and Janet R. Sawyer. "Vaginal Fistulas." *The American Journal of Nursing.* Lippincott Williams & Wilkins. Stable URL: http://0-www.jstor.org.rosi.unk.edu/stable/3421433. Accessed 11/30/2011.

Chen, C. Peter. "Caribbean Sea and Gulf of Mexico Campaigns: 16 Feb 1942 - 1 Jan 1944." *World War II Database.* Accessed at http://ww2db.com/battle_spec.php?battle_id=276 on March 8, 2012

Colburn, Cecil William. Correspondence. March, 1941–April, 1950.

Colburn, Hazel Izetta. Twenty-one ninety-minute interviews recorded between fall 1994 and spring 1995. Now housed in the Nebraska State Historical Society archives with a transcript.

Colburn, Nina. Genealogy notebooks accumulated from family bibles, interviews with family members and visits to the National Archives.

Commonwealth of Pennsylvania. Death Certificate. Ella May Ford. January 8, 1949.

Copley, Ella Mae Bowen Colburn. Phone conversation August 14, 1993.

Copley, Ella Mae Bowen Colburn. Remembered conversations over a period of decades.

Cressman, Robert J. "A Magnificent Fight: Marines in the Battle for Wake Island." *World War II Commemorative Series*. Washington, D.C.: Marine Corps Historical Center. 1992. Accessed online at http://www.ibiblio.org/hyperwar/USMC/USMC-C-Wake.html on March 8, 2012.

Dale, Raymond Elmer. *Otoe County Pioneers: A Biographical Dictionary*. Lincoln, Neb.: [s.n.] 1961-1965. Pp. 1194-1195, 1305, 2382-2384, 2470-2472.

"Death at the End of Convicts' Road." *The Nebraska State Journal*. Tuesday Morning, March 19, 1912.

"Death of Mrs. Hendricks Otoe County Pioneer." *The [Nebraska City] Daily Tribune*. Monday, January 8, 1906. Pp. 1.

"Desperadoes at Pen Take Warden's Life." *The Nebraska State Journal*. Friday Morning, March 15, 1912. Pp. 2.

"Douglas, Otoe County." *Nebraska our towns . . . East Southeast*. Project coordinator: Jane Graff. Seward, Nebraska: Second Century Publication Committee, 1992. Pp. 150-151.

"Early Settlers." *The Heritage of Blue Hill*. Blue Hill, Nebraska: The Blue Hill Bicentennial History Committee. 1977.

Eckert, Allan W. *A Sorrow in Our Heart*. New York, New York: Bantam Books. 1993.

Eiseley, Loren. "The Bird and the Machine." *The Immense Journey*. New York:Vintage Books, 1958. Pp. 179-193.

Eiseley, Loren. "The Slit." *The Immense Journey*. New York:Vintage Books, 1958. Pp. 3-14.

Elm Creek Precinct." *Standard Atlas of Webster County Nebraska*. Chicago, Illinois: Geo. A. Ogle and Co.

"Fruitless Search for Murderers Still On." *The Lincoln Daily Star*. Saturday Evening, March 16, 1912.

"General Summary (ies)." *Climatological Data, Nebraska Section*. January-June, 1928 Editions. Lincoln, Nebraska: U.S. Department of Agriculture, Weather Bureau. 1928.

Gribben, John. "Prologue: The Problem." *Schrödinger's Kittens and the Search for Reality: Solving the Quantum Mysteries*. Boston, Massachusetts: Little Brown and Co. Pp. 1-30.

Griswold, Sandy. Weekly sports columns. *Omaha World Herald*. 1890.

Goodman, Margo. Conversations both in person and by telephone in August/September, 1988.

Gutkind, Lee. *The Art of Creative Nonfiction*. New York, New York: John Wiley and Sons, Inc., 1997.

Hallowell, A. Irving. "Papers of Melville J. Herskovits: American Indians. White and Black: the Phenomenon of Transculturation." *Current Anthropology*. Vol. 4, No. 5 (Dec., 1963). Pp. 519-531.

Halevi, Yossi Klein. "Thin Places/Thick Realities." *On Being*. Interview with Krista Tippit. May 12, 2011. American Public Radio.

Haruf, Kent. *Plainsong*. New York, New York: Vintage Contemporaries. 1999.

Haynes, Edith Jones. "Wolf Creek Community." *Gleanings of Monroe County West Virginia History*. Ed. Charles B. Motley. Radford, Virginia: Commonwealth Press, 1973. Pp. 171-172.

Hedge Coke, Allison Adele. *Rock, Ghost, Willow, Deer*. Lincoln, Nebraska: University of Nebraska Press. 2004.

Helm, Thomas B. *History of Delaware County, Indiana: with illustrations and biographical sketches of some of its prominent men and pioneers*. Chicago : Kingman Brothers, 1881. Photocopy of page provided by Ball State University Archives.

Hiscox, Elizabyth, Cynthia Hogue and Lois Roma-Decley. "A Conversation with Martha Collins." *Writer's Chronicle*. May/Summer, 2011-11-09. Pp.

"Historical Sketch Twelfth Regiment Iowa Volunteer Infantry." *Roster and Record of Iowa Soldiers in the War of the Rebellion Together with Historical Sketches of Volunteer Organizations 1861-1866. Vol. III, 9th–16thRegiments–Infantry*. Des Moines: Emory H. English, State Printer. 1910. Pp. 529.

"Historical Sketch Twenty-Seventh Regiment Iowa Volunteer Infantry." *Roster and Record of Iowa Soldiers in the War of the Rebellion Together with Historical Sketches of Volunteer Organizations 1861-1866. Vol. III, 17th–31st Regiments–Infantry*. Des Moines: Emory H. English, State Printer. 1910. Pp. 1211.

Hodgson, Barbara. "The Search for Health: Opium's Role in the Evolution of Medicine." *In the Arms of Morpheus: The Tragic History of Laudanum, Morphine and Patent Medicines*. Buffalo, New York: Firefly Books. 2001.

Hoffert, Sylvia D. "Childbearing on the Trans-Mississippi Frontier, 1830-1900." *The Western Historical Quarterly.* Vol. 22, No.3 (Aug., 1991). Pp. 273-288. Publisher: Western Historical Association.

Holzimmer, Kevin C. "Walter Krueger, Douglas MacArthur, and the Pacific War: The Wakde-Sarmi Campaign as a Case Study." *Society of Military History.* http://www.jstor.org/stable/2944497. Captured: 21/12/2010.

Janifer, Howard. "Joseph's House Provides Home for Men with AIDS." *All Things Considered.* Interview with Daniel Zwerdling. January 8, 1995.

Kemper, General William Harrison. *History of Delaware County [Indiana].* Chicago: Lewis Publishing Company, 1908. Pp. 337-339.

"The Kentucky Coffee Tree: Gymnocladus dioicus (L.) K. Koch." *Plant Guide.* Published on-line by The U.S. Department of Agriculture, Natural Resource Conservation Service. http://plants.usda.gov/plantguide/pdf/cs_gydi.pdf. Captured: 11/21/2011.

Kittredge, William. "Owning it All." *Owning it All.* St. Paul, Minnesota: Graywolf Press. 2002. Pp. 57-72.

Klein, Jenifer. Conversation in August 14, 1993.

Klein, Jo Ann. Several conversations in November, 1992.

Klein, Ken. Several conversations in November, 1992.

"Lachesis." *Webster's New Universal Unabridged Dictionary.* New York: Barnes and Noble. 1996. Pp. 1073.

Land abstract. Southwest quarter, section two, township three, range ten.

Lansford. Bill. "Life in the Infantry." *The War.* PBS documentary online support site. Accessed October 13 at http://www.pbs.org/thewar/at_war_infantry.htm.

"Liver Cancer Treatment Information." Published by Cancer Answers.com. www.canceranswers.com/Liver.Cancer.html. Captured 11/9/2011.

Luttig, John C. *Journal of a Fur Trading Expedition on the Upper Missouri.* 1812-1813. Accessed online on 11/30/2011 at http://user.xmission.com/~drudy/mtman/html/Luttig/luttig.html.

Matties, Merrill J. "Elephants of the Platte." *The Great Platte River Road: The Covered Wagon Mainline Via Fort Kearny to Fort Laramie.* Lincoln, Nebraska: Nebraska State Historical Society, 1969. Pp. 61-102.

McKee, Jim. "The history of the Nebraska Industrial Home for unwed mothers." *The Lincoln Journal-Star*. On-line edition, Posted February 8, 2010.

Mendez, Joe. Former soldier with the 158th Regimental Combat Team, Headquarters Company. Telephone conversation 10/12/2011.

Meyer, Superintendent M. Evelyn. *Biennial Report of the Superintendent of the Nebraska Industrial Home, Milford, Nebraska.* For the Period ending June 30, 1923.

Mitchell, Robert D. "The Shenandoah Valley Frontier." *The Association of American Geographers*. Vol. 62, No. 3 (Sep., 1972), Pp. 161-186. Publisher: Taylor and Francis, Ltd.

Morton, Oren Frederic. "Monroe in the Revolution." *A History of Monroe County, West Virginia*. Dayton, Virginia: Ruebush-Elkins Co., 1916. Pp. 42-53.

Morton, Oren Frederic. "Ten Years of Indian War." *Annals of Bath County.* Staunton, Virginia: The McClure Company, Inc. 1918. Accessed on 01/14/11 at http://www.archive.org/stream/annalsofbathcoun00mort/annalsofbathco un00mort_djvu.txt

Morton, Oren Frederic. "Three Wars with the Indians."*A History of Monroe County, West Virginia*. Dayton, Virginia: Ruebush-Elkins Co., 1916. Pp. 33-41.

Morton, Oren Frederic. "The Swope Family."*A History of Monroe County, West Virginia*. Dayton, Virginia: Ruebush-Elkins Co., 1916. Pp. 494-.

Murray, Arhur. *How to Become a Good Dancer*. New York: Simon and Schuster, 1959.

Murphy, Linda. Conversations in August, 1988.

Murphy, Pat. "One Odd Shoe." *The Coyote Road: Trickster Tales*. Ed. Ellen Datlow and Terri Windling. New York, New York: Viking. 2007.

Native American Indian and Melungeon History-Genealogy. Accessed 05/20/2009 at http://mornstarz.blogspot.com/2008/04/4-thomas-pasmere-carpenter-corn-planter.html

O'Dell, Patricia. "Joseph's House Provides Home for Men with AIDS." *All Things Considered*. Interview with Daniel Zwerdling. January 8, 1995.

Patrick, Joe. The Bushmasters: Arizona's Fighting Guardsmen Online. 158th Regimental Combat Team (RCT) "Bushmasters" Forum within World War II Forums. Acessed 08/10/2010 at http://www.ww2f.com/land-warfare-pacific/23282-158th-regimental-combat-team-rct-bushmasters.html.

Phillips, Sidney. "Life in the Infantry." The War. PBS documentary online support site. Accessed October 13 at http://www.pbs.org/thewar/at_war_infantry.htm.

Pudup, Mary Beth. "The Limits of Subsistence: Agriculture and Industry in Central Appalachia." Agricultural History. Vol. 64, No. 1 (Winter, 1990), pp. 61-89.

Richardson, Robert H. Tilton *Territory: A Historical Narrative, Warren Township, Jefferson County, Ohio, 1775-1838*. Philadelphia : Dorrance, ©1977. Pp. 19.

Rowlandson, Mary. "A Narrative of the Captivity and Restoration of Mrs. Mary Rowlandson." *The Norton Anthology of American Literature: Sixth Edition, Volume A*. Ed. Nina Baym. New York, New York: W.W. Norton and Co. 2003. Pp. 308-340.

"Sassafras." *Rodale's Illustrated Encylopedia of Herbs*. Ed. Claire Kowalchik and William H. Hylton. Emmaus, Pennsylvania: Rodale Press, 1987. Pp.451.

Shaller, Susan. A Man Without Words. New York, New York: Summit Books. 1991.

Schmidt, Cindy. M.D., M.L.S. Reference Librarian, University of Nebraska Medical Center, McGoogan Library of Medicine. Ms. Schmidt helped me with research and summarized her sources in an email dated 10/14/2009.

Shankle, Glenn. "Landing at Lingayen Gulf" *Pacific Wrecks 1995-2011: 17 years preserving the living legacy of World War II*. http://www.pacificwrecks.com/people/veterans/shankle.html. Accessed 08/10/2011.

Sipe, C. Hale. *"Chapter XX:* Fort Ligonier and western Pennsylvania in the Revolutionary War (1782-1783)." *Fort Ligonier and its Times: A History of the First English Fort West of the Allegheny Mountains, and an Account of Many Thrilling, Tragic, Romantic, Important but Little Known Events in the Region Where the Winning of the West Began: Based Primarily on the Pennsylvania Archives and Colonial Records.* Harrisburg, PA: Telegraph Press, 1932. Pp. 537-538.

Sledge, Eugene. "Life in the Infantry." *The War*. PBS documentary online support site. Accessed October 13 at http://www.pbs.org/thewar/at_war_infantry.htm.

Smith, Dwight L. "Shawnee Captivity Ethnography." Ethnohistory. Vol. 2, No. 1(Winter, 1955). Pp. 29-41. Publisher: Duke University Press.

"Smith Tenders Services." *The Nebraska State Journal*. Sunday Morning, March 17, 1912.

Steele, Volney, M.D. *Bleed, Blister and Purge: A History of Medicine on the American Frontier.* Missoula, Montana: Mountain Press Publishing Company, 2005.

Sullivan, Gordon R., General, United States Army. *New Guinea: The U.S. Army Campaigns of World War II.* On-line brochure published by the U.S. Army Center of Military History. http://www.history.army.mil/brochures/new-guinea/ng.htm. Captured 12/21/2011.

"The Attack on Pearl Harbor." *Wikipedia:The Free Enclycopedia.* Accessed at http://en.wikipedia.org/wiki/Attack_on_Pearl_Harbor on March 8, 2012.

"The History Place: World War II in Europe. Timeline with photos and text." *The History Place.* 1996. Accessed online at http://www.historyplace.com/worldwar2/timeline/ww2time.htm on March 8, 2012.

"The Influenza Pandemic of 1918." Online article published by Stanford University at http://virus.stanford.edu/uda/. Accessed 12/01/2011.

"The Philippeans." *U.S. Army Campaigns of World War II.* Washington, D.C.: U.S. Army Center for Military History. Last updated October, 2003. Accessed online at http://www.history.army.mil/brochures/pi/PI.htm on March 8, 2012.

"Three are Killed in Prison Uprising." *The Lincoln Daily Star.* Thursday Evening, March 14, 1912.

Toffler, Alvin. *The Third Wave.* New York, New York: William Morrow and Company, Inc. 1980.

"Trail of Murderers Now Leads to Omaha." *The Lincoln Daily Star.* Sunday Morning, March 17, 1912.

Ulrich, Laurel Thatcher. *A Midwife's Tale: the Life of Martha Ballard, based on her Diary, 1785-1812.* New York: Alfred A. Knopf, 1990.

United States Census. 1930. Polk, Venango, Pennsylvania.

Ward, Superintendent Lena E. *Twelfth Biennial Report of the Nebraska Industrial Home at Milford, Nebraska.* Biennium Ending November 30, 1912.

Wilkinson, Charles. *Blood Struggle: The Rise of Modern Indian Nations.* New York: W. W. Norton, 2005.

Wexler, Laura. "Saying Good-Bye to 'Once Upon a Time,' or Implementing Postmodernism in Creative Nonfiction. " *Writing Creative Nonfiction.* Ed. Carolyn Forché and Philip Gerard. Cincinnati, Ohio: Story Press. 2001.

Made in the USA
Columbia, SC
15 November 2017